Practical Guide to SAP® Cost Center Accounting

John Pringle

Thank you for purchasing this book from Espresso Tutorials!

Like a cup of espresso coffee, Espresso Tutorials SAP books are concise and effective. We know that your time is valuable and we deliver information in a succinct and straightforward manner. It only takes our readers a short amount of time to consume SAP concepts. Our books are well recognized in the industry for leveraging tutorial-style instruction and videos to show you step by step how to successfully work with SAP.

Check out our YouTube channel to watch our videos at
https://www.youtube.com/user/EspressoTutorials.

If you are interested in SAP Finance and Controlling, join us at
http://www.fico-forum.com/forum2/
to get your SAP questions answered and contribute to discussions.

Related titles from Espresso Tutorials:

- Martin Munzel: New SAP® Controlling Planning Interface
  http://5011.espresso-tutorials.com
- Michael Esser: Investment Project Controlling with SAP®
  http://5008.espresso-tutorials.com
- Stefan Eifler: Quick Guide to SAP® CO-PA (Profitability Analysis)
  http://5018.espresso-tutorials.com
- Paul Ovigele: Reconciling SAP® CO-PA to the General Ledger
  http://5040.espresso-tutorials.com
- Tanya Duncan: Practical Guide to SAP® CO-PC (Product Cost Controling)   *http://5064.espresso-tutorials.com*
- Ashish Sampat: First Steps in SAP® Controlling (CO)
  http://5069.espresso-tutorials.com
- Marjorie Wright: Practical Guide to SAP® Internal Orders (CO-OM)
  http://5139.espresso-tutorials.com
- Ashish Sampat: Expert Tips to Unleash the Full Potential of SAP® Controlling   *http://5140.espresso-tutorials.com*
- John Pringle: Practical Guide to SAP® Profit Center Accounting
  http://5144.espresso-tutorials.com
- Janet Salmon & Claus Wild: First Steps in SAP® S/4HANA Finance
  http://5149.espresso-tutorials.com

John Pringle
Practical Guide to SAP® Cost Center Accounting

ISBN:	978-1-975731-19-9
Editor:	Christine Parizo
Cover Design:	Philip Esch
Cover Photo:	fotolia # 133098947 © bluedesign
Interior Design:	Johann-Christian Hanke

All rights reserved.

1st Edition 2017, Gleichen

© 2017 by Espresso Tutorials GmbH

URL: *www.espresso-tutorials.com*

Feedback
We greatly appreciate any feedback you may have concerning this book. Please send your feedback via email to: *info@espresso-tutorials.com*.

Table of Contents

Preface		**9**
1	**Introduction to Cost Center Accounting**	**11**
1.1	Business requirements for Cost Center Accounting	11
1.2	The concept of FI versus CO in SAP	13
1.3	The role of cost centers in SAP	17
1.4	New developments	17
1.5	Summary	25
2	**Master data in CCA**	**27**
2.1	Cost center	27
2.2	Cost center standard hierarchy	42
2.3	Cost center groups	45
2.4	Cost elements	50
2.5	Activity types	53
2.6	Statistical key figures	57
2.7	Summary	60
3	**Cost center planning in ECC**	**61**
3.1	Where cost center planning fits	61
3.2	Planning version concept in SAP	65
3.3	Cost input planning	68
3.4	Activity output and price planning	96
3.5	Statistical key figure planning	103
3.6	Planning aids	104
3.7	Summary	108
4	**Cost center planning in S/4 HANA**	**109**
4.1	Concept of BPC embedded planning	109
4.2	Planning areas in embedded planning	110

4.3	Planning functionality in S/4 HANA	111
4.4	Plan actual reporting with HANA	120
4.5	Summary	121

5 Cost center manual actual posting — **123**

5.1	Flow of actual values	123
5.2	Manual re-postings in CCA	129
5.3	Manual activity transactions	133
5.4	Actual statistical key figures	138
5.5	Manual cost allocations	139
5.6	Using BATCHMAN	140
5.7	Manual values in S/4 HANA	145
5.8	Summary	145

6 Periodic allocations — **147**

6.1	Why do allocations?	147
6.2	Actual cost allocations	149
6.3	Periodic activity allocations	153
6.4	Cycle overview	160
6.5	Overhead allocations	163
6.6	Accrual calculation	165
6.7	Transfer actual SKF values	169
6.8	Summary	172

7 Period end analysis and process — **173**

7.1	Period end analysis in CCA	173
7.2	Standard analysis	174
7.3	Target cost analysis for cost centers	176
7.4	Variance analysis	178
7.5	Actual price calculation	185
7.6	Marginal costing	190
7.7	Summary	196

8 Manufacturing and cost center accounting   **197**

8.1   Master data   197

8.2   Manufacturing planning scenario   200

8.3   Manufacturing execution scenario   209

8.4   Summary   219

9 Reporting in cost center accounting   **221**

9.1   Standard reporting   221

9.2   Report painter options   230

9.3   Summary   234

A The Author   **236**

B Index   **237**

D Disclaimer   **241**

Preface

Cost center accounting is likely the most used sub-module within SAP Controlling. The tight integration between Financial Accounting (FI) and Controlling (CO) in SAP requires us to direct most profit-and-loss postings to an object in CO. For most overhead-related costs, this cost object will ultimately be a cost center. Additionally, the cost center has a central role to facilitate both basic and advanced cost and management accounting functions within CO in planning, cost allocations, and reporting. The cost center can be a planning object, it can serve as both a sender and receiver in various allocations, and it is an object that commonly is reported on.

In reality, although Cost Center Accounting (CCA) is used heavily, its functionality is often under-used. Many companies using SAP only utilize CCA's most basic functions and often manually perform tasks or prepare analysis that could be automated. There are often many reasons for this including the "come back to it later" syndrome that occurs during an SAP project. Items that require more time to design or are perceived to be difficult get postponed. Often the intention is to come back later and look at these functions. Sometimes this happens; more often it does not. Another possibility is that the functionality may be useful but the process or setup is not well understood by the organization. Here, they might like to use it but lack the understanding.

I intend for this book to show both the basics of cost center accounting and many of the more advanced functions in planning, allocations, and reporting available within the module. Since SAP provides a wide range of functional options within its many modules and sub-modules, it will be true that not every organization will find all the cost center functions presented here applicable or even useful. However, I hope that by presenting all these options in some detail, some readers will want to explore them and perhaps introduce them into their organizations.

Acknowledgements

As with my last book, this is also dedicated to my wife Lynn and my children, Ness and John. I again want to thank Martin Munzel, Alice Adams, and all the people at Espresso Tutorials for the opportunity to share some of my SAP knowledge for a second time. I would also like to acknowledge two of my colleagues specifically for their help with sections of this book. Thanks to Jay Gandhi, master of and advocate for BPC planning. Jay reviewed and improved the chapter on cost center planning in S/4 and enhanced my knowledge of embedded BPC planning. I would also like to thank Matt Boyle, production planning consultant extraordinaire for his help in explaining and setting up the flexible planning and LTP scenario configuration. I am privileged to work with them and with many other talented and dedicated professionals at Illumiti on a day-to-day basis.

We have added a few icons to highlight important information. These include:

Tips

Tips highlight information that provides more details about the subject being described and/or additional background information.

Attention

Attention notices highlight information that you should be aware of when you go through the examples in this book on your own.

Finally, a note concerning the copyright: all screenshots printed in this book are the copyright of SAP SE. All rights are reserved by SAP SE. Copyright pertains to all SAP images in this publication. For the sake of simplicity, we do not mention this specifically underneath every screenshot.

1 Introduction to Cost Center Accounting

In this chapter, you will explore what a cost center is and why it is needed in SAP. To understand where cost centers fit within the organizational structures in SAP, you will need to know how and why SAP finance has been split into two general groupings, Financial Accounting (FI) and Management Accounting or Controlling (CO). Once you understand that, you will see where cost center accounting fits within the framework of controlling and understand the multiple functions available in Cost Center Accounting (CCA). Finally, you will explore changes we have seen recently in CCA in ECC 6 and S/4/HANA.

1.1 Business requirements for Cost Center Accounting

The term *cost center* generally is used within business and accounting literature to refer to a unit in an organization responsible for controlling costs only and has no responsibility for revenues, profits, or investment decisions. Most businesses will require cost centers in some form or another. These may be defined based on combinations of business function (finance, human resources), responsibility (management hierarchy), or location. Regardless of how they are defined, there will always be units within a business organization where the primary criteria for evaluating performance is based on cost control and cost management. This evaluation will typically take the form of measuring actual performance against a budget or a plan, and often the focus will be on reducing costs or maintaining costs at a particular level based on percentage of revenue or some other target. Often, the focus of this evaluation is on *overhead costs*, which are generally defined as any costs that cannot be directly traced to a product or output of the business. Often the outcomes of these cost evaluations will contribute to compensation equations or to significant business decisions such as whether to outsource entire business functions.

That deals with the high-level definition, but on a practical level, what should we consider a cost center to be? If you consider a typical business that manufactures and sells a product, you will see that there will be parts of the business responsible for revenue, profitability, and return on investment. These are the profit centers. You may also see that there are parts of the organization that are involved in manufacturing the product. These may be individual machines, groups of machines, groups of employees, or areas within the production facility. Sometimes these may be referred to as work centers or production cost centers. There will also be departments that, while not directly involved in production, will offer support services to the production facility like quality assurance, plant maintenance, and production supervision. Finally, there will be units within the organization that do not directly contribute to revenue or production but are still necessary to support the ongoing operations of the overall business. This group will include departments such as finance, human resources, information technology, and research and development.

In business, it is often common to equate the term *department* with the term *cost center*, and this is often valid, especially in the cases of support and administrative cost centers. However, this one-to-one mapping of a department to a cost center may not hold true on the shop floor of a production facility. Here, the entire production facility may be defined as a department from a management responsibility standpoint, so it may be necessary to define cost centers at a lower level such as a machine, group of machines, assembly line, or group of employees.

Within SAP, the functionality available in Cost Center Accounting (CCA) supports most business definitions and accounting requirements at a department or cost center level. So where does CCA fit within the SAP landscape? Functionally, it is one of the central sub-modules within the CO module. The functional sub-modules within CO can be roughly subdivided into three broad groups.

- ▶ Overhead cost controlling—primarily concerned with planning, tracking, and reporting overhead costs using the sub-modules CCA, Internal Orders, and activity-based costing.

- ▶ Product costing—primarily concerned with planning, tracking, and reporting product costs and production activities.

▶ Profitability management—primarily concerned with planning, tracking and reporting revenues and profits using the sub-modules Profitability Analysis and Profit Center Accounting (note that, since ECC5, profit center accounting may be part of the GL rather than part of CO).

Due to the integrated nature of SAP CO, there is considerable overlap between these areas, and the assignment of sub-modules to areas is arbitrary. For example, cost center accounting plays an important role in product cost planning, so even though it is not considered part of product costing, it would be almost impossible to perform standard costing without involving planning in cost center accounting. Similarly, I could have placed activity-based costing as part of product costing, but its primary function is the allocation of overhead costs, so it better fits within overhead cost controlling.

1.2 The concept of FI versus CO in SAP

Before delving deeply into the area of cost center accounting, it is important to understand the structure of SAP Finance and to recognize the differences between Financial Accounting (FI) and Controlling or Management Accounting (CO). Many computerized accounting systems are designed so that the general ledger serves as the repository for both financial and management accounting data. Often this is achieved by segmenting the GL account number to represent additional organizational units within the account number. This often results in extremely long GL account numbers and lengthy charts of account.

The original concept in SAP was that management accounting information should be separate from the general ledger and that the general ledger should support the strictly financial reporting requirements of the business for external needs. Meanwhile, management accounting would support internal management reporting needs. To achieve this, SAP devised separate organizational units within FI and CO. Since management accounting may be interested in tracking and reporting the flow of costs within an organization across legal entity lines, the primary organizational unit for CO, the *controlling area*, can exist at a higher level than the primary organizational unit for FI, the *company code*. For reporting purposes, the company code usually is defined at a legal entity level.

While it is possible to make a one-to-one assignment of a controlling area to a company code, the recommended approach is to have multiple company codes assigned to one controlling area. During the design phase of the implementation, it is a business decision to determine the organizational structure and to decide on the number of company codes and controlling areas and their assignments. There may be a number of business criteria affecting the organizational design of controlling areas and company codes, but there are a couple of technical limitations regarding the assignment that should be followed. Specifically, the operating chart of accounts should be common between the controlling area, and all company codes assigned to it should use the same fiscal year parameters.

Besides having separate organizational elements, FI and CO were designed to have separate master data elements. Within FI, the primary modules are General Ledger (GL), Accounts Payable (AP), Accounts Receivable (AR), and Asset Accounting (AA). Therefore, the key master data elements are GL account, vendor, customer, and asset. Conversely, CO largely is concerned with cost management within the organization, so its primary master data elements are cost elements, cost centers, internal orders, various forms of production orders, service orders, business processes, and profitability segments. Except for the cost element, all these master data elements can be referred to generically as cost objects. That is, they are objects where we can plan, receive, send, and report costs. In fact, the design of cost objects as master data objects fully supports the three primary functions of controlling in SAP:

- ▶ Planning
- ▶ Allocation
- ▶ Reporting

You will notice that posting is not one of the primary functions of controlling. This is because overall value cannot be created or reduced within CO. Postings that change the overall value of the organization will always flow into CO through FI. Transactions within CO only serve to move or allocate costs between cost objects and have no effect on the overall financial position of the enterprise. The determination of whether a through posting from FI occurs is determined by the master data in the chart of accounts as you will see in the next few paragraphs.

In the assignment of the company code to the controlling area, there is a common operating chart of accounts shared between FI and CO. Within FI, the elements in that chart of accounts are called *general ledger accounts*, while within CO, the elements are called *cost elements*. However, that is not the only difference, as not all elements within that chart will be used by both modules. If you look at Figure 1.1 you can see typical chart of account sections and whether they are used in FI, CO, or both. This is a typical example, but it may not be followed strictly in every situation.

Chart of Accounts	Financial Accounting	Controlling	Typical Cost Object
Balance Sheet	✓	✗	N/A
Revenue & Deductions	✓	✓ ✗	Project/Order/COPA
Cost of Sales (Std.)	✓	✗	N/A
Production accounts	✓	✓	Production Order
WIP Offset	✓	✗	N/A
Variances	✓	✓	COPA/Cost Center
SG&A Expenses	✓	✓	Cost Center/Internal Order
Non Operating Expense	✓	✓ ✗	Cost Center or no CO posting
Secondary Costs	✗	✓	All

Figure 1.1: Chart of account elements used by FI and CO

Balance sheet items do not exist in CO, while secondary cost elements (used for moving costs around within CO) do not exist in FI. Some of the other inclusions or exclusions will be determined by your business requirements or by technical limitations. For revenue accounts, if you are using costing-based COPA, the creation of revenue elements is not a technical necessity, as the revenue posting will flow there, anyway. If you are using another CO object to capture revenue such as a project or an order, then you will need a revenue element. In a costing-based COPA scenario with valuation, the cost of sales account posted by the *post goods issue* (PGI) transaction should not exist in CO. In that case, the cost of sales controlling posting to the profitability segment cost object will occur with the billing document, so having a CO posting occur at PGI would result in double counting the cost of sales in CO. In a manufacturing scenario, the process for determining unfinished work in production orders, known as WIP in SAP, results in a reclassification posting to move value from the income statement to the balance sheet at period end. This process is for reclassification for financial reporting purposes only, so the WIP offset account on the income statement should not exist as a cost element in CO. For expenses that fall in the non-operating category, I have seen different approaches. Some companies want all expenses to go to CO, so they create cost elements even for non-controllable expenses. Other companies will not create cost elements for these types of expenses and see them in FI.

In FI, the GL accounts technically are classified as either balance sheet or P&L. In CO, cost or revenue elements are classified as either primary or secondary, then further broken down by type. The primary cost or revenue elements are essentially extensions of the P&L general ledger accounts into CO. The existence of a primary cost element tells SAP that a posting to the equivalent GL accounts also requires a CO posting to an appropriate cost object. This is what determines whether a through posting from FI to CO will occur for a particular transaction line item. Automatic creation of the primary elements can be achieved through some configuration settings so that, whenever a GL expense or revenue account is created, a primary cost element is also created in the background.

The secondary cost element is created only in CO and will not exist in FI. The secondary cost elements are used for specific purposes within CO such as *activity allocation*, *results analysis*, *settlement*, *assessment,* and *overhead*. Secondary cost elements are created manually as needed since they are not linked to an existing GL account.

Secondary cost elements

 It is good practice to design the chart of accounts so that the secondary cost elements exist in their own range of account numbers. I have seen ranges of accounts starting with 8 or 9 being used to contain the secondary elements often. I also find it useful to build the cost element type into the number. For example, **921010** would be a secondary cost element of type **21**—used for settlement.

1.3   The role of cost centers in SAP

SAP offers several configuration and master data objects to model a business within the system. Objects defined in configuration such as the controlling area, company codes, plants, purchasing organizations, and sales organizations represent organizational elements that are relatively static. This is reflected because system configuration is required to change or add these elements. Other organizational units that may be more dynamic in nature such as cost centers, profit centers, and projects are represented by master data objects, which can be more easily added or changed. This book is specifically concerned with the functionality of cost centers.

It may be said that CCA is the most central module within controlling, and it would be hard to imagine an SAP implementation that does not make use of its functionality. The primary role of the cost center may be seen as a place where costs are incurred, but cost center accounting in SAP goes far beyond just the collecting and reporting of costs. Besides being a cost collector, the cost center serves as a sender of costs to other cost objects through various forms of allocations. The cost center also plays a key role in product cost planning and cost object controlling processes as a sender of overhead costs to both standard product costs and production cost objects.

In addition, the cost center is an object that can have a plan or a budget associated with it, and this allows it to be used in variance analysis in both a simple plan versus actual scenario, as well as in more complicated ways using targets, variance analysis, and marginal costing.

1.4   New developments

In the last few years, there have been several new products and new developments from SAP that either have or are likely to affect users of CCA functionality. The most dramatic of these changes has been the introduction of the so-called SAP Simple Finance and the subsequent introduction of S/4/HANA. Due to some confusion caused by SAP changing the name of certain products during the release cycle, I think it is important to offer clarity around these products. Currently, SAP is offering some of these products either as *cloud* offerings or as *on-premise* editions with different release schedules. The following relates to the on-premise offerings. Note that, for the S/4HANA products, the release numbers refer to the year and month of the release.

▶ SAP S/4HANA Finance—currently release 1605, previous release is 1503. The 1503 release was called SAP Simple Finance when it was released, and that name is still used in some documentation. This product contains the S/4 finance simplifications with a standard logistics solution.

▶ SAP S/4HANA—currently on release 1610, 1709 is upcoming, previous is release 1511. This product contains the S/4 finance simplifications along with simplified logistics.

▶ SAP ECC—current release ECC6 EHP8. My understanding is that *enhancement pack* 8 will be the last release of this product. This is the traditional SAP ECC product, and various options can be used with this product to take advantage of the performance improvements offered by the HANA database. However, this product will remain database agnostic, and you will not be required to use HANA.

When talking about simplifications in S/4HANA, SAP is primarily referring to simplifications of the database structure. However, these database simplifications will also lead to other simplifications in process and reporting. Due to the in-memory nature of the HANA database and some basic changes to the structure of the tables, the data extract performance of the HANA database is many times faster than a traditional database. The enhanced performance allowed by in-memory computing and the new table structure allows direct reporting access to line item tables and eliminates the need for totals tables and some indices. Tables such as GLT0, FAGLFLEXT, FAGLFLEXA, BSIS, BSAS, BSID, BSAD, BSIK, and BSAK have been eliminated and replaced by compatibility views with the same name. If you are migrating to S/4, the compatibility views will be created during the migration and will ensure that *database selects* in existing programs will still work.

One misconception about S/4HANA is that CO will no longer exist and will be incorporated into FI. I believe the reasons for this statement are due to the simplified table structure, specifically the introduction of the concept of the *universal journal* and to the elimination of the *cost ele-*

ment as a master data object. I will explain the universal journal concept first and then address the elimination of the cost element.

In traditional SAP ECC FI/CO, the transactions largely existed in different worlds. Even within FI, General Ledger (GL) and fixed asset transactions existed in different table sets. That meant sets of transaction, summary, and index tables for FI and other sets of tables for CO. In the S/4/HANA world, many of these tables in GL Accounting, Asset Accounting, Material Ledger, and CO have become redundant since the data became contained in one universal journal line item table called ACDOCA. The existing FI document header table, BKPF, remains as the header table for the universal journal. For those interested in exploring in more detail, there is a wealth of information available on the SAP Help Portal under the topic of "Migration to SAP Accounting powered by SAP HANA." Based on the material available there, I have prepared a simplified graphic of what has been replaced by ACDOCA (see Figure 1.2). For additional detail, you can refer to the SAP help source that was mentioned before.

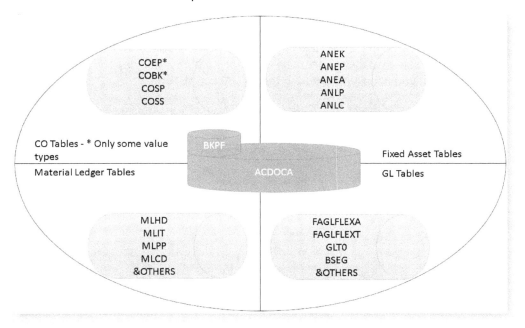

Figure 1.2: Universal journal structure

The most obvious benefits of the universal journal approach include:

▶ Elimination of data redundancy—data is stored once.

▶ Reduction of reconciliation between modules—one version of the truth.

▶ Multi-dimensional reporting on the universal journal (more on this later).

Besides introducing the universal journal, the second big change is the elimination of the cost or revenue element as a stand-alone piece of master data. As was discussed previously, the primary cost/revenue elements are in place to link the P&L general ledger accounts to controlling, and the secondary cost elements are used for forms of allocation within CO. In S/4HANA, the general ledger account now takes the combined role of GL account and cost element. The concepts of primary and secondary costs still exist and are seen in the **G/L Account Type** (see Figure 1.3). The different categories of cost element also still exist and are seen in a new section on the CONTROL DATA tab of the GL account master data (see Figure 1.4). The old cost element settings for record quantity unit of measure also are available in this section. The values that you can display in the *cost element category* will depend on the value that you initially selected in the **G/L Account Type**.

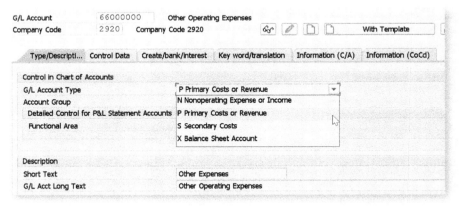

Figure 1.3: GL account type in S/4HANA

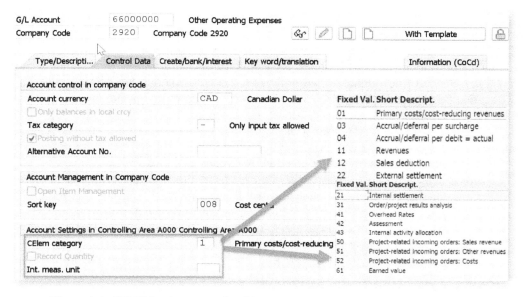

Figure 1.4: CELEM category on the GL account

These two major changes integrate FI and CO more tightly, but they do not mean that CO as a function will cease to exist. There will still be costing functions and management reporting requirements, such as variance analyses and overhead cost tracking, which will remain as CO functions, even if the table structure has evolved to allow much of the underlying data to reside in the same tables.

The implications on cost center accounting functionality of the universal journal and the elimination of the cost element are not apparent on the surface and should not affect most users. Many of the functions and master data elements in cost center accounting will continue to perform as before. The major exception will be in the area of planning. Many of the classic planning transactions in CO have been deactivated in S/4. The intent is to use SAP BPC for S/4 HANA Finance as the planning tool. This is an embedded BPC model type, which was previously known as Integrated Business Planning for Finance (IBPF). More detail on the S/4 HANA cost center planning functions will be provided in Section 4.4, where planning will be dealt with in more depth.

Coming back to multi-dimensional reporting, one of the major implications of being able to report against the ACDOCA line items is that you are no longer restricted in the characteristics that you can report against. In the traditional ECC product, the totals tables were largely pre-defined by SAP, so the number of summarized characteristics in tables such as GLT0 in the old GL or FAGLFLEXT was restricted to things like company code, business area, profit center, or segment. Even though new GL allowed some additional flexibility, the totals tables were limiting the ability to report out of ECC. With the universal journal and the ability to perform aggregations on the fly using HANA views in a tool such as *analysis for office,* you can present views or reports of the data summarized by any characteristic that is available within the universal journal. The following graphic (see Figure 1.5) is a representation of material available on the SAP help portal under the migration to S/4HANA section that was mentioned previously. It shows the increased flexibility provided by on-the-fly aggregation for reporting and analytics as opposed to the traditional ECC approach with pre-defined aggregates.

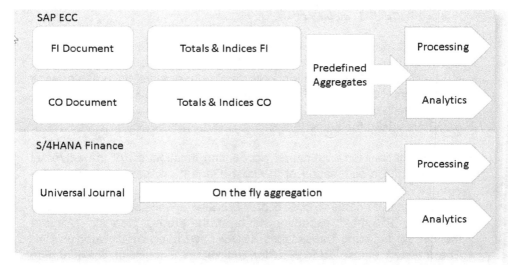

Figure 1.5: Aggregation in ECC versus S/4HANA Finance

Concurrent with the development of HANA and the S/4 products, SAP has also been focusing on the user experience. Traditionally, the SAP GUI was the primary interface between the user and the system. In in 2007, SAP introduced the *Net Weaver Business Client* (NWBC), which has evolved through various releases and is now called *SAP Business*

Client. The Business Client offers many functions and features not available in standard GUI, with the most relevant being the ability to run SAP's newer *Web Dynpro*-based applications. Web Dynpro is an SAP development environment that enables the developer to create applications using web browser-based technology. This has some impact on cost center accounting since several of the enterprise business functions delivered with the various enhancement packs in ECC6 include user roles and Web Dynpro-based transactions for cost center accounting. The most significant additions include Web Dynpro applications for cost center master data and hierarchies, versioning for cost center hierarchies with active and inactive versions, and enhanced Web Dynpro applications for planning.

Business function activation

Since the release of SAP ECC version 6.0, SAP has been releasing technical and functional upgrades through enhancement packs. These enhancement packs contain business functions that can be activated in the system if required. The business functions most relevant for cost center accounting are FIN_CO_CCMGMT and FIN_CO_CCPLAN, available since EHP6. Before activating business functions, users should thoroughly read the documentation and fully understand the implications of activating the function. Many business function activations cannot be reversed, and some will have a license impact for your SAP system.

An example of a Web Dynpro application for the cost center group maintenance is shown in Figure 1.6.

In 2013, SAP started designing and developing *Fiori* as a user interface. Initially, this was seen as a mobile strategy to redesign SAP transactions as apps to be rendered and run on mobile devices. This approach has evolved to the point where Fiori now is being promoted as the preferred user interface for S/4HANA. The Fiori interface uses a tile-based approach to present transactions to the users in a view called the Fiori Launchpad (see Figure 1.7). Sometimes, SAP has totally redesigned a transaction to become a Fiori app; in other cases, the Fiori tile is just a pointer to a standard SAP transaction or existing Web Dynpro application (see Figure 1.8). In CCA, many of the reports have been redesigned, as not all existing report painter based reports are supported in S/4 due to the changes in CO planning.

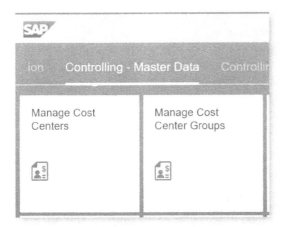

Figure 1.6: Cost center group Web Dynpro application

Figure 1.7: Fiori Launchpad with tiles

The design and release of Fiori apps is still ongoing, and more Fiori apps will be released by SAP. S/4HANA can be accessed through Fiori or through the Business Client, with Fiori being the recommended approach going forward. It is not recommended to use the standard SAP GUI to access S/4HANA systems since certain functions will now only be available through Fiori apps or Web Dynpro transactions and no longer accessible from the standard GUI.

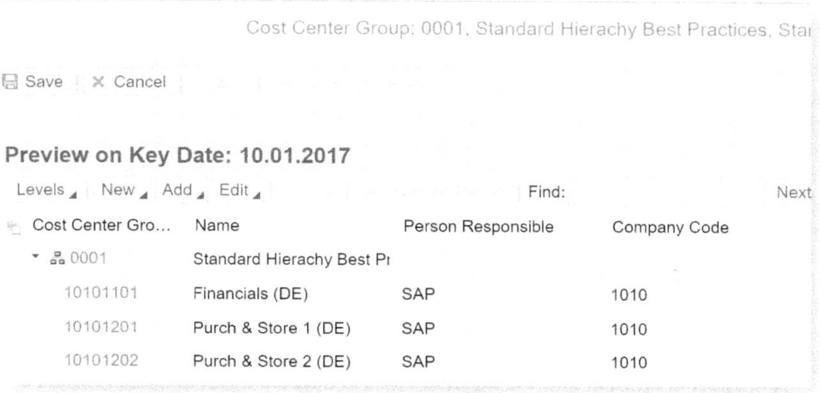

Cost Center Gro...	Name	Person Responsible	Company Code
0001	Standard Hierachy Best Pr		
10101101	Financials (DE)	SAP	1010
10101201	Purch & Store 1 (DE)	SAP	1010
10101202	Purch & Store 2 (DE)	SAP	1010

Cost Center Group: 0001, Standard Hierachy Best Practices, Star

Save   ✕ Cancel

Preview on Key Date: 10.01.2017

Levels   New   Add   Edit   Find: Next

Figure 1.8: Cost center group in Fiori

In summary, moving to an S/4HANA release and the new user experiences will impact SAP users in general and CCA users in particular. The general impact includes change management issues related to the new user interfaces and how this will affect day-to-day system interaction. More area-specific impacts are alterations in system functionality such as changes in master data functionality, using embedded BPC for planning, and new apps for reporting.

1.5 Summary

In this chapter, you have seen that CCA is one of the primary modules within SAP CO and that it is mostly concerned with managing overhead costs. You have learned about the two major sub-modules in SAP finance, FI and CO, and their respective roles. At a high level, you have seen where CCA fits in the CO module. Finally, you have seen some of the new developments in S/4HANA and in the newer SAP user experience provided by business client and Fiori, as well as how these changes may affect CCA.

2 Master data in CCA

One way of classifying data in SAP is to differentiate between items that are considered master data and items that are considered transactional data. In SAP, master data is relatively static data that is defined once and is shared throughout the application. Examples include vendors, customers, materials, general ledger accounts, cost centers, and profit centers. This master data then is used in transactional data such as invoices, accounting documents, and material movements. In an SAP implementation project, the structure and definition of master data should be thoroughly planned to reflect the needs of the business properly. Careful consideration should be given to such factors as numbering and naming the master data, permitted field values, and the ultimate reporting aims of the business. In this chapter, you will see the relevant master data available in CCA.

2.1 Cost center

As discussed in the previous chapter, the definition of the cost centers represents the organization from a cost control perspective. Once the master data is defined, the cost centers are arranged in a hierarchy to represent the structure of the enterprise from a cost control responsibility perspective. During the design of the system, the nature of that responsibility structure should be determined. On what parameters or criteria are the costs managed? Is it on a geographical basis, a functional basis, a product line basis, some other method, or a combination of some of the above? Usually a cost center should have an owner or manager to ensure that someone owns the responsibility for the plan and the costs.

As you will see, multiple views or hierarchies can be created using cost center groups to represent different ways of arranging the cost center structure. This concept will be discussed later in this chapter. At a minimum, you need to have a Standard Hierarchy, which needs to contain all the cost centers within the controlling area. Technically, the name of this hierarchy is defined first in the configuration settings and assigned to the controlling area before the cost center masters can be created.

The cost centers can be created either through the individual creation transaction code KS01 (see Figure 2.1) or directly within the standard hierarchy (this option will be shown later).

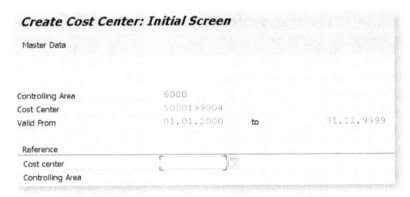

Create Cost Center: Initial Screen

Master Data

Controlling Area	6000
Cost Center	5000199004
Valid From	01.01.2000 to 31.12.9999

Reference

Cost center	
Controlling Area	

Figure 2.1: Create cost center initial screen

Set the controlling area

 Often, when entering transactions in the controlling module in SAP, you are presented with a preliminary screen asking you to enter the controlling area. Having to enter the controlling area constantly can become aggravating, especially when you may only be working with one area. The solution to this is to set your controlling area using transaction OKKS. Enter the controlling area that you work with and press the save button. The value is now stored in your user parameters and remains until you set it to a different value.

It is important to understand how you will name or number pieces of master data such as cost centers before you create them. Unlike some master data objects in SAP, a number range object does not drive cost center numbering. In fact, it is free form. You are limited by the field size

of up to 10 characters, and there are a few special characters such as *
that will be rejected; otherwise, you can use any alphanumeric combination you choose.

You should also know the cost center is specific to the controlling area
and not to the company code. This means it is not possible to have a
duplicate cost center identifier value within the same controlling area. For
example, you might have several company codes assigned to the same
controlling area, and you may have the same departmental function in
each of those company codes. As an example, in a legacy application,
you may have an HR department in two different companies, and this
legacy application will allow you to use the same department identifier in
each company. For instance, Human Resources might be department
100 in each of the company codes. In SAP, this will not work since we
cannot duplicate the identifier 100 in the same controlling area. In SAP,
you will need to work in another way. Perhaps by adding the prefix of the
company code or some other logic, you can build your cost center hierarchy without having duplicate numbers. You might have the logic that
the identifier 100 remains to mean Human Resources, but you add a
prefix to represent the company code so you would have cost centers
6000100 and 6100100. These kinds of thought processes need to occur
with cost center numbering in SAP.

When you have decided on your cost center number, go ahead with
transaction KS01. You will need to enter VALID FROM and TO dates. It is
important to understand that the cost center is considered a *time-based*
object in controlling, which means it is created with a validity period, and
you can create different data values for different periods.

In configuration, certain fields on the master data can be flagged as *time
dependent*, resulting in SAP storing a new master record whenever a
time-dependent field is changed on a cost center. The ability to create
time-based objects is a very important aspect of controlling since it allows you to view master data values at different periods. For example,
the person responsible for the cost center may change next year. If person responsible is a time-dependent field, then you will have a view of
the cost center master when Miles was the person responsible, and then
a new view starting when person responsible is reassigned.

Defining time dependent fields

 Since every change to a time-dependent field causes SAP to write a new master record for the data object being changed, you should be very careful in defining fields as time dependent in the system configuration. By defining many time-dependent fields, the data volumes can become large, and match-code searches can become confusing for the user, as a piece of master data with more than one-time range will appear multiple times in a match-code search. The SAP-delivered configuration should be sufficient for most situations.

The time dependency of other master data is checked when you assign a cost center to it, such as a profit center. For example, if you created a profit center to be valid from 01/01/2015 onwards, you cannot create a cost center assigned to that profit center with a valid-from date earlier than 01/01/2015.

Valid-from dates and other master data

 It is best to be aware of other master data requirements when you are setting up validity dates for cost centers, profit centers, and other CO objects. There may be re-quirements from other modules, such as HR or fixed assets, that the cost centers should exist for a certain time in the past to allow historical data to be loaded. It is good to know that before you create your cost centers and profit centers to avoid extra rework to extend the validity periods.

The final section on the initial screen allows you to use an existing cost center from the same or different controlling area as a template from which to copy your new cost center.

Copying master data

Many master data objects will have a COPY FROM or CREATE WITH REFERENCE option to allow you to use an existing piece of master data as a template for your new entry. This can significantly speed up the creation of new pieces of master data.

The most important information about the cost center is contained on the BASIC DATA tab. (see Figure 2.2).

Cost Center	5000199004		
Controlling Area	6000	Smarter Sisters Games	
Valid From	01.01.2000	to	31.12.9999

Basic data	Control	Templates	Address	Communication	History

Names

Name	US Corporate IT
Description	US Corporate IT

Basic data

User Responsible	
Person Responsible	Miles Cable
Department	IT
Cost Center Category	H
Hierarchy area	5000199
Company Code	6000
Business Area	
Functional Area	
Currency	
Profit Center	500040

Figure 2.2: Create cost center basic data

On this tab, you will define the **Name** and **Description** of the cost center. These are essentially a short text value and a longer text value to define the cost center name. You should maintain both values since some reports and evaluations will use the Name and others will use the Description, depending on the available space.

Other key fields on the BASIC DATA tab are **person responsible**; this is the person responsible for the results of the cost center, presumably the cost center manager. There is also **user responsible**, which links to the user master in the SAP system. This field is not mandatory since it is possible that the person responsible for the cost center does not exist as a user in the SAP system. The **department** field is a free text field that can be used to store an external department number. There is no validation on the entry in this field, so the user creating the cost center can enter any value they choose. This may be used to store a department identifier from pre-SAP systems which can be used as a cross reference.

The cost center category contains codes that have been created in the SAP configuration settings (see Figure 2.3). These can be used for a variety of control purposes, which we will explore later, and also populate default values into the cost center as it is being created. The category should relate to the function or purpose of the cost center. Ideally, each cost center should serve one primary function for example production or administration. If you are having trouble assigning categories to your cost centers because you think the cost center performs more than one function, then you may need to rethink your cost center design.

Cost center categories

CCtC	Name	Qty	ActPri	ActSec	ActRev	PlnPri	PlnSec	PlnRev	Cmmt	Func
A	Allocation Cost Pool				✓			✓		YB20
E	Development				✓			✓		YB50
F	Production/Plant	✓			✓			✓		YB20
G	Logistics				✓			✓		YB20
H	Service cost center	✓			✓			✓		YB40
L	Management				✓			✓		YB40
M	Materials				✓			✓		YB20
P	P Maintenance				✓			✓		YB20
S	Social				✓			✓		YB40
V	Sales/Marketing				✓			✓		YB30
W	Finance / Admin				✓			✓		YB40
X	Exploration				✓			✓		YB50

Figure 2.3: Cost center categories configuration

The field **Hierarchy node** makes the link between the cost center and its place in the standard hierarchy. The *hierarchy node* selected here is a *node* in the standard cost center hierarchy. The **company code** is the FI company code that the cost center is assigned to. This is a mandatory assignment, and a cost center can only be assigned to one company code at a time. This assignment is always time-dependent and can only be changed at the end of a fiscal year. The **business area** is an optional assignment in this case, as we are not using *business areas* in this system. The business area is another FI organizational object that can define separate areas of operations or responsibilities within an organization. The functionality and use of business area has been largely superseded by profit center and segment, although you might see business areas being used in industry-specific SAP solutions. Like the company code, the business area assignment is always time-based and also can only be changed at a fiscal year end.

During the creation of the cost center, the fields for **functional area** and **currency** will not be open for input. The *functional area* will default into the cost center based on the value assigned to the cost center category (see Figure 2.3) that you select. The currency will default into the cost center based on the configured local currency of the company code that you have selected. The functional area will become open during the creation of the cost center and can be changed from the default value. The currency on the cost center, which is known as the *object currency* in CO, cannot be changed to a value different from that of the assigned company code.

The final field on the basic data tab is the profit center. If you are using profit center accounting, either in the classic mode or as a scenario in the new general ledger, you will need to assign the cost center to a profit center. The purpose of assigning cost objects such as cost centers or orders to profit centers is to ensure that profit centers receive postings when the assigned objects receive postings and that users do not need to intervene manually. One assignment we do not see on the cost center is the *segment*. The segment is an organizational element that was introduced to SAP as part of the new GL. If you have not migrated to the new GL, you will not see the segment as a field in accounting postings, and you will not have to worry about it. If you have either migrated to the new GL or have always used new GL, then you may have the segment, and you will have considered how the segment is used in your organization. In a new general ledger system, the segment is assigned directly to the profit center, so it is unnecessary to also assign it on the cost center as the segment will be derived through the profit center assignment.

Additional parameter information is found on the CONTROL tab (see Figure 2.4).

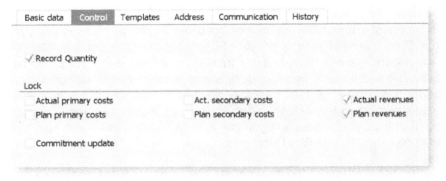

Figure 2.4: Cost center control tab

All the values on this tab will default into the cost center based on the cost center category selected on the BASIC DATA tab. If you look back at Figure 2.3, you will see that the settings for cost center category H have been adopted as defaults. These defaults can be changed, but it is rec-ommended to define the relevant categories and values so you don't need to manipulate these settings manually when creating cost centers.

The RECORD QUANTITY indicator on the cost center works in conjunction with the RECORD QTY indicator in the cost element (see Figure 2.5)

Cost Element	545010	Natural Gas
Controlling Area	6000	Smarter Sisters Games
Valid From	01.01.2010	to 31.12.9999

Basic Data	Indicators	Default Acct Assgnmt	History

Consumption quantities

✓ Record qty

Unit of Measure   M3

Figure 2.5 Qty indicator on the cost element

If both these indicators are checked, then in a posting involving the cost element and the cost center SAP will check whether you have entered a quantity and unit of measure in the posting. If the quantity is missing, there will be a warning message. In planning, using this combination of cost element and cost center, the system will enforce the unit of measure assigned to the cost element during the entry of the plan data.

Below the RECORD QUANTITY indicator in Figure 2.4 are the LOCK indicators. These indicate that the cost center is locked against the type of posting for which the indicator is checked. It is possible to lock the cost center against actual postings for primary costs, for secondary costs, and for revenues. It is important to note that even if the lock is inactive for actual revenues, the revenue posting will only be statistical to the cost center. In planning, it is also possible to lock against the same types of transactions. The last lock indicator is the COMMITMENTS UPDATE.

The term commitment in SAP generally means a contractual obligation for costs that will be incurred. It is possible to track commitments against many cost objects in SAP, including cost centers, internal orders, maintenance orders, production orders, and elements of projects such as work breakdown structures. Commitment management should be activated at the general controlling organization level in the system configuration (see Figure 2.6) before it can be activated for individual cost objects. Sometimes the activation of commitment tracking is activated on the master data for cost centers; other times, some additional configuration may be required.

Controlling Area	6000 Smarter Sisters Games
Fiscal Year	2007 to 9999
Activate Components	
Cost Centers	1 Component active
√ AA: Activity Type	
Order Management	1 Component active
Commit. Management	1 Components active
ProfitAnalysis	2 Component active for costing-based Profitability Analysis
Acty-Based Costing	Component Not Active

Figure 2.6: Commitment activation at controlling area

In most standard SAP systems, the types of obligations we see generating commitments in CO are cost object-assigned purchase requisitions and purchase orders from the materials management (MM) module. We will see examples of this later on when we discuss actual cost center posting.

The next tab on the cost center master contains links to *templates* that can be used to allocate planned or actual costs in SAP. Templates are sophisticated calculation tools primarily used in the *activity-based costing* component in SAP but can also be used in other modules such as cost center accounting and product costing to allocate planned or actual costs. You will notice on the template tab in Figure 2.7 that several templates can be assigned to the cost center for various purposes, such as *formula planning*. This functionality allows you to generate planned values in the cost center based on formulas defined in the template. In the cost center, you can assign formula planning templates for *activity-independent planning* and for *activity-dependent planning*.

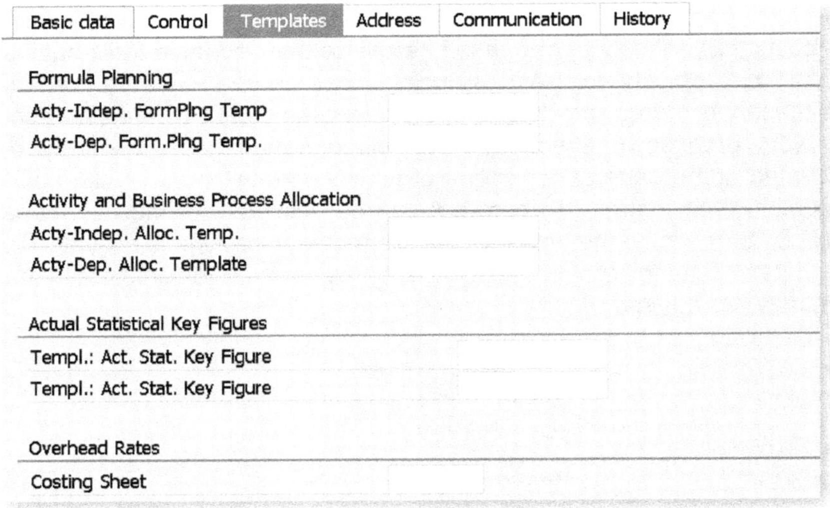

Basic data	Control	Templates	Address	Communication	History

Formula Planning

Acty-Indep. FormPlng Temp

Acty-Dep. Form.Plng Temp.

Activity and Business Process Allocation

Acty-Indep. Alloc. Temp.

Acty-Dep. Alloc. Template

Actual Statistical Key Figures

Templ.: Act. Stat. Key Figure

Templ.: Act. Stat. Key Figure

Overhead Rates

Costing Sheet

Figure 2.7: Cost center templates tab

Templates also can be assigned for actual activity and business process allocation. These templates would be used to allocate actual activity-independent or activity-dependent costs to the cost center periodically. It is also possible to assign two templates for actual statistical key figure calculation. Although the two fields have the same description, the first one is used for posting to a cost center, and the second one is for posting to a combination cost center and activity type.

The final possible assignment on the TEMPLATES tab is a *costing sheet*. The costing sheet is another allocation tool that is used primarily in product costing but can also be used as another method to move costs from a sending cost center to some other receiving cost object using percentage- or quantity-based overhead rates. By assigning a costing sheet on the cost center master, we are identifying the cost center as a receiving object for the overhead costs calculated by the costing sheet. If we were using actual overhead allocation and/or actual template allocation, then these would usually be periodic steps that would be run as part of the fiscal period closing process.

Template allocations

 The template allocation process is simply another way of moving costs around within SAP controlling. Although the tool is somewhat complex, the concept does not differ from other methods of cost allocation such as activity allocation, assessment, distribution, or settlement. Similar to the other forms of allocation, there will be cost objects that will send the costs, and there will be other cost objects that receive the costs. There also will be rules defining how much will be allocated from the senders to the receivers. The sender(s) and the rules are defined in the template. Then, the template is assigned to the receiving cost objects. If you keep this overall concept in mind, it will help when trying to design and use templates.

The next two tabs, ADDRESS and COMMUNICATION, allow you to enter the address, tax jurisdiction, language, telephone, fax, etc. for the profit center. If you are required to store this information at the cost center level, then the fields are available but not mandatory. The final tab, HISTORY, may become useful if you want to see who created the master data object or to see if any changes have been made to it.

Cost Center	5000199004	US Corporate IT	
Controlling Area	6000	Smarter Sisters Games	
Valid From	01.01.2000	to	31.12.9999

| Basic data | Control | Templates | Address | Communication | History |

History Data					
Created by		JPRINGLE			
on		02.02.2017		🔍 Change document	

Figure 2.8: Cost center history tab

The change document button (see Figure 2.8) will display all field changes to the master data (see Figure 2.9), and by clicking on the field, it will show the old and new values, who made the change, and when it was made (see Figure 2.10).

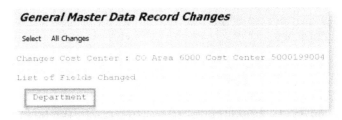

General Master Data Record Changes

Select   All Changes

Changes Cost Center : CO Area 6000 Cost Center 5000199004

List of Fields Changed

Department

Figure 2.9: Changed fields in the cost center

Changes Cost Center : CO Area 6000 Cost Center 5000199004

Date	Field Name	Valid From	Valid To	L	New Value	Old Value
02.02.2017	Department	01.01.2000	31.12.9999	EN	US IT	IT

Figure 2.10: Changed field detail

After you have created the cost center master using the transaction KS01, you can use transaction code KS02 to go back and make changes or transaction KS03 to display the master data. It is also possible to perform all these functions through the standard hierarchy, as you will see in the next section.

Once you have created your cost centers and started to use them, you may be interested in finding where your cost centers are used in allocations or in other master data elements. In the KS02 transaction, you can use the **where-used list** function that is accessed from the **environment** menu. (See Figure 2.11.) As an example, you can see what activity types are linked to this cost center through *activity planning*. Select the **where-used list** menu option, and then select the **activity types** option to get a report (see Figure 2.12). The **overall values** option gives a report on every area in one display.

If you are using the SAP business client with the cost center manager role provided in the FIN_CO_CCMGMT business function, or the FIORI app for manage cost centers to access the cost center master data, then the view will be slightly different and there will be some additional functionality. The approach using the business client will be shown; however, other than a few largely cosmetic differences in the search options and the screen layout, the FIORI app view is much the same. You will see the initial search screen for the Web Dynpro application in Figure 2.13

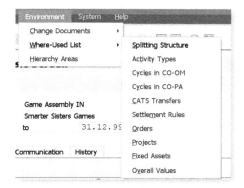

Figure 2.11: Cost center where-used

Display Activity Type Control Data

Controlling Area   6000   Smarter Sisters Game
Cost Center   5000101003 Game Assembly IN

ActTyp	Act. type short text	Year	Vsn	AllocCElem	Price ind.	
1000	Prod Labour	2016	0	943000	1	
1100	Prod Overhead	2016	0	943010	1	

Figure 2.12: Activity types used with cost center

Search: Cost Centers

Saved Searches:

· **Search Criteria**

Cost Center	is		
Cost Center Name	is		
Company Code	is	6000	

Maximum Number of Results   100

Search   Clear Entries   Reset to Default   Save Search As

Figure 2.13: Web Dynpro cost center search

The main thing to note is that the search is entirely flexible. There are three columns in the search: the field, the matching criteria, and the value being matched. Then to the right there are ⊕⊖ buttons that will allow you to add or remove search rows. Within both the field column and the matching criteria column, you can select values to build the search (see Figure 2.14).

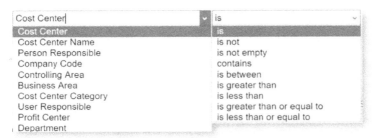

Figure 2.14: Flexible search selections

Once you run the search based on your inputted criteria, the results will be shown in a lower section of the screen (see Figure 2.15).

Figure 2.15: Results list for search

From the results list, you can select a cost center and click on the edit ✎ Edit button to open the cost center in edit mode or double click on the cost center name to open in display mode.

Figure 2.16: Web Dynpro view of cost center master

The first thing you will notice on the master data screen shown in Figure 2.16 is that the tabs are no longer present. Instead, we have stackable sections that can be opened and closed by a toggle ˀ button. These mostly correspond to the tabs that you see in the standard SAP GUI transaction. The major differences are:

▶ The original BASIC DATA tab has been split into two sections, GE-NERAL DATA and ORGANIZATIONAL UNITS.

▶ The HISTORY tab is now called COMPLIANCE.

▶ There is a new section for TRANSLATION AND LONG TEXT.

The addition of the translation section (see Figure 2.17) is a welcome feature since it was previously more difficult to maintain multiple language texts on the cost center master.

· **Translation and Long Text**

Insert

Language	Name	Description	Long Text
English	Finance - Corp	Corporate Finance	
French	Compt. financ.	Compt. financ.	
Spanish	Finanzas	Finanzas	

Figure 2.17: Cost center translation and long text

The **where-used list** is still available in the Web Dynpro application through a button, rather than through a menu. In addition, a **hierarchy**

area button will take you directly to the standard hierarchy node where the cost center is assigned (see Figure 2.18).

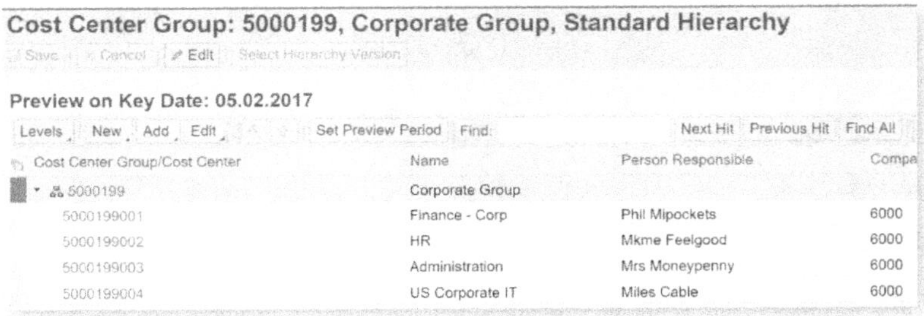

Figure 2.18: Hierarchy area

2.2 Cost center standard hierarchy

It is necessary to define a standard hierarchy for cost centers before you create the cost center master data. This is a hierarchy or tree structure that is assigned to the controlling area (see Figure 2.19). The hierarchy can take any form that you require to represent the structure of your organization. The hierarchy can be built by creating multiple levels known as nodes or groups. All of your cost centers must be assigned somewhere within the standard hierarchy.

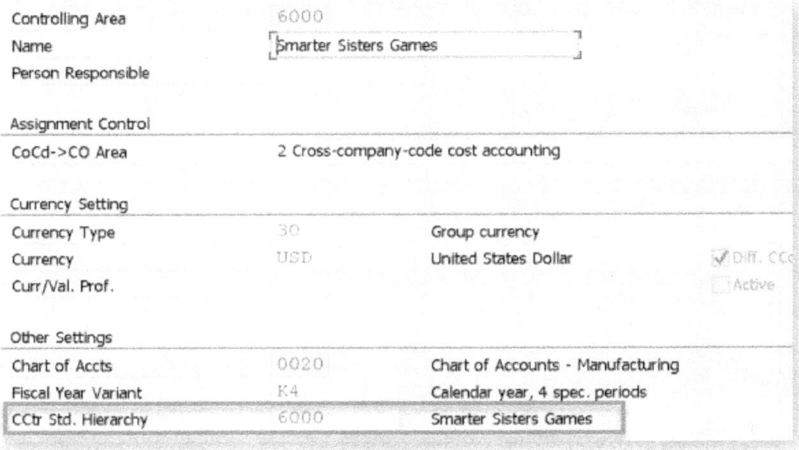

Figure 2.19: Controlling area settings assign hierarchy

The standard hierarchy is a particular type of cost center group that requires all the cost centers within the controlling area to be assigned to it. The overall hierarchy, and the groups within it, can be used functionally in SAP for planning, allocations, and reporting. If alternative groupings of cost centers are required for these functions, it is possible to create additional groups that are not linked to the standard hierarchy. This is shown in a following section on cost center groups.

The cost center standard hierarchy can be edited using transaction code OKEON and can be displayed using transaction OKENN (see Figure 2.20). You saw in the previous sections how to create, change, and display cost centers using transactions KS01, KS02, and KS03. These functions are also available directly in the standard hierarchy change transaction OKEON. Within this transaction, you use the create button 🗋 . to create cost center groups (nodes) or cost centers themselves (see Figure 2.21). The object is created relative to where you have your cursor positioned in the hierarchy. When you create a cost center in this way, you will not have to enter the hierarchy node on the screen as it will assume the value based on where your cursor is positioned in the hierarchy.

Standard Hierarchy for Cost Centers Change

Object Manager

as of   01.01.2017

Standard Hierarchy	Name	Activation status	Person responsible	Company code
6000	Smarter Sisters Games			
50001	US Group			
5000101	Indiana Plant			
5000101A	Board Games			
5000101001	Board Cutting Indiana	▣	Vincent Crane	6000
5000101002	Board Pasting Indiana	▣	Isaac Newton	6000
5000101003	Game Final Assembly Indiana	▣	Charles Dixon	6000
5000101004	Game Parts Bagging	▣	Al Crowley	6000
5000101B	Card Games			
5000101C	Video Games			
5000101Y	Plant Maintenance			
5000101Z	Plant Admin/Support			
5000102	Kentucky Plant			
5000103	Central Distriution Center			
5000104	Sales and Marketing			
5000199	Corporate Group			

Figure 2.20: Standard hierarchy framework

Lower-Level Group

Group at Same Level

Cost Center

     5000101A

Figure 2.21: Create options within OKEON

If you create your cost centers at an incorrect node of the hierarchy, you can use the mouse to drag and drop the cost center(s) or cost center group(s) into the correct position(s). Once you drag the profit center(s) to the correct node(s), you can organize them within the node(s) by using the MOVE ▲ ▼ buttons. When you drag and drop a cost center within the hierarchy, it will update the hierarchy node in the master data automatically, based on where you place the cost center.

Each node of the hierarchy is its own cost center group, and it is possible to see the history at each node within a hierarchy. On the basic data tab of the group, (see Figure 2.22) you can click on the change history 🗨 button to see what has happened to the group.

Basic data	Report information		
Group Name	5000199	Corporate Group	
Change Data			
Created By	JPRINGLE		
	📅 14.11.2016	🕐 11:00:45	
Last changed by	JPRINGLE		
	📅 02.02.2017	🕐 14:36:59	🗨

Figure 2.22: Cost center group basic data

Depending on the organization and how the standard hierarchy is used, the hierarchy can become large and complex. While every cost center must belong to the standard hierarchy and this rule is enforced, it is possible to create cyclical relationships within the hierarchy that cause an ambiguity. It is a good practice to run the ambiguity check occasionally to discover such errors. With your cursor on the top node of the hierarchy, select from the menu EXTRAS • AMBIGUITY CHECK to display any ambiguities (see Figure 2.23).

The standard hierarchy maintenance in the FIORI or business client interface is done through the cost center group maintenance transaction or app. Most of the functionality is similar to the regular SAP transaction, with a few additions. Similar to the cost center master, the cost center group now has a TRANSLATION AND LONG TEXT section. This makes it easier to maintain hierarchy node descriptions in multiple languages. Another change is that through versioning, hierarchies can be created in advance and set as inactive until you are ready to use them. Finally, a change request process has been provided to support changes to cost center master data in a manner compliant with the *Sarbanes-Oxley Act*.

Figure 2.23: Ambiguity check

2.3   Cost center groups

Groups of master data commonly are used within the SAP controlling module to aid with functionality in the areas of planning, allocations, and reporting. Within cost center accounting, you will likely group cost centers for three reasons:

▶   In planning to assist with plan data entry—pre-defined groups are easier to use than ranges of cost centers.

▶   In allocations—groups are useful in defining both senders and receivers in allocation cycles.

▶   In reporting—groups can be created for reporting requirements and saved for future use.

These groups, sometimes referred to as *alternative hierarchies*, share many of the characteristics of the standard hierarchy, but do not have to contain all the cost centers in the controlling area. The groups are created in transaction KSH1 and can contain any combination of cost centers organized in any manner (see Figure 2.24). In the following example, you want to group all the marketing cost centers in North America together to see a combined view of the marketing costs.

45

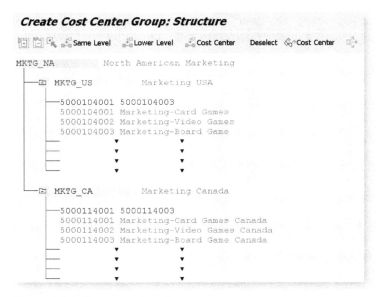

Figure 2.24: Create cost center group

Use groups in configuration

 It is generally a good practice to use groups in configuration rather than individual values or ranges. There are pieces of configuration where it is necessary to reference cost elements, internal orders, cost centers, or other CO objects. Often the configuration will give the option of referencing a range versus a group. Here, the group is usually the better option since it provides more future flexibility. If you configure a range, and new master data is added later that does not fall into the range, then a configuration change is required which will have to be transported through your system landscape to reach the production system. If you reference a group in the setup, since the group is master data, no configuration change and subsequent transports are required. The group can be adjusted to include the new data without significant delays.

The groups can be edited in transaction KSH2. In both KSH1 and KSH2, the same TOOLBAR is available. The group maintenance in KSH1 and KSH2 is not as user friendly and intuitive as the maintenance in the standard hierarchy. There is no drag-and-drop functionality or delete button. To delete items, you need to use the select ▧ button to mark the item; this will also open new options on the TOOLBAR. In Figure 2.25 I have added an incorrect cost center to my group and I want to remove it.

Figure 2.25: Remove unwanted item from the group

I have clicked on the item and pressed the select ▧ button. The selected item will appear highlighted in red. Now from the new TOOLBAR I can select the action that I want. Here, I want to remove the Corporate Canada cost center from the group. Therefore, I click the remove ▨ button and save the change. I could also use the INSERT options or move items to different places within the group structure.

The final button worth discussing for groups is the where-used ⬀ button. As mentioned, groups are used to support a variety of functions in SAP. They may be referenced somewhere in the system configuration or may be used in an allocation or within a report painter report. It is always useful to find out where a group is being used before changing it. To support this, SAP provides the where-used function. Clicking on the ⬀ button will allow you to select where you want to search for the use of the group (see Figure 2.26) and will return a report showing where the group is used based on the items you have selected. Figure 2.27 shows the group MKTG_NA is used in two allocation cycles and in a validation rule.

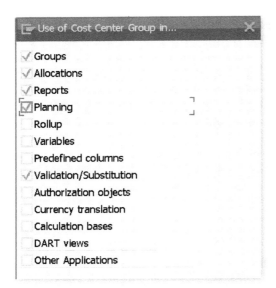

Figure 2.26: Selection for use of cost center groups

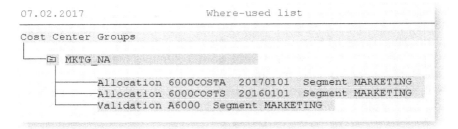

Figure 2.27: Where-used report for cost center groups

Moving cost center groups to another SAP system

 In an SAP implementation project, there are generally multiple systems involved. There will be at least a development system, a quality or test system, and a production system. Within the development and test systems, there may also be multiple clients such as a configuration client, a test client, and a sandbox client. It can be considerable effort to build your groups manually within each of these systems and clients. To assist, SAP has provided an export/import option for groups available under the EXTRAS menu. The group can be exported as a text file either to the SAP file system or to your computer (select the presentation server option), then imported into another SAP system or client. If you are just moving groups within the same client, then there is also a COPY FROM CLIENT option under the same menu.

The basic create, move, and remove functions shown in the cost center group are standard across all group transactions within the controlling module. The groups for other controlling objects such as *profit centers*, *cost elements*, *internal orders*, *activity types*, and *statistical key figures* can be manipulated in a similar manner to cost center groups.

The ambiguity check functionality we saw with the standard hierarchy is also available for cost center groups as are several other useful features. The first is the ability to copy a hierarchy with a suffix that can be done from transaction KSH1. It can be used to copy cost center groups or to make a time-based copy of the standard hierarchy. It may be most useful for those organizations that choose not to use the standard hierarchy for reporting purposes and maintain a lean standard structure. In those instances, cost center groups are used to represent the reporting structure of the business, and the standard hierarchy is treated as a necessary formality. Companies following this approach may make periodic copies of their reporting structure and then edit the copy to reflect changes in that structure. From the menu in KSH1, choose GROUP • COPY. Then, on the screen displayed in Figure 2.28, enter the group and the suffix. The copy results are shown in Figure 2.29.

Copy Cost Center Group: Initial Screen

Controlling Area	6000
Cost Center Group	6000
Copying with suffix	2017

Figure 2.28: Copy group with suffix

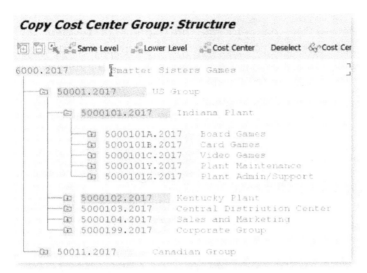

Figure 2.29: Group copied with suffix

If your copied group is supposed to contain all the cost centers in the controlling area, then you can use the menu option EXTRAS • CHECK AND HELP • CHECK COMPLETENESS to ensure that there are no missing cost centers. There is also a function under the same menu path to **delete unused groups.** This can be useful for cleaning up your hierarchies.

As we discussed in the previous section, in a FIORI or business client interface, all cost center group maintenance including standard hierarchy maintenance is done through the cost center group maintenance transaction or app.

2.4   Cost elements

The cost elements used in cost center accounting and other controlling applications are based on the *chart of accounts* assigned to the controlling area. If you are working in the ECC world, you can still speak of cost elements as distinct from GL accounts. In the S/4 HANA world, that distinction mostly has been removed. As you saw in Section 1.2, there are two broad types of cost element in controlling.

▶ Cost elements where transactions flow from financial accounting into controlling—these are known as primary cost elements.

▶ Cost elements used for moving costs around in controlling only—these are known as secondary cost elements.

Within the two broad groupings, the cost elements further are broken down by category. The category sub-divides the cost elements and determines their use. The categories available for primary cost elements are shown in Figure 2.30.

Category	Description	Use
1	Primary costs/cost-reducing revenues	Used for cost postings flowing from FI
3	Accrual/deferral per surcharge	Used for posting imputed costs during accrual calculations
4	Accrual/deferral per debit = actual	Used for posting imputed costs during accrual calculations
11	Revenues	Used to post revenues
12	Sales deduction	Used to post sales deductions like discounts or rebates
22	External settlement	Used to settle to objects outside CO such as balance sheet accounts

Figure 2.30: Primary cost element categories

The categories available for secondary cost elements are shown in Figure 2.31.

Category	Description	Use
21	Internal Settlement	Used to settle to objects within CO
31	Order/project results analysis	Used to store results analysis data on order/project
41	Overhead Rates	Used to allocate overhead costs
42	Assessment	Used to allocate costs during an assessment
43	Internal activity allocation	Used to allocate costs during an activity allocation
50	Incoming Orders Sales Revenue	Used for sales revenue for project related sales orders
51	Incoming Orders Other Revenue	Used for other revenue for project related sales orders
52	Incoming orders Costs	Used for costs from project related sales orders
61	Earned Value	Used for earned value analysis in project systems

Figure 2.31: Secondary cost element categories

The creation of primary cost elements can be tied to the creation of the underlying GL account so that the cost element creation is largely transparent to the end user. This is achieved through a configuration setting on the chart of accounts that specifies either manual or automatic creation of cost elements. In addition, the configuration settings for automatic generation of cost elements shown in Figure 2.32 assist with the assignment of the correct category to the cost element. If a GL account is created in a range defined in this screen, then the primary cost or revenue element will be created automatically with the correct cost element category.

Change View "Automatic Generation of Cost Elements:

New Entries

| Chart of Accts | 0020 |
| Description | Chart of Accounts - Manufacturing |

Automatic Generation of Cost Elements: Default Setting

Acct from	Account to	CElem cat.	Short Descript.
400000	439999	11	Revenues
440000	440000	1	Primary costs/cost-reducing revenues
500010	899999	1	Primary costs/cost-reducing revenues

Figure 2.32: Configuration auto generation of cost elements

Since secondary cost elements are not tied to any GL accounts, they must be created manually using their own transaction code, KA06. If primary cost elements are not created automatically, then transaction KA01 can be used. Both primary and secondary cost elements can be edited using the KA02 transaction.

The master data for the cost element is simple. Besides the name, description, and the cost element categories, there are only a few other fields worth mentioning. You saw the quantity indicators already in Figure 2.5, and the functionality was already discussed. There is an opportunity to assign default account assignment objects such as a cost center or an order directly to a cost element (see Figure 2.33). This is a very limiting way of assigning defaults since it defines one default object for the cost element for the entire controlling area. Assigning account assignment objects directly to a cost element rarely is used. The preferred approach is to assign default account assignment objects in the configuration transaction OKB9, where you can specify defaults in a more flexible manner by including other elements like a company code, profit center, or plant into the determination rule. Finally, there is a HISTORY tab which allows you to see the change history, similar to what is available on the cost center.

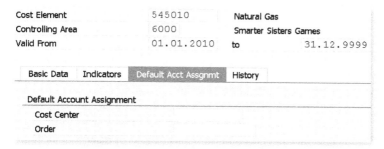

Cost Element	545010	Natural Gas
Controlling Area	6000	Smarter Sisters Games
Valid From	01.01.2010	to	31.12.9999

| Basic Data | Indicators | Default Acct Assgnmt | History |

Default Account Assignment
  Cost Center
  Order

Figure 2.33: Cost element default account assignment

2.5   Activity types

Before exploring the master data of the activity type, it is important to understand exactly why they are needed. Activity types are used to represent something that is done or provided by a cost center that can be defined in quantity terms. After the cost center, the activity type is probably the most important piece of master data in cost center accounting. It is what allows the integration of cost center accounting with many other modules in SAP such as product cost planning, production planning, and plant maintenance. The activity type carries the activity cost and quantity from the source cost center to the receiving object, thus allowing the absorption of labor and overhead costs by those objects. Probably the most common activity types are ones used to represent internal labor or machine time, but there are many other times where the use of activities may be appropriate to allocate costs.

For activities to be used, it is necessary for them to be assigned to the providing cost center and to have a planned unit price. The cost center assignment and creation of the price is done through activity output and price planning in cost center accounting. You will see how later when planning is discussed in Section 3.4.

Activities can be used in two types of allocations. The most common and easiest to understand is called *direct activity allocation*. This is where a cost center directly provides an activity to another object. Most often, this is a pull relationship where confirmation of a production order or plant maintenance order will pull activity quantities from the cost center associated with the appropriate work center. Direct activity allocations can also be created through posting time sheet entries in the *CATS* tool in SAP, as well as manually using transaction KB21N.

The second type of activity allocation is called *indirect activity allocation*. This is used when direct activity allocation is not possible but you still want to allocate costs and quantities from the sending cost center to the receiving objects. Indirect activity allocation is set up in a *cycle/segment* method similar to assessments and distributions; however, quantities as well as costs are allocated. You will see an example of how this works in cost center planning and in actual postings a little later in the book.

The activity type is created in transaction KL01 (see Figure 2.34). Similar to cost centers, activity types are time-based and may have a variety of validity periods if certain master data elements have changed. You can refer to Section 2.1 to refresh your memory on time-based master data.

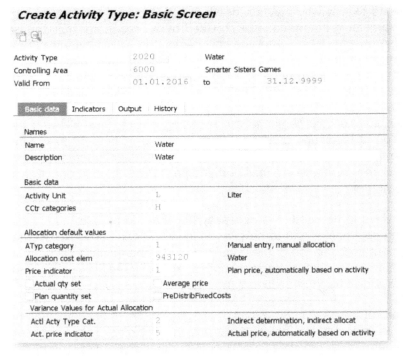

Figure 2.34: Activity type master

The activity type should be given a meaningful name and description. The activity unit should relate to the purpose of the activity. In Figure 2.34, I am creating an activity to allocate water costs from a general plant utilities cost center to production cost centers that actually use the water. It makes sense that water would be tracked in a volume unit such as liters or gallons. For activities that will be used in direct allocations through production task lists such as routings, it is important to ensure that the unit of measure on the activity is dimensionally consistent with the units of measure used in your task lists. For example, using H (hour) on an activity and MIN (minute) on a routing is okay, since they both belong to the time dimension, but using L (liter) on an activity and MIN (minute) on the routing would not work.

The field CCTR CATEGORIES can restrict the use of the activity type to only the categories of the cost center listed. Using a "*" in this field will mean that the activity can be used with all categories of the cost center. The fields ATYP CATEGORY (for planned activity) and ACTL ACTY TYPE CAT (for actual activity) relate to the use of the activity type in either direct or indirect activity allocation.

▶ Category 1 (manual entry, manual allocation) is the most commonly used. This is for direct activity allocations, for manual postings using KB21N, and for posting using timesheets (CATS).

▶ Category 2 (indirect determination, indirect allocation) is used in indirect activity allocation when the sender activity quantity can only be determined indirectly, either in the defined sender/receiver relationships, the receiver tracing factors, or based on fixed values in the allocation segments.

▶ Category 3 (manual entry, indirect allocation) is used in indirect allocation when the activities of the sending cost center are entered manually using the enter sender activities transaction KB51N. Then, these are allocated to receivers using tracing factors such as statistical key figures.

▶ Category 4 (manual entry, no allocation) only allows manual entry of activity values but cannot be used for allocation.

The activity type requires an ALLOCATION COST ELEMENT; this must be a secondary cost element with a category 43. In a manufacturing company using product costing, the cost elements used in activity allocation should be considered in the cost component structure that you will use for product costing.

There are two price indicator fields on the activity type. The first, simply called PRICE INDICATOR, is related to planned activity prices. The second, called ACT PRICE INDICATOR, is related to actual activity prices. There are various options for the PRICE INDICATOR and the ACT PRICE INDICATOR. These indicators control how the plan or actual activity price should be determined. For example, it might be calculated automatically by the system or determined manually, and the calculation could be based on the activity quantity or the capacity of the activity in the cost center.

- ▶ 1–Plan price, automatically based on activity
- ▶ 2–Plan price automatically based on capacity
- ▶ 3–Plan price Determine manually
- ▶ 5–Actual price, automatically based on activity
- ▶ 6–Actual price, automatically based on capacity
- ▶ 7–Manually determined for actual allocations

The decision here is whether you want the system to automatically calculate activity prices or calculate and enter them manually. If you want the system to calculate the prices, then you decide whether the denominator for the price calculation is based on activity (either planned or actual) or capacity. All other things being equal, capacity is less likely to change over time, so it will provide a more stable activity price. On the other hand, depending on the business, activity quantities may fluctuate and give a more variable monthly activity price. If you select manual determination, it is still possible to calculate activity prices that will not be used for allocation. These are called *purely iterative prices,* and there is a setting on the planning version that we will see in Section 3.2 to tell the system to calculate purely iterative prices.

There are four check boxes indicators in the default values section of the activity type. The AVERAGE PRICE indicator can be checked if you have not made the setting average activity price in the planning version and you want to define it at the activity type level. Refer to Section 3.2 to find more detail about planning version settings. The PLAN QUANTITY SET indicator means that you will need to set plan quantities manually and that these quantities will not be changed by plan reconciliation. The ACTUAL

QTY SET indicator means you may post manual actual activities in addition to any automatic activities that might be posted. The final indicator, PRE-DISTRIBUTION OF FIXED COSTS, is selected when the activity is used in marginal costing. This functionality will be described in Section 7.6.

These are all activity default values, which mean that they are used as the default settings for the activity during activity output and price planning. It is possible to override these defaults when you are actually entering plan values; however, this is very rarely done. It is more common to set up the activity type with the correct default values and use those in planning.

As with other CO master data, activity types can be placed in groups, and the groups can be used in planning, allocations, and reporting. The transactions for the activity type groups are KLH1 to create, KLH2 to change, and KLH3 to display. The functionality of activity type group maintenance is similar to cost center groups, so you can refer to Section 2.3 to refresh your understanding.

2.6 Statistical key figures

Statistical key figures (SKFs) can be created as master data in SAP Controlling and used to define some measurable value that you wish to attribute to a controlling object such as a cost center, profit center, or internal order. The figure should represent a statistic or numerical value beyond the currency amount posting that you wish to track for that cost object. Some examples of statistical key figures include headcount, number of computers, kilowatt-hours of electricity consumed, and number of purchase orders issued. The SKF will display on reports for the associated object and often is used as a factor to drive allocations.

Statistical key figure functionality is also available in the new GL, and SKFs can be posted against a variety of objects in the GL, including cost center, profit center, and segment. In the new GL, it is important to realize that planned and actual SKF postings from controlling objects will pass into the new GL based on real-time integration between FI and CO. This means you do not need to repeat SKF postings on the FI side if they are posted to the same SKF and cost object in CO.

The key role of statistical key figures in cost center accounting is their use as an allocation base or *tracing factor* within allocations. Additionally, they will also be reported on several standard SAP reports and could be used as the basis of analytical calculations, such as cost per employee

Regardless of where you are using the SKF, the master data only is created in one place with transaction KK01. The statistical key figure is created within the controlling area (see Figure 2.35) and is available for posting to objects assigned to that controlling area.

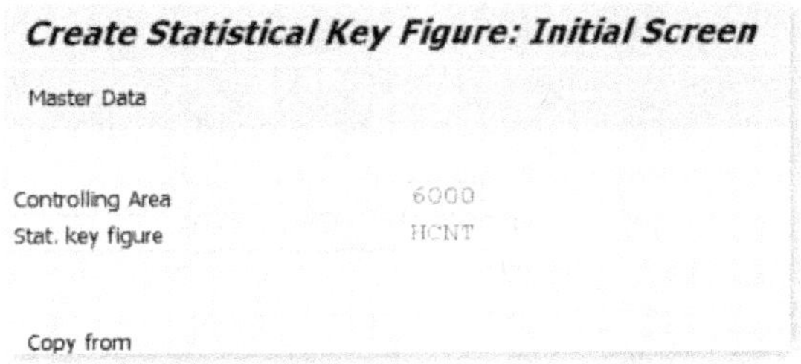

Create Statistical Key Figure: Initial Screen

Master Data

Controlling Area   6000
Stat. key figure   HCNT

Copy from

Figure 2.35: Create SKF initial screen

The SKF is a simple piece of master data with only a few fields to complete. You must give an alphanumeric identifier to the SKF. Then to create it, you must give it a name, assign a unit of measure based on the units available in your SAP system, and decide on whether the SKF will be treated as a fixed value SKF or a total values SKF.

The purpose or nature of the statistic that you are tracking should determine the fixed or total setting. The general definition is:

▶ The fixed value is carried over from the original posting to all subsequent periods in the same fiscal year. You only need to make a new posting if the value changes. This should be used for statistics that remain relatively constant over time, such as headcount.

▶ The total values amount does not transfer to the following period. Therefore, it needs to be entered every period. This is more useful for things like number of units produced in a period.

The LINK TO LIS button allows you to link a statistical key figure to a key figure in the *logistics information structure* (LIS). Click on the LINK button and then search by INFO STRUCTURE or by INFO SET. Then look in the selected application for the key figure to link to your SKF. Once you make the link, you will see it reflected in your SKF (see Figure 2.37). Once you have linked your SKFs, you can transfer the LIS values periodically to the SKFs in controlling. For a linked SKF, you can also to separate or break the link if it is no longer required.

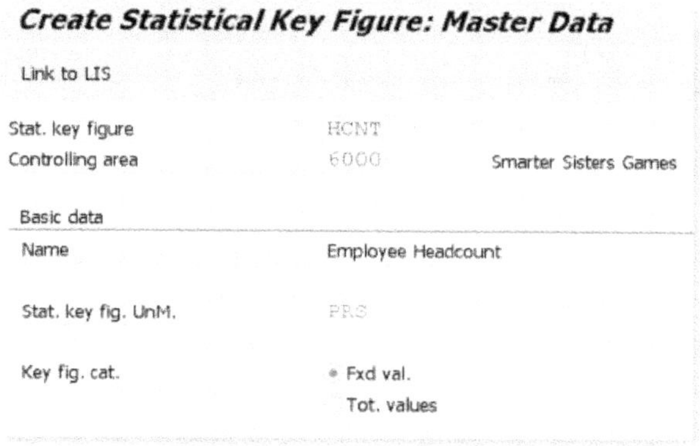

Create Statistical Key Figure: Master Data

Link to LIS

| Stat. key figure | HCNT | |
| Controlling area | 6000 | Smarter Sisters Games |

Basic data

Name	Employee Headcount
Stat. key fig. UnM.	PRS
Key fig. cat.	• Fxd val.
	Tot. values

Figure 2.36: Create SKF master data

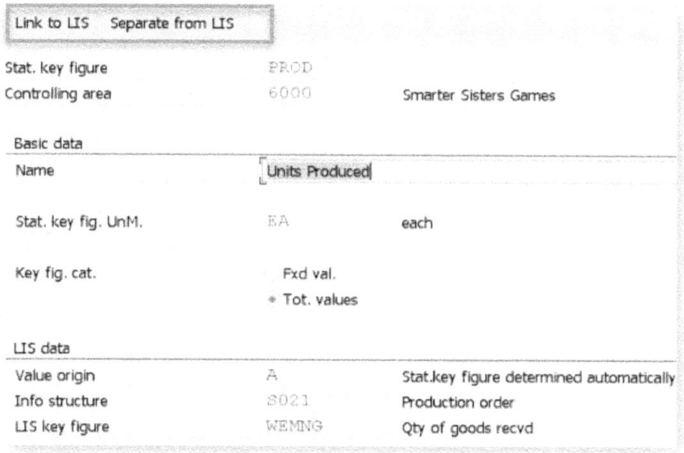

Link to LIS Separate from LIS		
Stat. key figure	PROD	
Controlling area	6000	Smarter Sisters Games

Basic data

Name	Units Produced
Stat. key fig. UnM.	EA	each
Key fig. cat.	Fxd val.
	• Tot. values

LIS data

Value origin	A	Stat.key figure determined automatically
Info structure	S021	Production order
LIS key figure	WEMNG	Qty of goods recvd

Figure 2.37: Link SKF to LIS

2.7 Summary

In this chapter, you have learned about the master data objects that are used within cost center accounting. You have learned about the concept of groups and hierarchies and how they may be used for planning, allocations, and reporting within SAP. You have also learned how to link a statistical key figure to a key figure in the logistic information system to allow for automatic updates of SKF values.

3 Cost center planning in ECC

This chapter will focus on the planning functionality in the SAP ECC release. You will learn how planning works in S/4/HANA in the following chapter. Here you will see how planning in cost center accounting fits into the overall planning cycle for an organization. You will learn about the basic concepts of planning in SAP, including versions, planner profiles, and layouts and how they can be used. Manual planning using planning layouts will be demonstrated, including how to upload plans from Excel using standard SAP functionality. You will also see plan integration with other cost objects, plan data transfer, and plan allocations. You will see in some detail how activity price planning works, including the concepts of plan cost splitting and plan price calculation and how this can function in a typical manufacturing company.

3.1　Where cost center planning fits

Most organizations go through an annual budgeting or planning cycle to forecast their revenues and expenses for the upcoming fiscal year. This planning cycle can involve several steps to get to the overall plan for the enterprise. Depending on the business, there will likely be a sales plan which will translate into planned revenue and cost of sales, and then there may be a production plan which will determine resource requirements and inputs for manufacturing. Finally, there will be an overhead plan incorporating input from overhead cost centers and human resources.

Ideally, you would build your overall plan without having to re-enter the same planning data into different modules within the system. It would make sense that all these planning pieces should be integrated and ultimately fed into an overall plan for the organization.

Since planning cycles can differ between organizations, the cycle presented in Figure 3.1 should be considered a generic example. The unique requirement of each enterprise means that there will have to be individual changes to the process in each company.

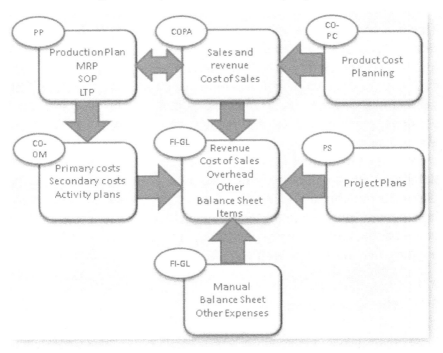

Figure 3.1: Generic planning cycle

The logical starting point for annual planning is the sales plan. The sales plan is usually defined by the sales department. This may be entered in the planning framework in COPA using transaction KEPM. This is where you define the characteristics that you wish to plan. There are many ways to define planning levels in KEPM. For example, you may want to plan sales quantity by sales organization, product, customer, and plant, or you may just want it by sales organization and product. Within costing-based COPA, it is possible to generate planned revenue and cost of sales numbers using valuation. The details of COPA planning are beyond the scope of this book and are discussed here only because they are part of the integrated planning cycle.

The sales plan can be transferred from COPA to *sales and operations planning* (SOP), where a rough-cut capacity plan can be executed. The production plan then is passed from SOP to *long-term planning* (LTP), where a planning run is carried out that will determine activity requirements at the production work centers based on the planned finished and semi-finished goods, as well as *planned independent requirements* for input materials. The activity requirements from the planning run in LTP can be transferred to activity planning in cost center accounting.

In the overhead management section of controlling, plans can be entered for either cost centers or internal orders that integrate into your overall GL plan. These would be the equivalent of departmental budgets and planning for small overhead projects. Plans entered into project systems at the WBS element level can also integrate with GL planning. Finally, manual planning in the GL can be used to plan additional revenue, expense items, or balance sheet items if required.

Our focus here is on the CO-OM piece of the planning cycle, but you will also see some of the key integration points with other planning elements. The purpose of cost center planning may vary among business types. In a manufacturing organization, cost center planning fulfills several goals:

- ▶ Set overhead cost targets for cost centers to allow for variance reporting.
- ▶ Allocate planned costs from support or overhead cost centers to production cost centers.
- ▶ Plan activity prices which will be used in product costing.
- ▶ Plan full or partial absorption of costs.

Within cost center accounting, there are three broad areas or objects where you can create plans to achieve the overall planning goals. First, there is *cost planning* for planning costs in cost centers. Cost planning can seem somewhat confusing since there can be many types and methods involved. Some parts of cost planning may be done manually, while other parts may be automatic. Within that split, we have further divisions between primary cost planning and secondary cost planning and then again between activity-independent and activity-dependent costs. You will see and understand each of these options later in this chapter. The second major area is *activity planning*, which includes activity output and price planning that can also have a manual and an automatic planning component. The final area is *statistical key figure planning,* where we can either manually plan statistical values for a cost center or automatically transfer them from LIS. The planned statistical key figures can then be used as tracing factors in planned cost allocations.

Planning versus budgeting

 What's in a word? SAP sometimes uses words or terms that have a specific meaning within the software but may be used in a different way within a business. One example is the use of budget. Many companies refer to their annual planning cycle as budgeting and call the plan that they create a budget. In SAP, this is called planning; budget has an entirely different meaning. Budgets are used primarily with internal orders and WBS elements to represent an approved spending limit for those objects. The budget amount is set at the level of the object and not at a cost element level. For orders and WBS elements, budgets can be subject to availability control, which can issue warnings or error messages based on the level of spending. Although it is possible to create a budget in cost center accounting, this is done rarely, and availability control is not available. If you wish to simulate availability control for cost centers, you can create a workaround using statistical internal orders with budgets linked to cost centers and activate the availability control on the statistical orders.

Within cost center planning, there should be a logical sequence to the planning activities. This sequence may vary from organization to organization, and the following is only a suggested flow.

1. Plan statistical key figures first because you may need to use them as tracing factors in planned allocations later.

2. Plan activity output quantities and capacities. If you are manually entering activity prices, then you can do it now, or you can calculate activity prices later.

3. Plan manual input costs.

4. Automatic cost planning and run plan assessments and distributions.

5. Automatic price planning.

The planning cycle may be iterative, and price planning may have to occur at different points for different cost centers.

3.2   Planning version concept in SAP

Throughout controlling, project systems, and in the new general ledger accounting, the concept of the *plan version* forms the basis of the planning concept. Versions make it possible to store different plans in parallel for the same controlling object. This allows you to maintain and report against different plans based on different conditions, such as a plan based on a favorable sales forecast versus a plan based on a more pessimistic sales forecast. Often, plan versions are used for storing forecasts. A business might start with an original plan and then every quarter update the plan based on history and a new projection, and store the result in a new plan version.

The plan versions are maintained at a general level (see Figure 3.2) for controlling and at a lower level for each controlling area, operating concern, and profit center accounting. Within the controlling area and profit center accounting, the plan version settings are also maintained by fiscal year.

General Version Definition

New Entries

Dialog Structure	General Version Overview				
General Version Definition	Version	Name	Plan	Actual	WIP/RA	Variance
· Settings in Operating Concern	0	Plan/actual version	✓	✓	✓	✓
· Settings for Profit Center Account	1	First Quarter Forecast	✓			✓
Controlling Area Settings	2	Second Quarter Forecast	✓			✓
· Settings for Each Fiscal Year	3	Third Quarter Forecast	✓			✓
· Delta Version: Bus. Transaction						

Figure 3.2: Plan versions at a general level

You must have one plan/actual version that can store both plan and actual data; after that, you can create as many other plan versions as you require. Additional plan versions must be created at the general level before they can be used in either controlling, COPA, or PCA. At the lower levels, you may use some of the plan versions maintained at the general level.

For planning in cost center accounting, you will focus on the versions for each controlling area. These have to be maintained at the controlling level and by fiscal year.

For each controlling area and year, you can maintain the control parameters in the version (see Figure 3.3). It is possible to lock the version by year, which is useful once you have finished your planning and want to prevent any further changes being made. The INTEGRATED PLANNING indicator controls whether line items are created for each change made to plan data and activates plan integration with other components such as profit center accounting. Finally, selecting the COPYING ALLOWED indicator allows you to use that version as a template when copying to another plan version.

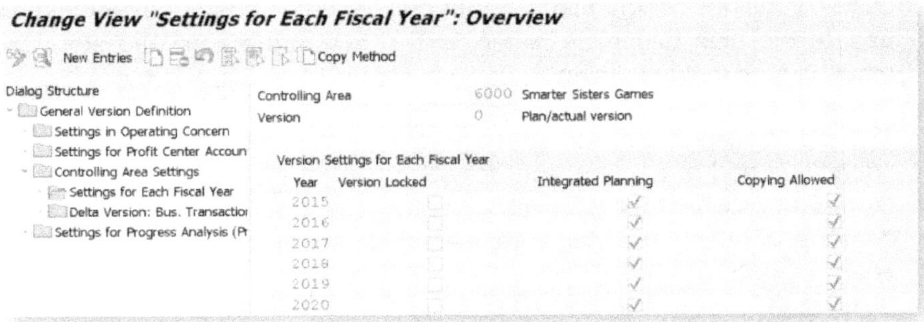

Figure 3.3: Plan version controlling area level

Within each fiscal year, there are some additional general planning settings and some settings specifically related to activity price planning and calculation (see Figure 3.4). The general planning settings are largely self-explanatory. The price calculation settings require more explanation since they control some of the behavior in automatic planning and actual activity price calculation.

In Section 2.5, you learned about the option to calculate purely iterative activity prices. This is controlled by the PURELY ITER PRICE check box. If you want the system to calculate activity prices even though you are maintaining the prices manually, you can select this option. The purely iterative prices are stored in parallel in the version but are not used for allocation.

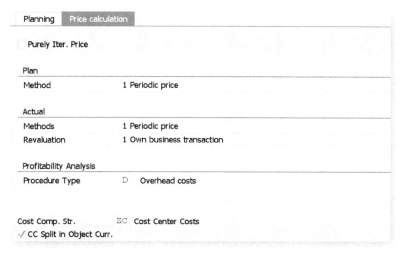

Figure 3.4: Plan version price calculation parameters

There are two price determination methods: one for plan, and the other for actual. The plan method has two options, **periodic price** or **average price**. The actual method has those two options, as well as a third based on **cumulative price**. These settings will affect how the plan and actual activity prices are calculated.

► Periodic Price—the costs in each period are divided by the activity quantities in that period to achieve a price. This can result in different prices for each period.

► Average Price—the costs for all periods are divided by the total activities for all periods; this results in a consistent activity price over all periods.

► Cumulative Price—this can be used for actual price calculation, takes the costs up to the current period, and divides by the activity quantities for that time to get a cumulative price.

The REVALUATION indicator is important since it controls whether actual activity revaluation is allowed and how the revaluation will post if you allow it. There are three options:

▶ Do not revalue—activities are not revalued with the actual price, and only the plan price will be used for activity prices.

▶ Own business transaction—the results from the actual activity revaluation will be posted in a separate transaction, allowing visibility to the original posting and the revaluation.

▶ Original business transaction—the original transaction is updated with the results of the revaluation; you will not see the revaluation separately from the original posting.

Depending on the receiving object, the actual revaluation will behave in a different fashion. For cost centers, business processes, and profitability segments, if the planning version is set for revaluation, then the revaluation will happen automatically during activity price calculation, and the options for own business transaction versus original business transaction will apply. For revaluation of all types of orders and WBS elements, the manual revaluation transaction must be used for the correct object.

3.3 Cost input planning

3.3.1 Manual cost input planning

Manual cost input planning is the foundation for cost center planning and is likely the function that is most used. Most organizations, if they want to be able to compare actual costs against plan costs, will engage in manual cost input planning. Some will only plan costs based on cost center and cost element. This is known as activity-independent planning. Others may also plan some costs using a combination of cost center, cost element, and activity type. This is known as activity-dependent planning. Manual planning can be carried out in both of these scenarios.

Manual cost planning implies loading plan values manually into SAP. This does not necessarily mean that users need to sit and key values into the system; manual planning also allows for uploading values from a spreadsheet as well as some plan copy functions. However, for manual planning to work, some basic configuration pieces need to exist. These are the *planning layouts* and the *planner profiles*. Planner profiles are assigned to *planning areas*, which are pre-defined in SAP. SAP provides a number of delivered planning layouts and planner profiles, some of which are shown in Figure 3.5. These should meet most needs; however, you may need to create custom profiles or layouts, which should be done by copying a standard delivered element and changing it to fit your needs.

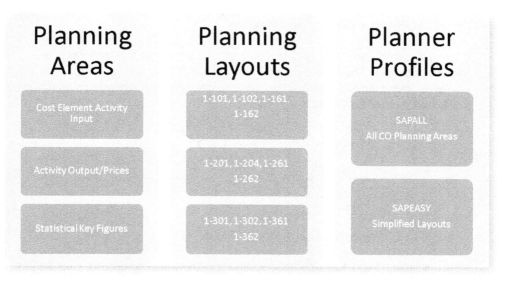

Figure 3.5: Standard manual planning elements in SAP

Regardless of whether you are doing manual planning for cost inputs, activity quantities and prices, or statistical key figures, layouts and profiles will be required. I will cover the fundamentals here, but be aware that the same principles will apply when looking at other manual planning areas.

Planner profiles are assigned to *planning areas* in SAP (Figure 3.6). In cost center accounting, there are three planning areas: cost elements/activity inputs, activity output/prices, and statistical key figures. The other areas relate to other CO objects such as orders or WBS elements. The assignment of planning areas to planner profiles is useful if you want to split the planning tasks between different users in your system, as the user can assign the planner profile.

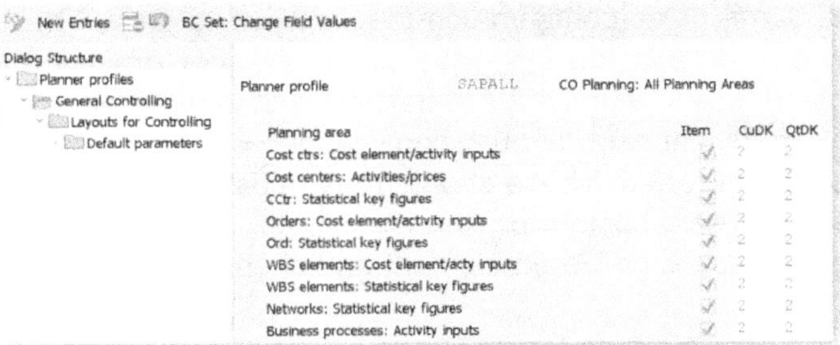

Figure 3.6: Planner profile and planning areas

Planning layouts are assigned to each planning area in a planner profile (see Figure 3.7). The layout determines the fields that are present when you enter the planned values. The layouts are created and edited using the *report painter* functionality in SAP.

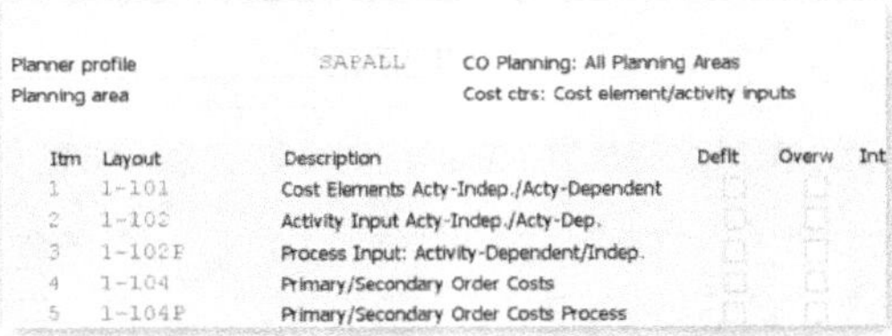

Figure 3.7: Planning layouts assigned to profile SAPALL

The important thing to know about creating planning layouts is that all the characteristics you require for planning must be defined somewhere in the layout. They are defined as either *variables*, *sets*, or *fixed values* in the lead columns in your layout (see Figure 3.8), defined in the general data section of the report (see Figure 3.9), or used in one of the key figure columns (see Figure 3.10).

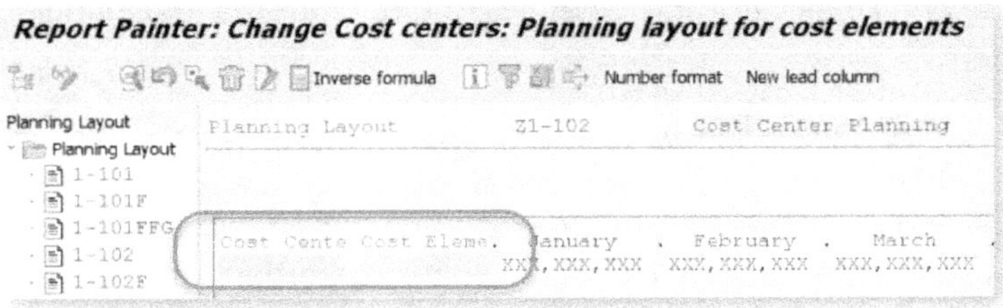

Figure 3.8: Planning layout lead columns

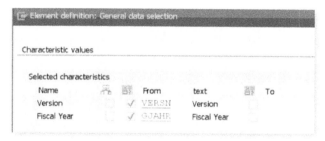

Figure 3.9: Planning layout general data selection

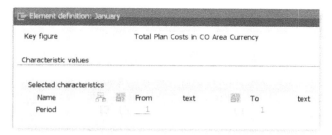

Figure 3.10: Characteristic assigned to key figure

Once you have created a planning layout, you will assign it to a planner profile before you can use it. Refer to Figure 3.7.

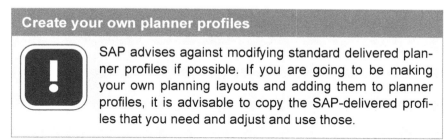

Whether you have created your own planner profile or are using a standard SAP-delivered one, there are some settings to be aware of which will affect the functionality of the assigned layouts (see Figure 3.11).

Itm	Layout	Description	Deflt	Overw	Integrated E...	File descri...
1	Y1-101	Best Practices Cost Elements Planning	✓	✓	✓	
1	Y1-101-A	Best Practices Cost Elements Planning	✓	✓		
1	Z1-102	Cost Center Planning		✓	✓	

Planner profile   YBALL_01   BP planning with Excel (reduced)
Planning area   Cost ctrs: Cost element/activity inputs

Figure 3.11: Plan layout settings in planner profile

Here, you have an INTEGRATED check box. This does not have anything to do with integrated planning; instead, this activates Excel in your planning layout. With integrated Excel, you open your planning layout in an Excel worksheet layout rather than in a standard planning screen. Integrated Excel is also the starting point for creating the file descriptions and templates to be used in a flexible Excel upload of plan data. This function is generic across CO modules and can be used for all planning functions for cost centers, internal orders, statistical key figures, activity types, COPA, and more.

Since this function can be so useful, it is worth showing the steps in detail. The first step is to check the integrated Excel box associated with your planning layout. Next, select the layout, go to the DEFAULT PARAMETERS sub-dialog, and enter some selection variables (see Figure 3.12). It is better to run this with the following option selected: • Form-Based. Select the overview button 🔍 and open the layout in Excel format. You will receive a message about the file description being generated, and then you will see the layout in Excel (see Figure 3.13). You may have to accept macros or otherwise change some security settings in Excel if it does not open immediately.

Cost Element/Activity Input Planning: Init. Scr

🔍 ⓘ Layout   ⓘ Profile

Layout	Z1-102	Cost Center Planning
Variables		
Version	0	
Fiscal Year	2017	
Cost Center	5000199003	
Cost Center	5000199003	
Cost Element	540000	
Cost Element	599999	

Figure 3.12: Enter parameters

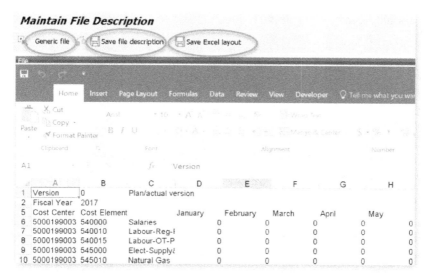

Figure 3.13: Microsoft Excel layout

You will notice three buttons in the layout. The first is used to generate a *generic file*. This is the link between the physical file and the generated file description. In uploading files, the system looks for files containing the generic file name. The generic file should consist of a fixed part that will be common to all the physical files to be imported and then a "*" representing a variable portion, and then the file extension, which may be .txt or .csv (see Figure 3.14).

Figure 3.14: Generic file name

To complete the process, click on the SAVE FILE DESCRIPTION button and then on the SAVE EXCEL LAYOUT button. Use the FILE • SAVE AS or the [F12] key in the Excel sheet to save a template copy of the layout locally. When you back out of the layout and the parameter screen, it is not necessary to save the default parameters unless you want them to appear as defaults in manual planning. When you go back to the layout view, you should now see the file description linked to the planning layout (see Figure 3.15).

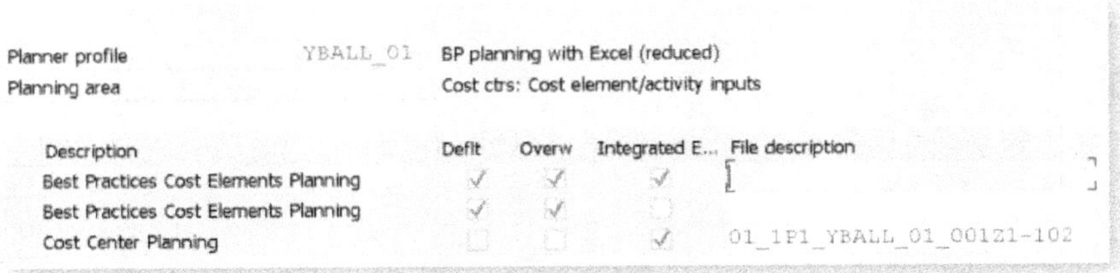

Planner profile		YBALL_01	BP planning with Excel (reduced)			
Planning area			Cost ctrs: Cost element/activity inputs			
Description		Deflt	Overw	Integrated E...	File description	
Best Practices Cost Elements Planning		✓	✓	✓		
Best Practices Cost Elements Planning		✓	✓			
Cost Center Planning				✓	01_1P1_YBALL_01_001Z1-102	

Figure 3.15: File description in the planning layout

You can use the template that you saved locally to fill with planned values and upload into SAP. You have to un-protect the spreadsheet and remove any total rows that have been inserted by SAP. To upload, first populate the file with plan data and save as either a .txt or .csv file, depending on what you selected previously in the generic file. Next, from within an SAP cost center planning transaction such as KP06, use the menu to select EXTRAS • EXCEL PLANNING • UPLOAD to import your plan (see Figure 3.16). You have the option to upload a single file or all files in a directory. SAP will look for all files in the directory containing the generic file name and will import them. You also have to select the FILE DESCRIPTION associated with your layout. There may be multiple options available, so it is important to select the correct file description. It must be the same as the one generated (as seen in Figure 3.15)

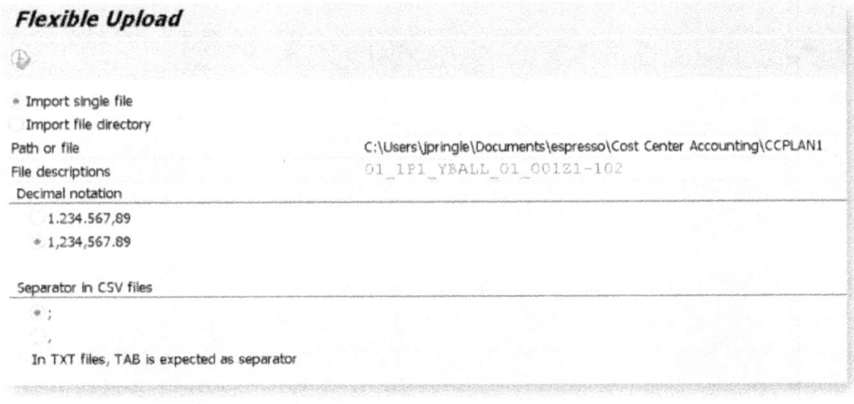

Flexible Upload

• Import single file	
Import file directory	
Path or file	C:\Users\jpringle\Documents\espresso\Cost Center Accounting\CCPLAN1
File descriptions	01_1P1_YBALL_01_001Z1-102
Decimal notation	
1.234.567,89	
• 1,234,567.89	
Separator in CSV files	
• ;	
In TXT files, TAB is expected as separator	

Figure 3.16: Upload from Microsoft Excel

Execute the upload by pressing the ⊕ button. There will be a message telling you whether the upload was successful or not (see Figure 3.17). The planned data from your spreadsheet should now be posted in cost center accounting.

Figure 3.17: Flexible upload message

If you have problems with the upload

There is a lot of useful information on possible issues that might cause errors in an Excel upload in SAP note 319713 – Error with Excel upload—possible causes. If you get an error message with your upload, this note likely will explain the underlying issue. This note also outlines what you need to do if you make changes to a layout and need to regenerate the file layout and the generic file name.

Similar Excel upload functionality can be used for activity output/price planning and statistical key figure planning; all that is needed is a planning layout and a planner profile configured to allow it.

You can build Excel layouts to load activity-independent and activity-dependent costs. You can also load these costs manually using transaction KP06 (see Figure 3.18). Layout 1-101 can be used for both activity-dependent and independent costs. Costs that are activity-independent only require a cost element and a cost center for planning; the activity field should be left blank. Activity-independent costs are always considered to be *fixed costs* in SAP since there can be no variability by activity quantity.

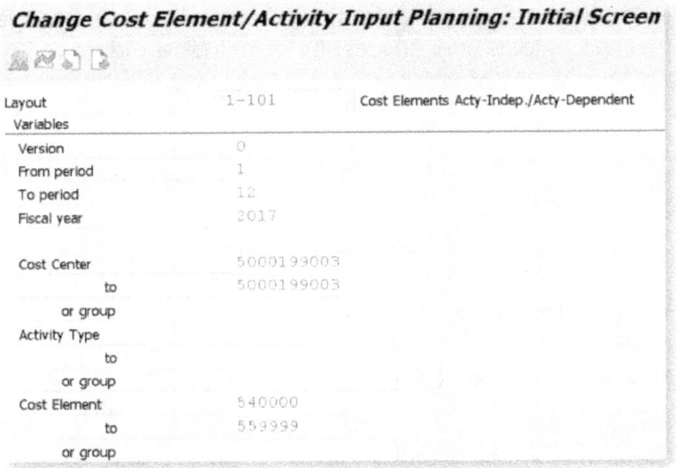

Change Cost Element/Activity Input Planning: Initial Screen

Layout	1-101	Cost Elements Acty-Indep./Acty-Dependent
Variables		
Version	0	
From period	1	
To period	12	
Fiscal year	2017	
Cost Center	5000199003	
to	5000199003	
or group		
Activity Type		
to		
or group		
Cost Element	540000	
to	559999	
or group		

Figure 3.18: KP06 initial screen

From the initial screen, you can access the overall planning view (see Figure 3.19) by clicking on the ▨ button.

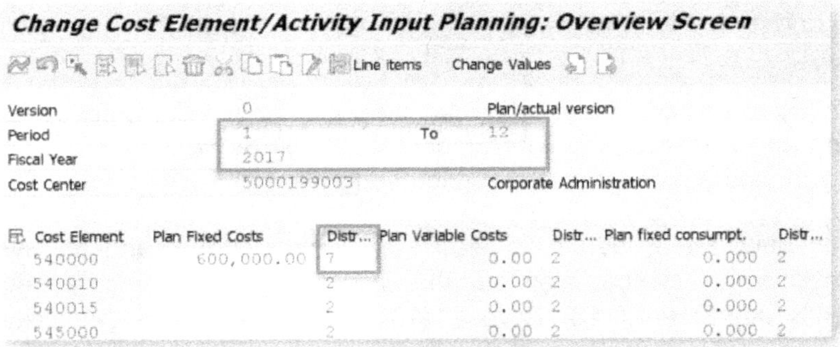

Change Cost Element/Activity Input Planning: Overview Screen

Line Items   Change Values

Version	0		Plan/actual version	
Period	1	To	12	
Fiscal Year	2017			
Cost Center	5000199003		Corporate Administration	

🔢 Cost Element	Plan Fixed Costs	Distr...	Plan Variable Costs	Distr...	Plan fixed consumpt.	Distr...
540000	600,000.00	7	0.00	2	0.000	2
540010		2	0.00	2	0.000	2
540015		2	0.00	2	0.000	2
545000		2	0.00	2	0.000	2

Figure 3.19: Activity-independent planning overview screen

Here you can enter the overall planned values for the periods selected on the initial screen. Note that since we did not specify any activities in the selection, we can only enter fixed costs. You also have the opportunity to select a distribution key. This key defines how the overall value that you entered will be distributed over the individual fiscal periods. I have chosen a distribution key that distributes based on the number of days in the period, and you can see the result of viewing the period screen after clicking on the ▨ button (see Figure 3.20).

Version	0	Plan/actual versio
Fiscal Year	2017	
Cost Center	3000199003	Corporate Adminis
Cost Element	540000	Salaries

Per... Text	Plan Fixed Costs	Plan Variable Costs
1 January	50,958.90	0.00
2 February	46,027.40	0.00
3 March	50,958.91	0.00
4 April	49,315.06	0.00
5 May	50,958.91	0.00
6 June	49,315.07	0.00
7 July	50,958.90	0.00
8 August	50,958.90	0.00
9 September	49,315.07	0.00
10 October	50,958.91	0.00
11 November	49,315.07	0.00
12 December	50,958.90	0.00
* Pe	600,000.00	0.00

Figure 3.20: KP06 Period view

You can also edit values in the period view, and they will be updated in the overall view. Using the flexible Excel upload process or some custom developed program would be the preferred approach for loading cost center plans, but KP06 can be useful for making edits to already loaded values.

Activity-independent costs can still be used in plan activity price calculation but must be assigned to the activity type through a cost splitting structure in configuration. Costs assigned this way will show up as a part of the fixed portion of the activity price once it is calculated.

Activity-dependent cost planning can be used when the costs in a cost center can be directly attributed to an activity produced by that cost center. You can again use KP06 with layout 1-101 to perform activity-dependent primary cost planning. You need to plan activity-independent and activity-dependent costs separately, even though you use the same transaction, so you will need to run the transaction more than once. On the initial screen for KP06 (see Figure 3.21), the only difference is that you enter activity types or an activity type group in your selection.

Use groups for planning

It is good practice to use groups for planning. Cost center groups can be used to group similar cost centers with similar planning requirements. Cost element groups can be used to separate costs that require activity-dependent planning from those that don't, and activity type groups can be used to make planning selection easier.

Layout	1-101	Cost Elements Acty-Indep./Acty-Dependent
Variables		
Version	0	Plan/actual version
From period	1	January
To period	12	December
Fiscal year	2017	
Cost Center	5000101905	Plant Utilities Indiana
to	5000101905	Plant Utilities Indiana
or group		
Activity Type		
to		
or group	UTILITIES	Utilities
Cost Element		
to		
or group	UTILITIES	Utilities

Figure 3.21: KP06 initial screen activity-dependent planning

The activity-dependent costs can be divided into fixed and variable portions.

Change Cost Element/Activity Input Planning: Overview Screen

Line items   Change Values

	Version	0		Plan/actual version
	Period	1	To	12
	Fiscal Year	2017		
	Cost Center	5000101905		Plant Utilities Indiana

Activity	...	Cost Element	Plan Fixed Costs	Distr...	Plan Variable Costs	Distr...	Plan fixed consumpt.	Distr...	Plan vbl consumption	Distr...	Unit	Q	L
2000		545000	250,000.00	7	750,000.00	7		2		2	KWH	✓	
		545010		2		2		2		2	M3	✓	
		545200		2		2		2		2	L	✓	

Figure 3.22: Activity-dependent cost planning overview screen

It is also possible to manually plan activity-independent and activity-dependent secondary costs. These would represent costs provided as an activity from another cost center that should be included in your cost center's plan. For example, the information technology cost center provides support services to other cost centers in the plant, and you want to reflect the use of those services in the other cost centers. SAP provides the standard layout 1-102 for this purpose (see Figure 3.23). For secondary cost planning, it is necessary to identify the sending cost center and activity type, as well as the receiving cost center and possibly activity type. In this case, the secondary costs that you are planning will be activity-independent, so you will leave the receiving activity type blank on the initial screen.

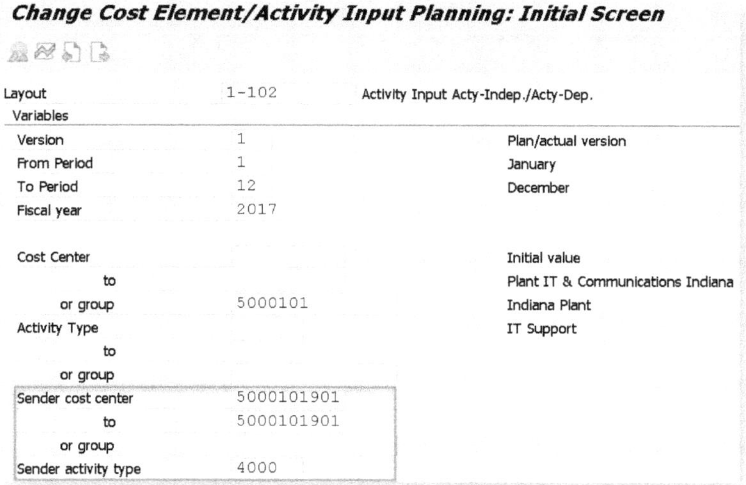

Change Cost Element/Activity Input Planning: Initial Screen

Layout	1-102	Activity Input Acty-Indep./Acty-Dep.
Variables		
Version	1	Plan/actual version
From Period	1	January
To Period	12	December
Fiscal year	2017	
Cost Center		Initial value
to		Plant IT & Communications Indiana
or group	5000101	Indiana Plant
Activity Type		IT Support
to		
or group		
Sender cost center	5000101901	
to	5000101901	
or group		
Sender activity type	4000	

Figure 3.23: Secondary cost planning initial screen

On the overview screen (see Figure 3.24), you will see that the plant finance cost center is planning to use 1,200 hours of IT service provided by the sending IT cost center. The prerequisite for this is that the IT service activity already has some planned output values: capacity, activity quantity, or a planned price, in this case, $75 per hour.

Change Cost Element/Activity Input Planning: Overview Screen

Version	1		Plan Version: 1
Period	1	To	12
Fiscal Year	2017		
Cost Center	5000101902		Plant Finance Indiana

Sender Cost C...	Sender ...	Plan fixed consumpt.	Distr...	Plan vbl consumption	Distr...	Unit	Plan fixed costs	Plan Variable Costs	Alloc. cost ele...
5000101901	4000	1,200	2	0	2	H	90,000.00	0.00	943400

Figure 3.24: Secondary cost planning overview screen

The result of this planning is that the activity input and output is posted to the sending cost center and activity type, while the activity input is posted to the receiving cost center using the secondary cost element (see Figure 3.25).

Display Plan Cost Line Items for Cost Centers

Master Record

Year	frm	To Period	Cost Center	Cost Element	CO object name	Acty Type	Cost element name	Total val. rep.crcy	Tot. F&V qty	UM
2017	1	12	5000101901	943400	Plant IT & Comm IN / IT Support	4000	IT Support	0.00	0	H
2017	1	12	5000101901	943400	Plant IT & Comm IN / IT Support	4000	IT Support	90,000.00-	1,200-	H
2017	1	12	5000101901	943400	Plant IT & Comm IN / IT Support	4000	IT Support	90,000.00	1,200	H
2017			5000101901		Plant IT & Comm IN / IT Support			0.00	0	H
2017	1	12	5000101902	943400	Plant Finance IN		IT Support	90,000.00	1,200	H
2017			5000101902		Plant Finance IN			90,000.00	1,200	H
								90,000.00	1,200	H

Figure 3.25 : Results of secondary cost planning

Many receiver cost centers may plan to get services from the IT cost center. If they all engage in secondary cost planning, we will see all the activity that they have planned as a scheduled activity output in the IT cost center. See this by displaying the activity price planning for the IT cost center in transaction KP27 (see Figure 3.26).

Display Activity Type/Price Planning: Overview Screen

Line items

Version	2		Plan Version: 2
Period	1	To	12
Fiscal Year	2017		
Cost Center	5000101901		Plant IT & Communications Indiana

Activity ...	Plan Activity	Distr...	Capacity	Distr...	Unit	Variable price	Pla...	Alloc. cost ele...	T	EquiNo	Scheduled Activity
4000	6,000				2	H	75.00	1	943400	1	1	5,480

Figure 3.26: Scheduled activity in cost center

This scheduled activity may differ from the activity output that is planned by the IT department. They are planning 6,000 hours, which is what they need to recover their costs; however, the cost centers that are planning to use the IT services only require 5,480 hours in total. In this situation, you can run the plan reconciliation transaction KPSI to reconcile the activity output plan with the secondary cost planning (see Figure 3.27).

Controlling Area	6000	Smarter Sisters Games
Version	2	Plan Version: 2
Fiscal Year	2017	
Period	001	to 012
Cost center group	6000	
Processing status	TestRun	

Processing completed without errors

Display status	Total for all per.					
OTy	Object	Name	AUn	Total plan activity	New plan activity	Activity difference
ATY	5000101901/4000	Plant IT & Comm IN	H	6,000	5,480	520-

Figure 3.27: Plan reconciliation

Now the plan activity in the IT cost center will be adjusted to 5,480 hours, and the department manager will need to determine what to do to recover the costs (see Figure 3.28). This may mean that the activity rate of $75 per hour needs to be increased, or it may mean that the departmental costs will have to be reduced. Plan reconciliation is an important step in activity planning and is a prerequisite for other functions. Many of the period end analysis steps you will see in Chapter 7 will require fully reconciled plans to provide meaningful results.

Cost Centers: Actual/Plan/Variance	Date: 21.02.2017	Page: 2 / 3

Cost Center/Group	5000101901		Plant IT & Comm IN	Column: 1 / 2
Person responsible:	Lucius Fox			
Reporting period:	1 to 12 2017			

Cost Elements	Act. Costs	Plan Costs	Var. (Abs.)	Var. (%)
540000 Salaries		450,000.00	450,000.00-	100.00-
* Debit		450,000.00	450,000.00-	100.00-
943400 IT Support		411,000.04-	411,000.04	100.00-
* Credit		411,000.04-	411,000.04	100.00-
** Over/Underabsorption		38,999.96	38,999.96-	100.00-

Figure 3.28: Under-absorption of IT costs

A final form of manual planning supported in SAP is called dependency planning. Here, activity-dependent and activity-independent costs can be determined from a calculation or a dependency. The calculation can be based on an activity type or a statistical key figure. This type of planning can be useful if there is a direct relationship between the statistic and the cost being planned. For example, many office or administrative expenses vary based on the number of employees. In this case, the organization plans for $25 per month per employee for office expenses (see Figure 3.29). The dependency planning is carried out using transaction KP06 and the planner profile SAPR&R with the layout 1-1R2.

In the period screen, (see Figure 3.30) you can see that the planned amount of $25 per employee is multiplied by the planned headcount of eight to calculate a monthly planned cost.

Version	1		Plan Version: 1
Period	1	To	12
Cost Center	5000101902		Plant Finance Indiana
Fiscal Year	2017		

Cost Element	R. Depend...	Fxd dependency ...	Distr...	Var. depend. price	Distr...	Depend...	Dependency srce ...	Unit	Plan Fixed Costs	Distr...
581130	2 HCNT	25.00	2	0.00	2	00001		96	PRS	2,400.00	2

Figure 3.29: Dependency planning overall

Version	1	Plan Version: 1
Cost Center	5000101902	Plant Finance Indiana
Fiscal Year	2017	
Cost Element	581130	Office Furniture & Supplies

Per...	Text	R. Depend...	Fxd dependency ...	Depend...	Dependency srce ...	Unit	Plan Fixed Costs
1	January	2 HCNT	25.00	00001	8	PRS	200.00
2	February	2 HCNT	25.00	00001	8	PRS	200.00
3	March	2 HCNT	25.00	00001	8	PRS	200.00
4	April	2 HCNT	25.00	00001	8	PRS	200.00
5	May	2 HCNT	25.00	00001	8	PRS	200.00
6	June	2 HCNT	25.00	00001	8	PRS	200.00
7	July	2 HCNT	25.00	00001	8	PRS	200.00
8	August	2 HCNT	25.00	00001	8	PRS	200.00
9	September	2 HCNT	25.00	00001	8	PRS	200.00
10	October	2 HCNT	25.00	00001	8	PRS	200.00
11	November	2 HCNT	25.00	00001	8	PRS	200.00
12	December	2 HCNT	25.00	00001	8	PRS	200.00
*Pe					96		2,400.00

Figure 3.30: Dependency planning periods

In practice, I do not see many companies using dependency planning even though it could be useful. Often it is easier to perform the dependency calculation in an Excel model and just load the result into SAP using a flexible Excel upload.

In many organizations, the extent of cost planning is activity-independent primary cost planning. This approach provides only the most rudimentary reporting and analysis such as basic actual/plan/variance reports. To achieve more meaningful analysis the use of activity-dependent planning and secondary cost planning should also be considered.

3.3.2   Automatic cost input planning

In addition to the manual cost planning methods that you have seen, there are also several automatic planning methods available for cost planning. You will usually want to consider a combination of manual and automatic planning methods in your overall planning solution.

The following methods are provided for automatic planning:

▶ Template planning, also called formula planning

▶ Planned accrual calculation

▶ Planned overhead calculation

▶ Planned distribution

▶ Planned periodic re-posting

▶ Planned assessment

▶ Planned indirect activity allocation

In Section 2.1, you saw that templates can be assigned on the cost center master and learned a little about their purpose. Now you will see some more detail on how templates can be used in formula planning. The templates can be created in transaction CPT1 and are always created with reference to an *environment*. The environments relate to the area where the templates will be used and define the functions available for calculation within the template. For cost center planning, the relevant environments are CPD, used for activity-dependent formula planning, and CPI, used for activity-independent formula planning.

As an example, you will see a rather simple template that will calculate planned values based on some formulas involving statistical key figures. In the template shown in Figure 3.31 there are two calculation rows; one is related to salaries, and the other is for wages. For the salary, simply multiply the planned value of an SKF called HCNT—headcount by another SKF called AVESAL—average salary. You can maintain the planned values for these in SKF planning manually. For the wages (formula not shown) expense, you multiply the SKF for headcount by another SKF for hourly wage times the number of hours in the month.

| Template | ZCCPL1 | CCA Planning Template |
| Environment | CPI | Activity indep. cost ctr planning |

Template overview : display

Type	Object	Description	Plan costs per	Planned quanti	Activation condition
Calculation Row	SALARIES	Salaries		StatKeyFigureC	
Calculation Row	WAGES	wages		StatKeyFigureC	
Cost Element	540000	Salaries	CalculationRow		CostCenterCategory
Cost Element	540010	Labour-Reg-Pr	CalculationRow		CostCenterCategory

Planned quantity per period   + - * / ( )

```
StatKeyFigureCostCenter( FiscalYear = CurrentFiscalYear,
                         CostCenter = CostCenter,
                         ActivityType = '',
                         StatisticalKeyFigure = HCNT,
                         Version = CurrentPlanVersion )
* StatKeyFigureCostCenter( FiscalYear = CurrentFiscalYear,
                           CostCenter = CostCenter,
                           ActivityType = '',
                           StatisticalKeyFigure = AVESAL,
                           Version = CurrentPlanVersion )
```

Figure 3.31: Template for CCA formula planning

The cost element row determines the planned amount to be placed in the selected cost elements. I am planning cost element 540000 for salaries and 540010 for production labor. You simply reference the amount from the relevant calculation row, which is an annual value, and divide by 12 to get the monthly costs (see Figure 3.32).

Plan costs per period   + - * / ( )

```
CalculationRowValue( CalculationRowName = 'SALARIES' )
/ 12
```

Figure 3.32: Cost element row for salaries

The activation condition can be used to tell the system when to use particular lines. In this case, you only want to calculate wages for cost centers with category "F" and salaries for all other cost centers. You can create a rule in each cost element line to achieve this (see Figure 3.33). In the cost element 540000 line, you would create an activation condition if the cost center category does not equal "F," and in the 540010 line, you would create an activation if the cost center category equals "F."

Figure 3.33: Activation condition in template

To use the template in *formula planning,* it must be assigned appropriately to your cost centers on the TEMPLATES tab of the master data. Refer to Figure 2.7 if you do not recall where this is. You can now run transaction KPT6 to execute formula planning. You can execute this based on a variety of selection criteria, and it will calculate formula planning for the cost centers with templates assigned. (See Figure 3.34).

Formula Planning: Results

Cost Center	Cost Element	FixValue COCurr
5000101001	540010	864,000.00
5000101002	540010	798,720.00
5000101003	540010	552,960.00
5000101004	540010	288,000.00
5000101100	540010	750,720.00
5000101110	540010	576,000.00
5000101200	540010	307,200.00
5000101900	540000	300,000.00
5000101901	540000	390,000.00
5000101902	540000	519,999.96
5000101903	540000	350,000.04
5000101904	540000	110,000.04
5000101905	540000	180,000.00
5000103001	540000	756,000.00
		6,743,600.04

Figure 3.34: Formula planning results

Similar to dependency planning, I find formula planning to be used very little in cost center accounting. This is likely due to the complex nature of the template and because it is often easier to perform many of the planning calculations in a spreadsheet prior to loading the data into SAP. The same may also be true of the planned accrual calculation and the planned overhead calculation.

The accrual calculation in CO is used to automatically post *imputed costs* or *accruals* to posting periods throughout the year in situations when the actual cost outlay may just be in one or two periods. A good example is where bonus pay may only be paid out at year end but you want to reflect a portion of it monthly in the cost centers to avoid wide cost fluctuations in one period. The accrual method can be used in actual posting and in planning.

Accrual calculation requires a type of calculation tool called an *overhead structure*, which is similar to the *costing sheet* used in overhead calculation (see Figure 3.35).

Overhead structure		YBL	Sum wages and salaries			
Rows						
Row	Base	O/H Rate	Description	Fr.	To	Credit
110	Y-B1		Wages			
120	Y-B2		Salaries			
190			Sum wages and salaries	110	120	
210		Y-Z1	Vacation Time	190	190	Y11
220		Y-Z2	Bonus Accrued	190	190	Y12
230		Y-Z3	Sick leave accrued	190	190	Y13

Figure 3.35: Overhead structure

The components of the overhead structure are similar to the components of a costing sheet. These components are setup separately and are brought together in the overhead structure. The BASE defines the values that the overhead or accrual will be calculated from. In the example, these are wages and salaries. The O/H RATE defines the percentage of the base that will be calculated as overhead or accrual. Finally, the credit defines the object to receive a credit posting and the cost element being used in the posting. For an accrual calculation, this will be a primary cost element type 3; for an overhead allocation with a costing sheet, we use a secondary cost element type 41. Refer back to Section 2.4 if you need to review cost element types.

You can use transaction KSA8 to run the planned accrual calculation. This will calculate the accrual and will post monthly using the cost elements and partner object defined in the credit assigned to the overhead structure (see Figure 3.36).

Planned overhead calculation works in a similar manner, except that you need to assign the costing sheet to the cost center on the TEMPLATES tab. The costing sheet has similar elements to the overhead structure; you need to define the base, the overhead rates, and the credit. The transaction for planned overhead is KSP4, and the result will be similar to the plan accrual, except that the posting will use a secondary cost element.

You will see more about costing sheets in Section 8.3 when the actual manufacturing period end process is explained.

Plan Accrual Calculation for Cost Centers

Cost Center	Partner Object	Cost Element	Val/COArea Crcy
5000101001	ORD 9ABONUS	540500	60,480.00
	ORD 9ABONUS	540510	86,400.00
	ORD 9ABONUS	540520	25,920.00
5000101002	ORD 9ABONUS	540500	55,910.40
	ORD 9ABONUS	540510	79,872.00
	ORD 9ABONUS	540520	23,961.60
5000101003	ORD 9ABONUS	540500	38,707.20
	ORD 9ABONUS	540510	55,296.00
	ORD 9ABONUS	540520	16,588.80
5000101004	ORD 9ABONUS	540500	20,160.00

Figure 3.36: Results of plan accrual

The most used automatic planning methods tend to be the planned allocations. These include planned distribution, planned periodic re-posting, planned assessment, and planned indirect activity allocation. These methods all use the *cycle* and *segment* approach to allocations, so once you understand the basics of that, you will be able to set up and run all four as you require.

Planned allocations are particularly useful for moving support costs to the manufacturing cost centers to support plan activity price calculation and to understand the over/under-absorption of overheads. They are also useful for distribution of shared costs based on some fixed or variable factor.

The planned distribution and planned periodic re-posting are allocations using the originally posted or planned primary cost elements. This may be useful to allocate certain shared costs that were originally planned or posted to one cost center. An example of this might be rent costs that may have been coded to one cost center for convenience and then allocated based on some factor such as square footage to other cost centers. The major difference between distribution and re-posting is how the totals tables are updated. A distribution will update the sender cost center as a partner in the totals table while a reposing will not. Because of this, the re-posting will save memory and may have faster run times, but the tabulated records will be less complete.

Build a cost map

 When working with allocations and cost flows, it is useful to build a cost map or cost model. This can be done in a flowcharting tool such as Visio or even in Excel. Map out all your cost centers and link them with arrows represen- ting the allocations. I like to use color-coding to differen- tiate different types of cost movements. In a manufacturing company, all the absorbable costs should flow to the production related cost centers. Often, I will also reference the cost elements being used a- long with activity types. The map will serve as a useful reference to trace issues when you actually run your allocations.

As an example of a distribution, you may have an advertising cost center that is shared between the three marketing cost centers for the different product lines that were sold. The idea is to distribute the cost of that ad- vertising cost center to the marketing cost centers based on the number of advertisements that they require. This value is tracked in a statistical key figure.

Plan distribution cycles are created in transaction KSV7 and can be edit- ed in KSV8. Depending on your system setup, these may not be open in your production system, and you may have to make changes in your development system and move them to production. It is also possible to have these transactions opened in production with the help of a *basis* resource.

In general, the allocation cycle has a header (see Figure 3.37) to which you attach segments as needed. The key indicator here is the ITERATIVE check box. This is important if the cost center(s) that you are allocating from are also receivers in the cycle. The iterative flag will ensure that those cost centers are emptied. If you want a portion of the costs to re- main in the sending cost center, then you can un-check this.

You then use the ATTACH SEGMENT button to add the first segment. The segment defines the senders and receivers as well as the *tracing factors* to be used in the allocation.

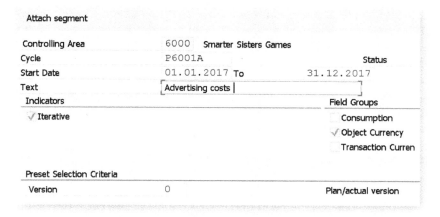

Figure 3.37: Distribution cycle header

Controlling Area	6000	Smarter Sisters Games	
Cycle	P6001A	Advertising costs	
Segment Name	ADVERT	Advertising	Lock

Segment Header | Senders/Receivers | Sender Values | Receiver Tracing Factor | Receiver Weighting Factor

Sender values

Sender rule	1 Posted amounts	⌄	
Share in %	100.00 %		
○ Act. vals	◉ Plan vals		

Receiver tracing factor

Receiver rule	1 Variable portions	⌄	
Var.portion type	6 Plan Stat. Key Figures		⌄
Scale Neg. Tracing Factors	1 No scaling		⌄

Figure 3.38: Distribution segment header

The segment has a number of tabs and is somewhat dynamic in that some of the options will change depending on the selection of the tracing factor. The tracing factor is selected on the SEGMENT HEADER (see Figure 3.38). The following options are available as tracing factors:

- ▶ Variable portions
- ▶ Fixed amounts
- ▶ Fixed Percentages
- ▶ Fixed Portions

The most flexible of these is the **variable portions** option since it allows you to base the allocation on values from outside the segment. All the fixed options require you to maintain amounts within the segment and therefore are less useful when the tracing factor values are likely to change over time. If you select the **variable portions** option, then you will need to select the **var portion type**. This defines what the tracing factor will be. There are many options but the most common are based on amounts and statistical key figures.

Once you have set the segment header, you should define the SENDERS/RECEIVERS. Here you define the sending cost centers or groups and the sending cost elements. Since this is a distribution, you should only select primary cost elements in the SENDER section. Then you define the receiving objects or groups (see Figure 3.39)

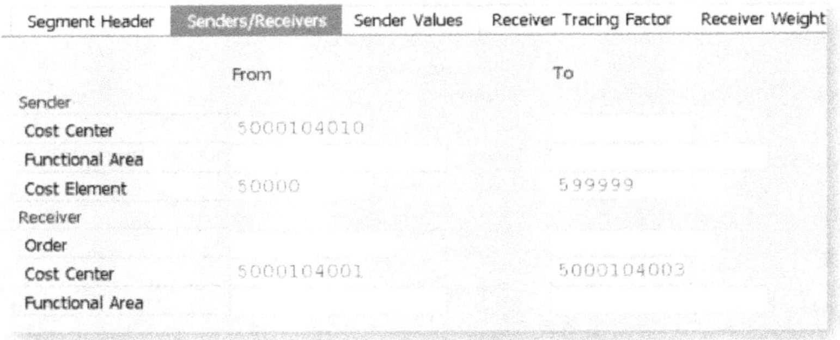

Segment Header	Senders/Receivers	Sender Values	Receiver Tracing Factor	Receiver Weight
	From		To	
Sender				
Cost Center	5000104010			
Functional Area				
Cost Element	50000		599999	
Receiver				
Order				
Cost Center	5000104001		5000104003	
Functional Area				

Figure 3.39: Distribution senders and receivers

In the case of allocation using a tracing factor, you will need to maintain values on the RECEIVING TRACING FACTOR tab (see Figure 3.40). Depending on the VAR PORTION TYPE, the values that you enter here may appear different from mine. Since you are using plan statistical key figures as the basis for your allocation, you should the SKF for number of adds placed as the tracing factor.

The plan distribution can be run from transaction KSVB (see Figure 3.41). You can select the **from and to** periods and the **fiscal year**. I am only going to run the cycle that just was created, but you can run more than one cycle at a time by adding more to the CYCLE list. The results are shown in Figure 3.68. All the cycle/segment type allocations can be reversed by pressing ⬆ + F8 while you are on the initial screen.

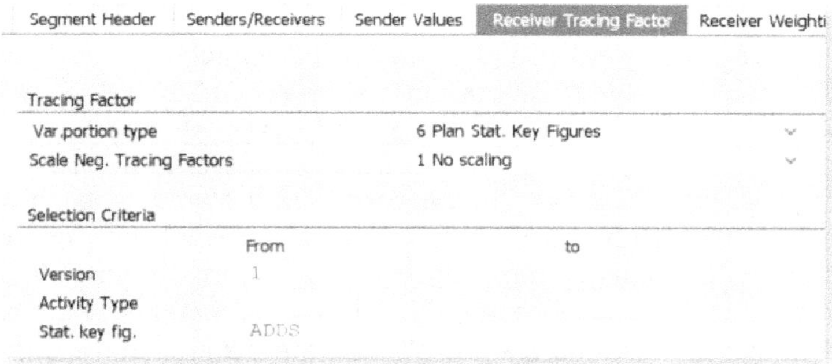

Segment Header	Senders/Receivers	Sender Values	Receiver Tracing Factor	Receiver Weighti

Tracing Factor

Var.portion type	6 Plan Stat. Key Figures	⌄
Scale Neg. Tracing Factors	1 No scaling	⌄

Selection Criteria

	From	to
Version	1	
Activity Type		
Stat. key fig.	ADDS	

Figure 3.40: Distribution receiver tracing factor

Execute Plan Distribution: Initial Screen

Settings

Parameters

Controlling Area	6000	Smarter Sisters Game
Period	1 To	12
Fiscal Year	2017	

Processing

Background Processing

✓ Test Run

✓ Detail Lists   List selection

Cycle	Start Date	
P6000A	01.01.2017	Advertising costs V1

Figure 3.41: Execute plan distribution

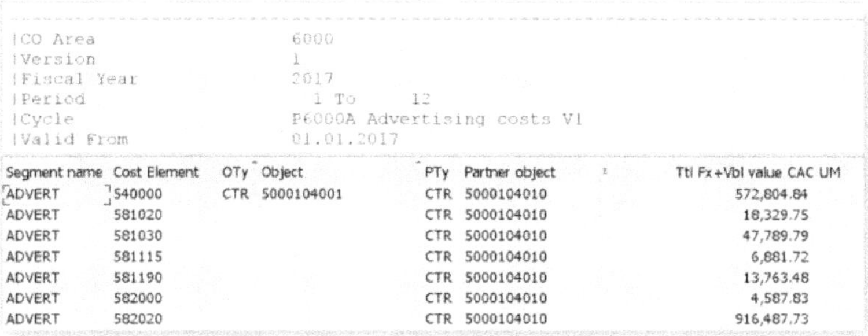

CO Area	6000
Version	1
Fiscal Year	2017
Period	1 To 12
Cycle	P6000A Advertising costs V1
Valid From	01.01.2017

Segment name	Cost Element	OTy	Object	PTy	Partner object	‡	Ttl Fx+Vbl value CAC UM
ADVERT	540000	CTR	5000104001	CTR	5000104010		572,804.84
ADVERT	581020			CTR	5000104010		18,329.75
ADVERT	581030			CTR	5000104010		47,789.79
ADVERT	581115			CTR	5000104010		6,881.72
ADVERT	581190			CTR	5000104010		13,763.48
ADVERT	582000			CTR	5000104010		4,587.83
ADVERT	582020			CTR	5000104010		916,487.73

Figure 3.42: Results of plan distribution

91

As mentioned, the cycle setup and running of the planned periodic re-posting is very similar to what you just saw for distribution. The transaction codes for planned periodic re-posting are KSW7 and KSW8 to create and change the cycle and KSWB to execute the allocation.

Assessments are allocations that use secondary cost elements to move the costs between cost objects. This is useful if you want the primary costs to remain on the sending cost center and you want the costs from the sending cost center to be allocated in a more summarized manner. An example of this is when you want to allocate the plant cafeteria costs to the production cost centers using one secondary cost element to represent the nature of the sent costs. As a prerequisite, you will require a secondary cost element type 42 to represent the cafeteria costs. The planned assessment cycle is created using transaction KSU7. The process is much the same as you saw for distribution. The major difference on the SEGMENT HEADER tab is the addition of the ASSESSMENT COST ELEMENT (see Figure 3.43). All the other fields on this tab work the same way as the distribution cycle.

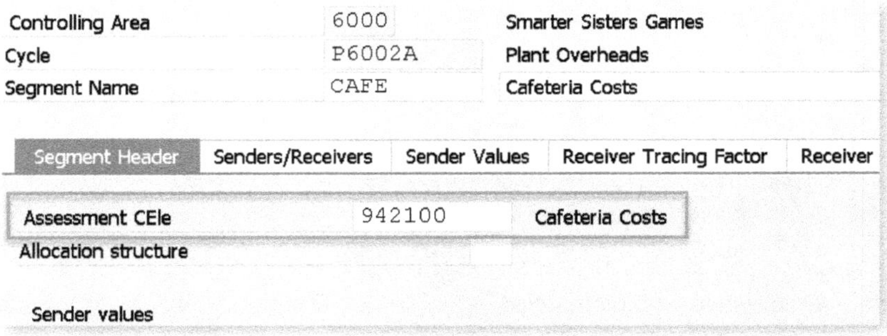

Controlling Area	6000	Smarter Sisters Games
Cycle	P6002A	Plant Overheads
Segment Name	CAFE	Cafeteria Costs

Segment Header	Senders/Receivers	Sender Values	Receiver Tracing Factor	Receiver

Assessment CEle	942100	Cafeteria Costs
Allocation structure		

Sender values

Figure 3.43: Assessment cycle – assessment cost element

The other tabs in the assessment cycle segments will be similar to what you saw in the distribution. The assessment is run using transaction KSUB, and the results can be seen in the receiving cost centers (see Figure 3.44). Note that the costs are transferred using a single secondary cost element per segment.

```
Cost Centers: Actual/Plan/Variance      Date: 27.02.2017           Page:     2 /   3

                                                                  Column:    1 /   2
Cost Center/Group            6001PROD                Plant 6001 Production
Person responsible:               *
Reporting period:             1  to    12   2017
```

Cost Elements	Act. Costs	Plan Costs	Var.(Abs.)	Var.(%)
540010 Labour-Reg-Productn		4,137,600.00	4,137,600.00-	100.00-
540500 Vacn Pay Accrual		289,632.00	289,632.00-	100.00-
540510 Bonus Accrual		413,760.00	413,760.00-	100.00-
540520 Sick leave accrual		124,128.00	124,128.00-	100.00-
942100 Cafeteria Costs		364,500.00	364,500.00-	100.00-
942110 Plant Finance Costs		716,399.88	716,399.88-	100.00-
942120 Plant General Admin		465,000.12	465,000.12-	100.00-
943400 IT Support		180,000.00	180,000.00-	100.00-
* Debit		6,691,020.00	6,691,020.00-	100.00-
** Over/Underabsorption		6,691,020.00	6,691,020.00-	100.00-

Figure 3.44: Result of assessment in receiving group

The final planning allocation is called planned indirect activity allocation. This is similar to assessments since it also uses a secondary cost element, in this case type 43, but also requires a sending activity type in addition to a sending cost center. The indirect activity allocation moves quantities of an activity between cost centers, and it requires that an activity cost should already exist if the value is to be determined. The secondary cost element used in the allocation is derived based on the activity being used. The indirect activity allocation cycle is created using transaction KSC7 and changed using KSC8. The cycle segment format is similar to the other planned allocations you have seen.

On the segment header, you will need to pay special attention to the RULE (see Figure 3.45). The value that you select here will be determined by the settings on the activity type master data. Refer back to Section 2.5 to review activity type settings. This rule determines how the activity quantities on the sender will be determined. There are three options:

▶ Posted quantities—this means that planned activity quantities should have been posted on the combination of the sender cost center and activity type prior to running the allocation cycle. For planning, this would have been done in transaction KP26. You would use this rule if the activity type category on your activity type is set to **manual entry, indirect allocation**. The posted quantities can be allocated based on your selected tracing factor.

► Fixed quantities—this means that you will enter the sending quantities manually within the allocation segment.

► Quantities calculated inversely—this means that the sending activity quantities will be calculated based on the receivers in the allocation cycle. The activity type category for this should be **indirect determination, indirect allocation**.

The receiver tracing factor serves the same purpose as it does in the distribution or assessment cycles. Even though this is an activity allocation, it is not necessary to use planned or actual activity as the receiver tracing factor. The purpose of the tracing factor is to define some relationship that serves to map the allocated costs to the receivers. This may be planned activity, planned statistical key figure values, or planned amounts. The key thing is that it serves as a realistic factor for basing the cost allocation.

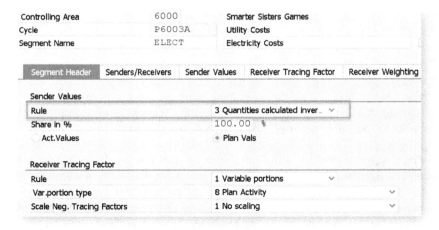

Figure 3.45: Indirect activity allocation segment header

In this allocation, the quantities will be calculated inversely, based on the receiver's relationship with the tracing factor **plan activity**.

On the SENDER/RECEIVERS tab, you need to select the sending **cost center**(s) and also the sender **activity types** (s). In the example in Figure 3.46 the sender cost center is the utilities cost center, and the activity type 2000 is electricity. The receiver is the group of production cost centers.

	From	To	Group
Segment Header	Senders/Receivers	Sender Values	Receiver Tracing Factor	Receiver Weighting Factors
Sender			
Cost Center	5000101905		
Functional Area			
Activity Type	2000		
Receiver			
Order			
Cost Center			6001PROD

Figure 3.46: Indirect activity allocation senders/receivers

The activity that is to be used as the tracing factor is selected on the RECEIVER TRACING FACTOR tab (see Figure 3.47). In this case, activity 1100—machine time is used as the tracing factor. The business feels that the number of machine hours planned on each production cost center is a reasonable predictor of the number of KWH of electricity that each will use.

Segment Header	Senders/Receivers	Sender Values	Receiver Tracing Factor	Receiver W
Tracing Factor		
Var .portion type	8 Plan Activity	
Scale Neg. Tracing Factors	1 No scaling	
Selection Criteria		
	From	to
Version	1	
Activity Type	1100	

Figure 3.47: Indirect activity allocation receiver tracing factor

In all types of allocation cycles, it is possible to modify the sender or receiver amounts by some manually entered factors. These are entered on the SENDER VALUES and the RECEIVER WEIGHTING FACTORS tabs. This functionality is easy to understand, and I have not provided screenshots of those tabs.

The planned indirect activity allocation is run from transaction KSCB. This is similar to the execution transaction of the other three methods. There are two results from this. First, if we are updating the activity quantity of the sender, then we should see the planned activity quantity reflected (see Figure 3.48).

95

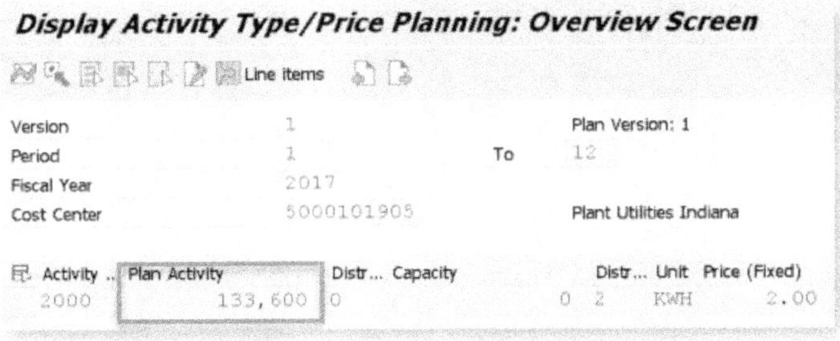

Display Activity Type/Price Planning: Overview Screen

Version	1		Plan Version: 1	
Period	1	To	12	
Fiscal Year	2017			
Cost Center	5000101905		Plant Utilities Indiana	

Activity ..	Plan Activity	Distr...	Capacity		Distr...	Unit	Price (Fixed)
2000	133,600	0		0	2	KWH	2.00

Figure 3.48: Plan activity updated by allocation

We should also see the cost of the activities reflected on the receiving cost centers (see Figure 3.49).

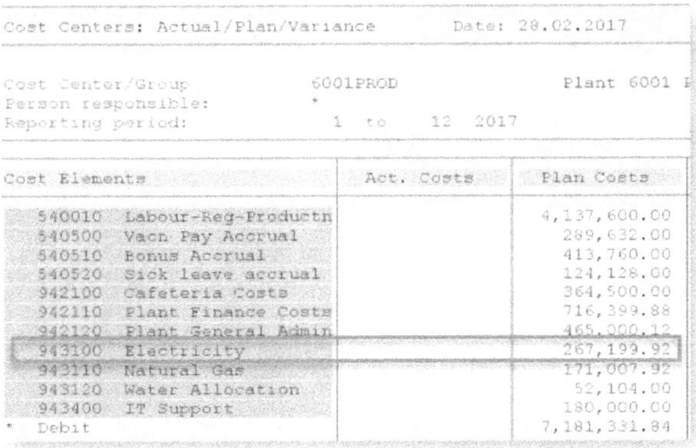

```
Cost Centers: Actual/Plan/Variance          Date: 28.02.2017

Cost Center/Group          6001PROD              Plant 6001
Person responsible:           *
Reporting period:           1  to   12   2017

Cost Elements                      Act. Costs        Plan Costs
   540010   Labour-Reg-Productn                     4,137,600.00
   540500   Vacn Pay Accrual                          289,632.00
   540510   Bonus Accrual                             413,760.00
   540520   Sick leave accrual                        124,128.00
   942100   Cafeteria Costs                           364,500.00
   942110   Plant Finance Costs                       716,399.88
   942120   Plant General Admin                       465,000.12
   943100   Electricity                               267,199.92
   943110   Natural Gas                               171,007.92
   943120   Water Allocation                           52,104.00
   943400   IT Support                                180,000.00
 * Debit                                            7,181,331.84
```

Figure 3.49: Activity allocation on receiving group

3.4 Activity output and price planning

In a manufacturing company, activity output and price planning will play a key role in the product costing function. This largely involves setting the prices of the activities used by the production work centers and having them reflected in the standard costs of the products once they have been calculated. Some companies simply calculate activity rates manually outside of SAP and enter the prices manually into the system through transaction KP26; others make more use of the integrated functionality of SAP to plan activity output quantities based on production planning and to automatically calculate activity prices based on those quantities and the values from cost planning.

One of the concepts in standard cost setting is that all the costs of production including support and overhead costs should be attributed to the products being made. This is the concept of *full absorption costing*. This is shown in a rather simplified context in Figure 3.50. This concept applies both to planning in SAP and to tracking actual costs. First, the primary and secondary costs of the support cost centers are allocated to the production cost centers. This commonly is done using an assessment, but sometimes other forms of allocation are also used. The goal is to allocate all the costs so that the *over/under-absorption* in the sending cost centers becomes zero.

The production cost center will incur its own direct costs as well as receiving allocations from the support cost centers. The planned or actual activity output from the production cost centers will update the product costs or, for actual postings, a production cost object such as a production order. In planning, the goal should be to determine activity prices so that, based on the level of output, the planned over/under-absorption in the production cost centers becomes zero. This ensures that the products are absorbing all the required values into their standard costs. In the case of actual postings, the debits to the production object will occur at the planned rates, but you will see later that it will be possible to revalue these objects based on calculated actual rates. Any balance at the end of a production order is considered variance and can be analyzed during the period end process for *cost object controlling*.

Support Cost Centers	Production Cost Centers	Production Object
Debits	**Debits**	**Debits**
Primary Costs	Primary Costs	• Materials In
• Salaries	• Wages	• Activities In
• Other Support Costs	• Other Direct	• Overheads In
Secondary Costs	Secondary Costs	**Total Debits**
• Allocations in	• Allocations in	Credits
Total Debits	**Total Debits**	• Materials Out
Credits	**Credits**	**Total Credits**
• Allocations Out	• Activities Out	**Variance**
Total Credits	**Total Credits**	
Over/Under Absorption	**Over/Under Absorption**	

Figure 3.50: Absorption costing in SAP

Manual price and output planning is simply carried out using transaction KP26 and the standard layout 1-201. Here you can simply enter the price, which can be split into fixed and variable portions, or you can also enter the plan activity quantity as well as the capacity (see Figure 3.51). The price entered will be the used for product costing based on the activity price settings on the valuation variant. Period specific values can be entered or displayed by clicking on the ✍ button.

Version	0		Plan/actual version								
Period	1	To	12								
Fiscal Year	2017										
Cost Center	5000102200		Video Game Assembly Kentucky								

Activity ... Plan Activity		Distr... Capacity		Distr...	Unit	Price (Fixed)	Variable price	Price unit	Pla...	P... A...	Alloc. cost
1000	15,000 2		18,000	2	H		30.00	00001 1			943000
1100	15,000 2		18,000	2	H		40.00	00001 1			943010
*Activ	30,000		36,000								

Figure 3.51 : Manual activity type price planning

If you enter a price and an activity quantity, then an equivalent plan credit will be posted to the cost center (see Figure 3.52).

Cost Centers: Actual/Plan/Variance		Date: 09.05.2017		Page: 2 / 3
				Column: 1 / 2
Cost Center/Group	5000102200		Video Game Assem KY	
Person responsible:	Nathan Rambo			
Reporting period:	1 to 12 2017			

Cost Elements	Act. Costs	Plan Costs	Var.(Abs.)	Var.(%)
943000 Production Labour		450,000.00-	450,000.00	100.00-
943010 Machine Time		600,000.00-	600,000.00	100.00-
* Credit		1,050,000.00-	1,050,000.00	100.00-
** Over/Underabsorption		1,050,000.00-	1,050,000.00	100.00-

Figure 3.52: Plan credits from activity price/output planning

A more integrated scenario for activity price and output planning involves sales planning feeding long-term production planning that, in turn, can automatically create planned activity quantities for the relevant cost center/activity type combination. In conjunction with this, cost planning is occurring for the production cost centers. Activity-dependent and independent costs are being planned, and applicable overhead costs are being assessed into the cost centers. With activity quantities and costs in place, it is possible to have SAP calculate the planned activity price.

This would be a relatively simple thing if all the planned input costs were activity-dependent since there would be a direct relationship between the planned activity, the input cost, and the activity quantity. However, this is rarely the case, as the input plans usually are comprised of a combination of activity-dependent and activity-independent costs, and there are sometimes multiple activities being output by each cost center.

To calculate an activity price, all the input costs in the cost center should be associated to an activity. If this is not done directly through activity-dependent planning, then it needs to be done using either *equivalence numbers* or *plan cost splitting*. This is shown conceptually in Figure 3.53.

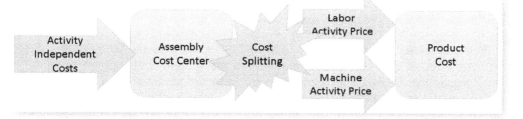

Figure 3.53: Plan cost splitting

Splitting by equivalence numbers is the simplest option since it does not require additional system configuration. You can enter the equivalence numbers during planning in transaction KP26 (see Figure 3.54).

Version	0		Plan/actual version										
Period	1	To	12										
Fiscal Year	2017												
Cost Center	5000105100		Card Game Assembly Missouri										

Activity ... Plan Activity		Distr... Capacity		Distr... Unit	Price (Fix...	Variab...	Price unit	Pla...	P...	A...	Alloc. cost ele...	T	EquiNo
1000	28,200	2		2	H			00001	1		943000	1	2
1100	24,000	2		2	H			00001	1		943010	1	5
*Activ	52,200		0										7

Figure 3.54: Equivalence numbers in planning

Plan cost splitting will then split all the planned activity-independent costs based on the ratio of the equivalence numbers (see Figure 3.55). With this option, there is no need to assign a *splitting structure* to the cost center. SAP will always split using equivalence numbers if you do not configure and assign a splitting structure. In reality, splitting based on a splitting structure is usually the preferred method since you are able to directly link groups of cost elements to activity types. In addition, once the splitting structure is defined, the splitting is carried out automatically based on the configuration, whereas the equivalence numbers will need to be maintained manually every time you change your planning.

Plan Cost Splitting: List

Display status   Total for all periods

Cost Object	Cost Elem.	Name	Partner object	Resource	Planned (COArCurr)	Crcy
CTR 5000105100	540000	Salaries				USD
ATY 5000105100/1000	540000	Salaries			171,428.52	USD
ATY 5000105100/1100	540000	Salaries			428,571.48	USD
CTR 5000105100	550110	Facility Costs				USD
ATY 5000105100/1000	550110	Facility Costs			6,857.16	USD
ATY 5000105100/1100	550110	Facility Costs			17,142.84	USD
CTR 5000105100	551155	Rental Costs				USD
ATY 5000105100/1000	551155	Rental Costs			8,571.48	USD
ATY 5000105100/1100	551155	Rental Costs			21,428.52	USD
**					654,000.00	USD

Figure 3.55: Split by equivalence numbers

As mentioned, the other option is to split based on cost element. For this, you need to define a splitting structure in the system configuration using transaction OKES. The same splitting structure can be used for both plan cost splitting and actual cost splitting. Once the splitting structure is defined, you need to assign it to the cost centers that will need cost splitting using the configuration transaction OKEW.

The configuration of the splitting structure consists of a number of related components. First, there is the overall definition of the structure shown in Figure 3.56.

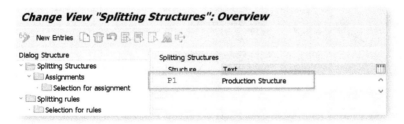

Figure 3.56: Splitting structure overall definition

Once you have created the overall structure definition with text, you need to define the assignments. You should create one assignment for each activity type. (See Figure 3.57). In this case, there are two activities, labor and machine time, so two assignments are defined.

Structure Name		P1	Production Structure		
Assignments					
Assgnmnt	Text			Rule	Text
1	Labor			P1	Production
2	Other			P1	Production

Figure 3.57: Splitting structure assignments

Next, for each assignment, you need to define the source cost elements and the activity type (see Figure 3.58). Here you can assign ranges, cost elements, or preferably cost element groups to an activity type.

Structure Name		P1	Production Structure	
Assignment		2	Other	
Splitting Rule		P1	Production	
Controlling Area		6000	Smarter Sisters Games	
Selection for assignment				
Field Label	From Value	To Value		Group
Cost Element				OTHER
Activity Type	1100			

Figure 3.58: Cost elements and activity type for each assignment

The final required step in OKES is to create the splitting rule. This involves creating a rule and assigning a pre-defined method (see Figure 3.59). For actual and plan cost splitting, the method will usually be by activity quantity or planned activity quantity. Once the rule is defined, it can be tied to the assignments that were created in Figure 3.57.

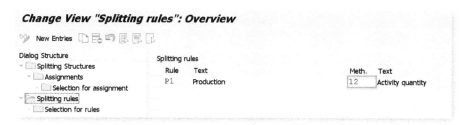

Figure 3.59: Create splitting rule

The next piece of configuration assigns the splitting structure to the cost centers using transaction OKEW. On the initial screen, you select the cost centers and versions that you want to assign. Once you get past the initial screen, you will see something like Figure 3.60. You will see all the created splitting structures, and you will see the unassigned cost centers. To assign a cost center to the splitting structure, simply click the check box next to the cost center, then select the splitting structure and click the ⬚ button. The cost center(s) will now be assigned to the splitting structure (see Figure 3.61).

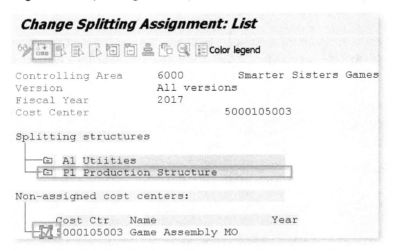

Figure 3.60: Splitting structure before cost center assignment

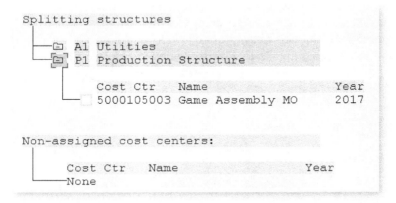

Figure 3.61: Splitting structure after cost center assignment

Once this configuration is in place, you can perform plan activity price calculation using plan cost splitting. Run transaction KSPI to calculate the planned activity prices. This transaction will carry out the splitting and the price calculation together. If you need to see the splitting as a sepa-rate step, you can run planned splitting independently using transaction KSS4 and then run planned price calculation. This is usually not neces-sary, so just KSPI is being run in this example. The first screen is simply the selection of cost centers. After that, you can see the plan price calcu-lation (Figure 3.62).

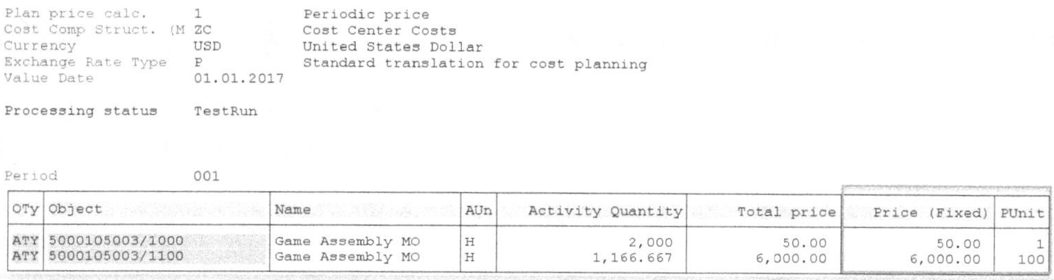

```
Plan price calc.      1            Periodic price
Cost Comp Struct. (M  ZC           Cost Center Costs
Currency              USD          United States Dollar
Exchange Rate Type    P            Standard translation for cost planning
Value Date            01.01.2017

Processing status     TestRun


Period                001
```

OTy	Object	Name	AUn	Activity Quantity	Total price	Price (Fixed)	PUnit
ATY	5000105003/1000	Game Assembly MO	H	2,000	50.00	50.00	1
ATY	5000105003/1100	Game Assembly MO	H	1,166.667	6,000.00	6,000.00	100

Figure 3.62: Activity prices automatically calculated

Some things to note:

▶ The per-unit price is the total price divided by the price unit. In Figure 3.62, the per-unit activity price of activity 1100 is $60 per hour since the price unit is 100.

▶ The price calculation from activity-independent costs will always result in a fixed price.

▶ If you want a variable portion in the price, you need to do activi-ty-dependent planning and plan variable input costs in the cost center.

In Chapter 8, you will see the integration of cost center accounting with production planning and product cost planning in more detail and see a further example of planned activity price calculation.

3.5   Statistical key figure planning

As you saw in Section 2.6, the statistical key figures exist to capture plan and actual values for any non-monetary statistics you need to capture. The statistical key figure values can be used simply for reporting or, as we have seen, as tracing factors in allocation cycles. To plan statistical key figures, you use transaction KP46. These can be planned directly in SAP and can be uploaded using the flexible Excel method if you have built the corresponding layouts and assigned them correctly to the planner profile. There are three standard layouts provided for SKF planning:

▶ 1-301– Statistical Key Figures: Standard

▶ 1-302 – Stat. Key Figures: Activity-Dependent

▶ 1-303C – Statistical Key Figures: Central

As you can see from the layout, it is possible to plan or post SKF values on a combination of cost center and activity, but this is not something that I have seen in practice. I will just plan headcount for my cost centers using layout 1-303C where you can enter the plan values for the cost centers in a list format (see Figure 3.63).

Version	2		Plan Version: 2
Period	1	To	12
Fiscal Year	2017		
Stat. key fig.	HCNT		Employee Headcount

Cost Center	T	Current Plan Value	Distr...	Maximum plan value	Distr...	Unit
5000101001	1	8	2		2	PRS
5000101002	1	12	2		2	PRS
5000101003	1	5	2		2	PRS
5000101004	1	9	2		2	PRS

Figure 3.63: SKF Planning

Once you have saved the plan values, they will be available for use in cost center reports and in allocation cycles.

3.6 Planning aids

SAP offers a number of transactions to aid with planning. There are two copy functions, copy plan to plan, and copy actual to plan. There is also a transaction to revalue plan values based on percentages, and there are some transactions to transfer values from other SAP modules.

The copy plan to plan transaction, KP97, can be used to copy plan values based on periods, fiscal years, and versions (see Figure 3.64). The option SELECT PLAN DATA allows you considerable control over the type of plan data to be copied. You can choose to copy only certain plan data such as activity-independent primary costs and statistical key figures, or you can choose to copy all plan data. In KP97, you specify the TEMPLATE or source to copy and the TARGET to receive the copy.

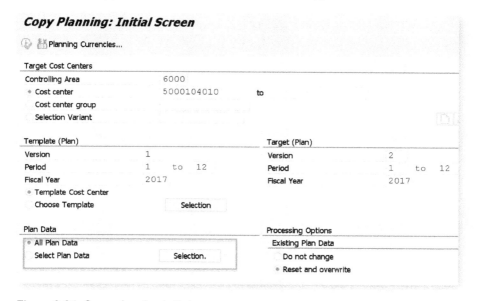

Figure 3.64: Copy planning initial screen

The transaction KP98 allows you to copy actual data to plan versions. This is useful if you want to copy a prior year actual into an upcoming plan year or if you want to copy a range of actual periods into a forecast version to give you a version that has year-to-date actuals and remaining plan. The selection screen and function of KP98 is almost identical to KP97.

The transaction KSPU allows you to perform a plan revaluation. There are two steps to this process. First, you define the revaluation, and then you run the revaluation. Multiple revaluation rules can be processed in one run. To create or change a revaluation, you select EXTRAS • REVALU-ATION • CREATE from the menu within transaction KSPU. On the initial screen, you will enter the name, fiscal year, and version for the revaluation and then go to the create screen (see Figure 3.65). Here you should enter a description, the cost centers or cost center group, and the cost element group. By clicking on the DEFINITION button, you can define the revaluation factors for each cost element in the group (see Figure 3.66). The revaluation factor can be positive or negative and can vary depending on the periods. Use the NEXT COST ELEMENT button to define rules for further cost elements.

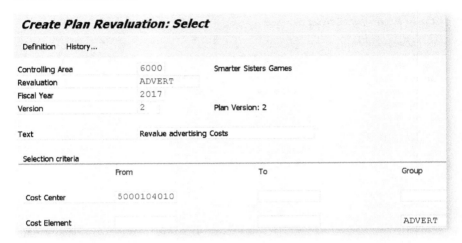

Figure 3.65: Create revaluation initial screen

Figure 3.66: Plan revaluation definition

Once the revaluation definitions have been created, they are run from the initial screen of KSPU. The result of the revaluation can be seen in the plan line items (see Figure 3.67).

Year	frm	To Period	Cost Element	Cost Center	Cost element name	Cost element descr.	Σ	Total val. rep.crcy
2017	1	12	540000	5000104010	Salaries	Salaries		1,500,000.00
2017	1	12	540000	5000104010	Salaries	Salaries		52,684.92
2017				50001040 △			•	1,552,684.92
△							• •	1,552,684.92

Figure 3.67: Plan revaluation posting

One of the most useful transfer functions is a report to transfer planned depreciation from the fixed asset module to cost center planning. This is straightforward since each asset is linked directly to a cost center from the asset master data. The transfer can also include anticipated depreciation from planned capital investments including *appropriate requests, WBS elements,* and *investment internal orders.* The report transaction is S_ALR_87099918; there are a number of selection criteria that can be selected, including whether to include various investment management objects. Once you run this, you will see planned depreciation costs included in the cost centers (see Figure 3.68).

```
Period Breakdown: Actual/Planned        Date: 24.02.2017          Page:      2 /    2

                                                                 Column:    1 /    1
Cost Center/Group        5000103100         Trucking Fleet
Person responsible       Willie Coyote
Cost Element/Group       640000            Depreciation Expense
Fiscal Year              2017
```

Periods	Act. Costs	Plan Costs	Var.(Abs.)	Var.(%)
1 January		38,333.33	38,333.33-	100.00-
2 February		38,333.34	38,333.34-	100.00-
3 March		38,333.33	38,333.33-	100.00-
4 April		38,333.33	38,333.33-	100.00-
5 May		38,333.34	38,333.34-	100.00-
6 June		38,333.33	38,333.33-	100.00-
7 July		38,333.33	38,333.33-	100.00-
8 August		38,333.34	38,333.34-	100.00-
9 September		38,333.33	38,333.33-	100.00-
10 October		38,333.33	38,333.33-	100.00-
11 November		38,333.34	38,333.34-	100.00-
12 December		38,333.33	38,333.33-	100.00-
* Total		460,000.00	460,000.00-	100.00-

Figure 3.68: Results of planned depreciation transfer

3.7 Summary

In this chapter, you have learned about cost center planning in SAP. You have seen where cost center planning fits in a typical overall planning cycle. You have gained some appreciation of the integrated nature of planning in SAP and now understand the three main areas of planning: cost input planning, activity output/price planning, and statistical key figure planning. You should now understand the distinction between activity-dependent and activity-independent cost planning and know the implications of using one versus the other. You have seen how to perform manual planning for each of these areas as well as some automatic methods. Finally, you have learned about some tools to aid with planning such as plan copy, plan revaluation, and planned depreciation transfer.

4 Cost center planning in S/4 HANA

In this chapter, you will see how cost center planning is carried out in S/4 HANA (1610 on premise). The basic concepts of embedded planning including the use of analysis for office as a planning front end will be covered. You will get some idea about what is currently available for cost center planning in S/4 and what is still in process. This is not intended to be a guide to setting up BPC or to provide an in-depth review of all the features of embedded planning. The intention is just to give a flavor of how cost center planning looks and behaves in S/4 HANA.

4.1 Concept of BPC embedded planning

Embedded planning is the preferred approach for basic CO planning in S/4 HANA. In this case, embedded means using BPC functionality to plan with an *analysis for office* layout as a front end. This functionality is designed to replace some of the manual planning steps within the SAP ERP component. At this time, not all the planning functions are available in embedded BPC, so it is necessary to perform a sort of hybrid planning (see Figure 4.1).

	Manual Planning	Copy to ERP	Planned Allocations	Copy from ERP	Update Planning
Tool	Analysis for Office/BPC	Analysis for Office/BPC	ECC Planned Allocations	Analysis for Office/BPC	Analysis for Office/BPC
Data Stored in	BPC Tables	ERP Tables	ERP Tables	BPC Tables	BPC Tables
BPC Area	A00 or A01	A09		A09	A00 or A01

Figure 4.1: Embedded planning for cost centers

The manual plan entry can be carried out in the analysis for office Excel workbook and saved. At this point, the saved data only resides in BPC; there are no planning values in the ERP system. There are currently no functions to perform planned allocations within embedded BPC so it is

necessary to copy the planned data into ERP to run the planned allocations. Once these have been run, the allocated plan can be copied back
into BPC. The copy from and to functions are run in a separate BPC area
and workbook from the one that you used to enter the data. Once you
have copied the allocated plan back into BPC, you can make edits and
go through the cycle again if required.

Currently, the process of manual plan entry is supported for activity-
independent primary cost planning

4.2 Planning areas in embedded planning

Prior to using embedded planning, you must have analysis for office
installed on your computer, and a number of technical and configuration
steps have to be completed. Analysis for office is a SAP-provided add-in
for Microsoft Excel which can be used for ad hoc reporting as well as
planning.

Description	Technical Name
Balance Sheet Planning on Periods	/ERP/SFIN_AA1_WB01
Balance Sheet Planning on Years	/ERP/SFIN_AA0_WB01
Cost Center Activity Planning	/ERP/SFIN_A03_WB01
Cost Center Fixed Consumption Planning	/ERP/SFIN_A03_WB10
Cost Center Planning On Periods	/ERP/SFIN_A01_WB01
Cost Center Planning On Years	/ERP/SFIN_A00_WB01
Functional Area Planning On Periods	/ERP/SFIN_A81_WB01
Functional Area Planning on Years	/ERP/SFIN_A80_WB01
Internal Order Planning On Periods	/ERP/SFIN_A11_WB01
Internal Order Planning On Years	/ERP/SFIN_A10_WB01
Market Segment Planning On Periods	/ERP/SFIN_A51_WB01
Market Segment Planning On Years	/ERP/SFIN_A50_WB01
P&L Planning On Periods	/ERP/SFIN_A91_WB01
P&L Planning On Years	/ERP/SFIN_A90_WB01
Plan Data Transfer for Cost Centers	/ERP/SFIN_A09_WB01
Plan Data Transfer for Cost Centers (Group Crcy)	/ERP/SFIN_A09_WB02
Plan Data Transfer for Internal Orders	/ERP/SFIN_A19_WB01
Plan Data Transfer for Internal Orders (Group Crcy)	/ERP/SFIN_A19_WB02
Plan Data Transfer for Projects	/ERP/SFIN_A29_WB01
Plan Data Transfer for Projects (Group Crcy)	/ERP/SFIN_A29_WB02
Profit Center Planning On Periods	/ERP/SFIN_A71_WB01
Profit Center Planning On Years	/ERP/SFIN_A70_WB01
Project Planning On Periods	/ERP/SFIN_A21_WB01
Project Planning On Years	/ERP/SFIN_A20_WB01
Sales Planning on Periods	/ERP/SFIN_A51_WB02

Figure 4.2: Areas and workbooks in BPC planning

SAP provides a number of pre-defined planning areas and workbooks (see Figure 4.2). It may also be possible to have custom areas and workbooks built by a BPC expert. Note that the areas available for cost center planning are A00, A01, A03, and A09, and there may be more than one workbook available per area.

You will either use area A00 or A01 to enter the plan data manually. Area A00 allows planning on an annual basis, while A01 provides twelve periods for a fiscal year. The A09 area is used for copying the plan data to and from SAP ERP.

4.3   Planning functionality in S/4 HANA

Embedded planning functionality in S/4 begins with entering the manual plan data. The area A01 will be used; this allows planning by individual period in the fiscal year. As I mentioned, analysis for Office is an add-in to Excel. If you have this installed, either you will have an icon like 🔲 or you will launch it from your Windows start menu. Launching this will start Excel with some additional tabs and functions (see Figure 4.3).

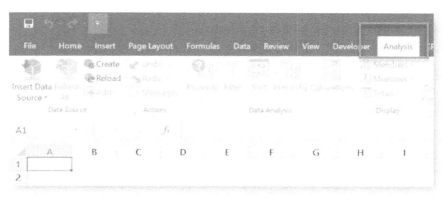

Figure 4.3: Analysis tab in Excel

To find the planning areas, you will go to the FILE menu and select ANALYSIS • OPEN WORKBOOK • OPEN WORKBOOK FROM SAP NETWEAVER PLATFORM (see Figure 4.4).

111

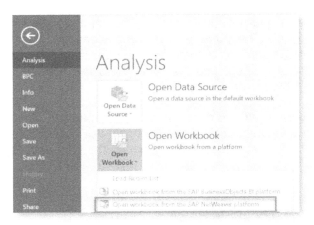

Figure 4.4: Open analysis workbook

Here you will be prompted to log in to an SAP system, so select the system, and login. You will then see the open document screen, and you can use the search function with the search word **planning** to display the screen from Figure 4.2. Here you select the area and workbook that you want to use.

Once you select the workbook, you will be prompted for parameters such as **fiscal year**, **category**, **company code,** and **cost centers** (see Figure 4.5). Complete all required parameters and click **OK**. Note that the CO concept of plan version does not appear here. The category in BPC can be thought of as similar to the version in ERP, and it is possible to configure various categories for other purposes such as different forecasts.

* Fiscal Year	2018	
* Category	BUD	
* Company Code	1000	
Cost Center	5000199001	
	5000199002	

Figure 4.5: BPC plan selection parameters

Figure 4.6: New plan in BPC

You will notice that, if you plan for a year where there are actual values in the prior year, then this layout will bring those actuals into a column in the workbook. You can then use the button Copy Actual to Plan to populate the planned values based on the prior year actuals (see Figure 4.7). Notice that when you do this, it will bring the correct actual period values into the periods, not simply divide the total actual value by twelve.

Figure 4.7: Copy actual to plan

Even if you are not starting from prior year actuals, you can still distribute the plan from an annual value, use Excel formulas in cells, and perform a plan revaluation based on a factor. In Figure 4.8 the plan values have been entered in the total plan column for 2017. By clicking on the recalculate button, you can distribute this plan to each period (see Figure 4.9).

113

Prompt Variables	Save	Clear Plan		Back to Saved State		Copy Actual to Plan		Recalculate	

Fiscal Year	2017
Category	BUD
Company Code	1000
Cost Center	5000199001
GL Account Hierarchy	
GL Account / GL Account G	
Currency	USD

			[+] Total Actual 2016	[-] Total Plan 2017	Period 1	Period 2	Period 3
Cost Center	G/L Account		$				
5000199001 Corporate Finance	581030	Consultants		24,000.00	0.00	0.00	0.00
	581130	Office Furn & Suppl		12,000.00	0.00	0.00	0.00

Figure 4.8: Enter a new plan

			[+] Total Actual 2016	[-] Total Plan 2017	Period 1	Period 2	Period 3
Cost Center	G/L Account		$	$	$	$	$
5000199001 Corporate Finance	581030	Consultants		24,000.00	2,000.00	2,000.00	2,000.00
	581130	Office Furn & Suppl		12,000.00	1,000.00	1,000.00	1,000.00
	Result			36,000.00	3,000.00	3,000.00	3,000.00

Figure 4.9: Recalculated plan

You can enter or edit values directly in the period columns and then re-calculate to update the total plan; alternatively, you could enter a formula in the total plan column and recalculate to push the values to the periods. Generally, standard Excel functions like copy and paste can be used to populate cells. If you do not want to plan by period, there is another area and worksheet available to plan by fiscal year.

Once you have entered the plan values for your cost centers and saved them in BPC, you can copy those values back into the ERP system to perform allocations. The planning area A09 is used to copy values to and from ERP. You will follow similar steps to get to the planning area and the parameters (see Figure 4.10). Here you will see this version because you are going to be copying values from the selected **category** in BPC to a selected plan **version** in ERP.

Figure 4.10: Parameters for area A09

The layout of this sheet is different (see Figure 4.11) from the A01 work-sheet; there are some different button options, and all the planning data is presented in single columns, not a column by period. When you first open this workbook, it will show the values stored in BPC for the selected cost centers and GL accounts. These are displayed in the AMOUNT BPC column. When you click on the **copy BPC to ERP** button, the values will be copied into the AMOUNT ERP column (see Figure 4.12). You then need to click to the **save data** button to start the actual transfer.

Plan Data Transfer for Cost Centers

System: DE3 - Client: 20 - User: jpnngle

| Prompt Variables | Copy BPC to ERP | Copy ERP to BPC | Save Data |

Fiscal Year	2018
Posting Period	1 - 12
Category	BUD
Version	0
Cost Center	5000199001; 5000199002; 5000199003; 5000199004; 500019
GL Account Hierarchy	
GL Account / GL Account Gr	
Currency	USD

Figure 4.11: Copy BPC to ERP worksheet

Deb/Cred Ind	CO	Cost Center	G/L Account	Posting period	Amount BPC $	Amount ERP $	Quantity BPC	Quantity ERP
D		5000199001	0010/540000	1	16,711.23	16,711.23	0	0
				2	18,966.60	18,966.60	0	0
				3	19,440.88	19,440.88	0	0
				4	17,746.60	17,746.60	0	0
				5	19,461.47	19,461.47	0	0
				6	18,263.75	18,263.75	0	0
				7	21,589.68	21,589.68	0	0

Figure 4.12: Amount going to ERP

The transferred data will be visible in any of the ERP cost center reports showing planned data (Figure 4.13).

Cost Centers: Actual/Plan/Variance	Date: 15.03.2017	Page: 2 / 2
		Column: 1 / 2
Cost Center/Group	5000199001	Finance - Corp
Person responsible:	Phil Mipockets	
Reporting period:	1 to 1 2018	

Cost Elements	Act. Costs	Plan Costs	Var. (Abs.)	Var. (%)
540000 Salaries		16,711.23	16,711.23-	100.00-
581030 Consultants		6,016.04	6,016.04-	100.00-
581705 Audit fees		3,008.02	3,008.02-	100.00-
* Debit		25,735.29	25,735.29-	100.00-

Figure 4.13: Plan values transferred from BPC

As mentioned, automatic allocation functionality is not currently part of embedded planning, so this must be done in ERP. If you are using statistical key figures as tracing factors in your allocations, these must also be planned in ERP, as there is not currently a standard worksheet for that in BPC.

In this company, all the office rent costs have been planned to the Corporate Administration cost center (see Figure 4.14), and a planned distribution will be used to allocate the rent to the other corporate cost centers. The actual mechanics of the distribution cycle will not be shown here as you have already seen that in the previous chapter, and there is no significant change in the functionality in S/4.

Now it is possible to go back to embedded BPC and copy these distributed values back into the BPC plan. Again, the A09 area will be used, and you will enter similar parameters as before. Now you will see some values in the AMOUNT ERP column that do not exist in the AMOUNT BPC column (see Figure 4.16). These values represent any planned allocations posted in ERP such as assessments or distributions. The values shown in Figure 4.16 are the credit values to the sending cost center. If you were to scroll further down in the worksheet, you would see corresponding debit values in the receiving cost centers.

				Column: 1 / 2
Cost Center/Group	5000199003		Corporate Admin	
Person responsible:	Mrs Moneypenny			
Reporting period:	1 to 12 2018			

Cost Elements	Act. Costs	Plan Costs	Var.(Abs.)	Var.(%)
540000 Salaries		63,865.01	63,865.01-	100.00-
581100 Office Rent		1,200,000.00	1,200,000.00-	100.00-
581130 Office Furn & Suppl		22,808.95	22,808.95-	100.00-
581190 Travelling & Accom		18,347.49	18,347.49-	100.00-

Figure 4.14: Planned rent before distribution

After the distribution, the rent has been allocated to four additional cost centers in addition to corporate administration (see Figure 4.15).

581100	Office Rent	CTR	5000199001		215,672.16-	215,672.16-
581100	Office Rent	CTR	5000199002		168,224.28-	168,224.28-
581100	Office Rent	CTR	5000199003		258,806.64-	258,806.64-
581100	Office Rent	CTR	5000199004		125,952.60-	125,952.60-
581100	Office Rent	CTR	5000199005		431,344.32-	431,344.32-
				·	1,200,000.00- ·	1,200,000.00-
Distribution				· ·	1,200,000.00- · ·	1,200,000.00-

Figure 4.15: Office rent planned distribution

Figure 4.16: BPC amounts in ERP

Clicking the **copy ERP to BPC** button will bring the amount into the AMOUNT BPC column, and then clicking **save data** will update the BPC plan.

Deb/Cred Ind	CO	Cost Center	G/L Account	Posting period	Amount BPC	Amount ERP	Quantity BPC	Quantity ERP
					$	$		
C		5000109003	0010/581100	1	-100,000.00	-100,000.00	0	0
				2	-100,000.00	-100,000.00	0	0
				3	-100,000.00	100,000.00	0	0
				4	-100,000.00	-100,000.00	0	0
				5	-100,000.00	100,000.00	0	0
				6	-100,000.00	100,000.00	0	0
				7	-100,000.00	-100,000.00	0	0
				8	-100,000.00	-100,000.00	0	0

Figure 4.17: ERP amount copied to BPC

The plan integration functionality appears to work within BPC, similar to ERP. If you look at one of the planning areas for profit center planning such as A71, you will see that amounts that were planned on the cost centers flowing into the related profit center plan. The same will be true if you use the A91 area, which provides P&L planning by company code, similar to new GL planning in ERP.

Profit Center		G/L Account		[+] Total Actual 2017	[-] Total Plan 2018	Period 1	Period 2	Period 3	Period 4
				$	$	$	$	$	$
1000	Profit Center 1000	Audit fees	581705	41,056.10	41,056.10	3,008.02	3,417.59	3,499.37	3,194.39
		Bank Charges	700610	63.66					
		Communications	581020	123,578.81	115,595.68	8,469.25	9,622.41	9,852.64	8,993.98
		Computer S/Hardware	581025	59,695.54	59,695.54	4,373.66	4,969.18	5,088.07	4,644.64
		Consultants	581030	206,569.43	185,903.87	13,473.93	15,308.52	15,674.81	14,308.73
		Donations	581700	1,414.18					

Figure 4.18: Profit center plan in BPC

Coming back to cost center planning, there are three new planning areas added in the 1610 release in addition to the ones that you have seen already in 1511.

The area A03_WB10 called *cost center fixed consumption planning* is a layout where you can enter sender and receiver cost centers and the costs being moved, which are essentially fixed amount transfers between cost centers. This somewhat duplicates a planned allocation but is extremely manual, and there are no rules or tracing factors. The system reads actuals based on sender receiver relationships and includes manual activity-independent cost allocations as well as distributions, assessments, and periodic re-posting in the prior year actual column. The values that you post or change here show up in the A09 area as an amount in BPC but do not get transferred to ERP when the transfer is run. Changes made with this transaction will remain in BPC planning only.

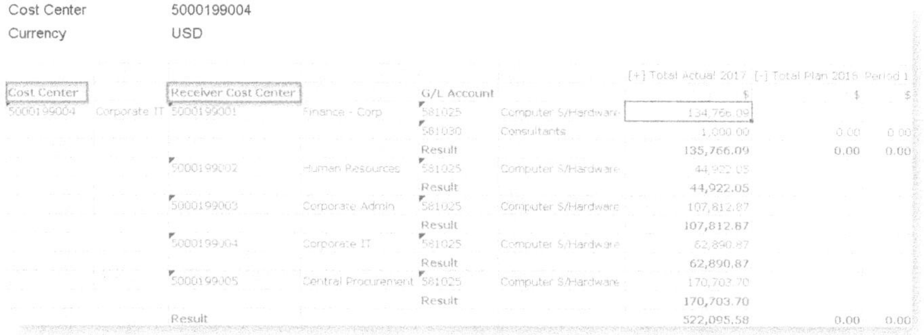

Figure 4.19: Cost center plan fixed consumption

The next new area provided in 1610 for cost center planning is A03_WB01, which is used for cost center activity planning. In this case, there are two tabs provided. One tab is for activity price planning (see Figure 4.20), and the second is for activity quantity planning (see Figure 4.21).

Figure 4.20 : Activity price plan in BPC

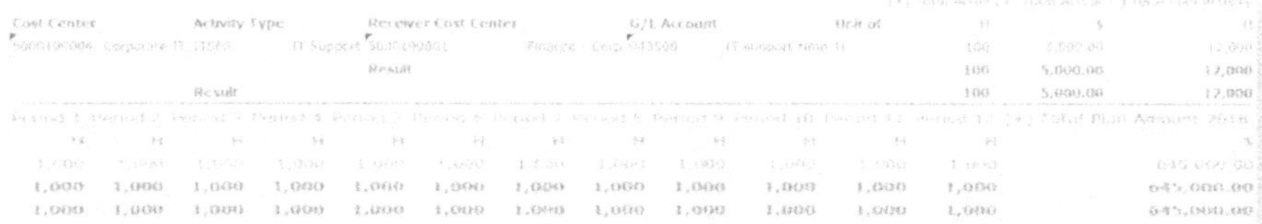

Figure 4.21: Activity quantity plan in BPC

The values from the first tab and the quantities from the second tab are used to determine the TOTAL PLAN AMOUNT for the year. Again, these values do not get transferred back to ERP when you run the plan transfer.

The final planning area available now is called cost center cost simulation and uses planning area A02. This can be used to simulate the effects of various allocations scenarios with the BPC plan.

4.4 Plan actual reporting with HANA

One of the most basic things that cost center managers will require is the ability to compare their actual results versus their plan. In SAP ECC6 and prior releases, there were a number of delivered reports to do this. Now with embedded planning, the idea is that BPC will be the system of record for the plan data, and the actual data will reside in the ERP system. This means that plan data may be either incomplete or non-existent in the ERP system, making the old ECC reports useless.

To remedy this, SAP has come up with a number of reports linking plan data from BPC and actual data from ERP. These are accessed through Fiori tiles. In Section 1.4, you learned that Fiori is the new preferred user interface for S/4. There are a number of reporting tiles available, and two of the most relevant for cost center accounting are shown in Figure 4.22.

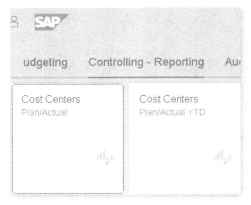

Figure 4.22: Fiori key cost center reports

A sample of the output from the plan/actual report is shown in Figure 4.23. There are a number of formatting options available, as well as the ability to download to Excel.

									Fiscal Year	Category	Posting Period	Company Code	Functional Area	Seg
2017		BUD		001		1000			

Cost Center Hierarchy	Cost Center / Cost Center Group	Cost Center	GL Account Hierarchy	GL Account / GL Account Group
		5000199001		

Data Analysis   Graphical Display   Query Information

Filter ∨   Sort ∨   Hierarchy ∨   Drilldown ∨   Display ∨   Measures ∨   Totals ∨

	G/L Account		Actual Amount	Plan Amount	Difference	%-Difference
	Assessment	942100	$ 3,457.49	$ 6,186.67	$ -2,729.18	-44.11 %
	Audit fees	581705	$ 3,008.02	$ 3,000.00	$ 8.02	0.27 %
	Computer S/Hardware	581025	$ 1,131.12	$ 2,000.00	$ -868.88	-43.44 %
Finance - Corp	Consultants	581030	$ 6,016.04	$ 2,000.00	$ 4,016.04	200.80 %
	Office Furn & Suppl	581130		$ 1,000.00	$ -1,000.00	-100.00 %
	Salaries	540000	$ 16,711.23	$ 17,000.00	$ -288.77	-1.70 %
	Result	Result	$ 30,323.90	$ 31,186.67	$ -862.77	-2.77 %
Result	Result	Result	$ 30,323.90	$ 31,186.67	$ -862.77	-2.77 %

Figure 4.23: Fiori cost centers plan/actual

4.5   Summary

You have seen some of the functionality available for cost center planning in S/4 HANA using embedded BPC. This chapter has just scratched the surface and has only focused on cost centers using "out of the box" functionality. I expect that the range of planning options and the functionality available with this tool will expand with upcoming releases of the software.

5 Cost center manual actual posting

In this chapter, you will understand the flow of actual values from other SAP ECC modules into CCA, including commitments from Materials Management. You will see how manual postings such as reporting costs or re-posting line items work CCA. You will learn how to perform manual activity allocations and actual statistical key figure postings and how to perform manual cost allocations. Finally, you will learn how to set up and use an Excel template to use the BATCHMAN transaction to upload many actual postings to CCA.

5.1   Flow of actual values

The main thing to understand is that original primary cost actual postings in CCA are always a result of business transactions being completed in other modules (see Figure 5.1).

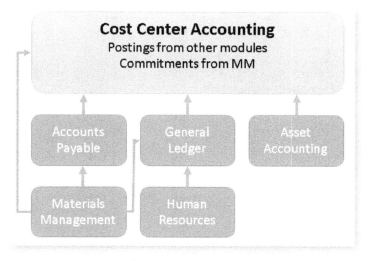

Figure 5.1: Actual primary cost flow to CCA

Any business transaction that has a bearing on costs will be posted to a primary cost element in the original transaction. As you saw earlier, the postings to a primary cost element will require the presence of a cost object in the posting. Generally, this will be a cost center, but in some instances, it may be another object such as an internal order or a WBS element.

All the primary postings will either originate in FI or flow through FI before they get to CCA. Postings from MM many be specifically directed to cost centers by selecting the account category "K" on the purchase order line (see Figure 5.2). Account assigned purchase orders can be created with reference to a material master or simply as text items. In either case, the value of the purchased item will post as a cost to the cost center and not to inventory (see Figure 5.3).

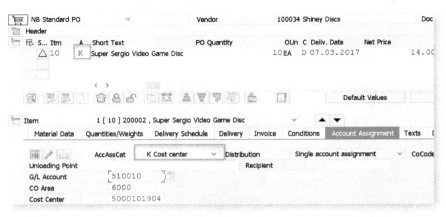

Figure 5.2: Account assigned purchase order

Document Number	5000000002	Company Code	6000	Fiscal Year	2017
Document Date	07.03.2017	Posting Date	07.03.2017	Period	3
Reference		Cross-Comp.No.			
Currency	USD	Texts exist		Ledger Group	

CoCod	Item PK	Account	Description	Amount	Currency	Cost Center	Profit Center	Material
6000	1 81	510010	Consump-Semi Fin	140.00	USD	5000101904	500050	200002
6000	2 96	211200	Gds Recd / Inv Recd	140.00-	USD		500050	200002

Figure 5.3: Goods receipt to a cost center posting

Even in the case of inventory purchase orders, it may still be possible to have some cost center postings occurring. In cases where *purchase price variances* (PPV) are being generated, either at the *goods receipt* transaction or the *invoice receipt* transaction, the variance amount will be posted to a primary cost element and will require assignment to a cost object in controlling. Since these accounting postings happen automatically because of a MM business transaction, there is no opportunity for the user to assign a cost center to the posting manually. In cases like this, the cost center is automatically determined from settings in the configuration transaction **OKB9—default account assignment** (see Figure 5.4).

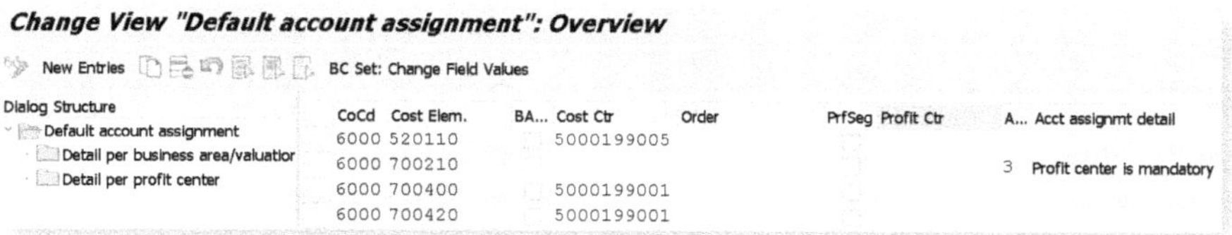

Figure 5.4: Default account assignment in CO

The most basic setting is to assign one default cost center per company code and cost element, as in the case of cost element 520110 in Figure 5.4, but there is also the possibility of further refining the assignment either on the basis of profit center or business area/valuation area (plant). For cost element 700210, the profit center is used to determine the default cost center (see Figure 5.5); it is also possible to use business area or valuation area (plant) in a similar fashion.

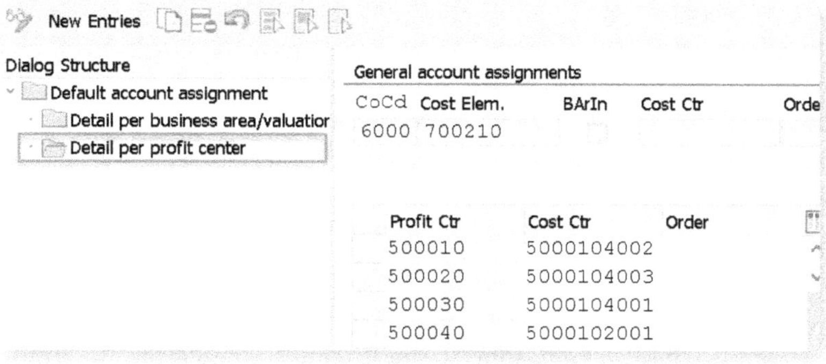

Figure 5.5: Default account assignment by profit center

If you post a goods receipt for a purchase order where a price variance is expected, you will see that the PPV posting uses the OKB9 setting to determine the correct cost center (see Figure 5.6).

125

Data Entry View							
Document Number	5000000004	Company Code		6000		Fiscal Year	2017
Document Date	07.03.2017	Posting Date		07.03.2017		Period	3
Reference		Cross-Comp.No.					
Currency	USD	Texts exist				Ledger Group	

CoCod	Item	PK	Account	Description	Amount	Currency	Cost Center	Profit Center	Material
6000	1	89	131000	Inventory-RawMat	102.50	USD		500050	100134
6000	2	96	211200	Gds Recd / Inv Recd	110.00-	USD		500050	100134
6000	3	86	520110	Purchase Price Var	7.50	USD	5000199005	500040	100134

Figure 5.6: Goods receipt with PPV

It is important to configure entries in OKB9 for all cost elements where automatic postings may occur. Commonly these will be accounts for price variances, exchange rate differences, inventory adjustments, and other small differences. If you have missed a cost element in the configuration and you try to process a business transaction that triggers a posting to that cost element, you will see the error shown in Figure 5.7.

Typ	Item	Message text
※		Account 530000 requires an assignment to a CO object

Figure 5.7: Missing account assignment error

Objects in controlling can also receive and report *commitment* postings, which flow from the MM module. The commitment is a reflection of a future cost coming from either an account assigned *purchase requisition* or *purchase order*. You can refer back to Section 2.1 to see how commitment management is activated in the controlling area and the relevant settings on the cost center.

In a manufacturing company, most commitments will be created from purchasing documents dealing with goods or physical items. These types of commitments are converted to actual costs when the purchasing items that created them are received or invoiced. This is known as a *quantity-based commitment*. The situation with service procurement is somewhat different, especially with the use of the service entry sheet functionality. Here, the quantity on the PO line for the service is always 1, and the receipt is value-based. This scenario is handled as a *value-based commitment*. The purchase order line quantity would be fully received with the first service receipt, and this would lead to incorrect conversion of commitment to actual values when there are still remaining values to receive.

The selection of value-based versus quantity-based commitment is controlled by configuring the units of measure in SAP. The unit of measure "AU" is used for services in SAP, and you can see that it is flagged for value-based commitment (Figure 5.8). You will find that most of the other units of measure in the system do not have this flag checked, so they are used for quantity-based commitments.

Int. meas. unit	LE		
Display		Measurement unit text	
Commercial	AU	Activity unit	
Technical	AU	Activ.unit	
Decimal places			
float. point exp.			
		ALE/EDI	
		ISO code	C62
Conversion		Primary code	
Numerator	1		
Denominator	1		
Exponent	0	Application Parameters	
Additive constant	0.000000	√ Commercial meas.unit	
Decimal pl. rounding	3	√ Value-based commt	
Unit of meas.family			

Figure 5.8: Commitment control on unit of measure

Even if the goods receipts or invoice receipts have not been completed, the system can reduce the commitment values to zero in certain situations. This makes sense if the purchase order line is cancelled or if the purchase order is considered completed, even if there are still open quantities. Setting the **delivery completed** or the **final invoice** indicator on the PO line will set the remaining commitment value to zero. Marking a PO line or a purchase requisition line for deletion will similarly set the commitment value to zero. Converting a purchase requisition to a purchase order will transfer the commitment; it will cease to be a commitment related to a purchase requisition and will become one related to the purchase order.

There are varieties of standard cost center reports, which will show actual, plan, and commitment values, as well as a transaction to display commitment line items, KSB2. Additionally, you can display the commitment from within the purchasing document by selecting the menu option ENVIRONMENT • AC COMMITMENT **documents** (see Figure 5.9).

CO Commitments For Purchase Requisition 10000052

Ref. Tr	RefDocNo	RfItm	Name	Cost Element	Year	Per	Value/LC	Total Quantity	Object identification
PREQ	10000052	10	services	581030	2017	3	19,000.00	1	CTR 6000/5000199005
PREQ	10000052	20	Support	581030	2017	3	2,000.00	10	CTR 6000/5000199001

Figure 5.9: Commitments for a purchase requisition

If you are using payroll in SAP, you will see payroll postings coming from HR through FI and into cost centers. Even if you are not using SAP payroll, it is likely that you will have developed an interface from your payroll system to post the periodic payroll journals to FI and CO.

A final group of actual postings will be those coming from asset accounting into cost centers. Every month, a portion of the value of the fixed assets within the company needs to be expensed to reflect the use of those assets. This process, called *depreciation*, results in primary cost posting to cost centers. Each fixed asset that the company owns is assigned directly to a cost center when the asset is created (see Figure 5.10). The field called COST CENTER is the one that receives the depreciation and any write-off or other postings from the asset. The RESP COST CENTER is not used for depreciation posting.

Asset	20013	0	Production Machine	
Class	2000		Machinery - Fixed	C

General	Time-dependent	Allocations	Origin	Net Worth Tax	Deprec. Areas

Interval from 01.01.1900 to 31.12.9999

Cost Center	5000101200	Video Game Assembly
Resp. cost center	5000101200	Video Game Assembly
Activity Type	1100	Machine Time
Plant	6001	Indiana Mfg Plant

Figure 5.10: Cost center on asset master

It is also possible to post depreciation to a combination of cost center and activity type if you identify the activity type on the asset master. This is only possible if you activate the setting ACCOUNT ASSIGNMENT ACTIVITY

TYPE on the ACTIVATE COMPONENTS section of the controlling area configuration (see Figure 5.11).

Controlling Area	6000 Smarter Sisters Games	
Fiscal Year	2007 to 9999	
Activate Components		
Cost Centers	1 Component active	∨
✓ AA: Activity Type		

Figure 5.11: Activate account assignment activity type

This may be useful if you want to post costs directly to a combination of cost center and activity, as in a production environment where the production machine depreciation may post to the production cost center and the machine activity type. The results of the periodic depreciation run, transaction AFAB, are shown in Figure 5.12. Each asset will create a cost posting to its assigned cost center.

Asset	Acct.d	Cost Center	Profit Ctr	Name	Description	Σ	Amount TBP Σ	Plannned Amount Σ	Amt Posted Σ	Cumul.Amt C
20014	160020	5000101001	500040	Production Line 1	Ordinary deprec.		17,361.11-	208,333.33-	0.00	17,361.11- L
20015		5000101002	500040	Production Line 2			5,972.22-	71,666.67-	0.00	5,972.22- L
20016		5000101003	500040	Production Line 3			3,611.11-	43,333.33-	0.00	3,611.11- L
20017		5000101004	500040	Production Line 4			1,666.67-	20,000.00-	0.00	1,666.67- L
20018		5000101100	500050	Production Line 5			10,069.44-	120,833.33-	0.00	10,069.44- L
20019		5000101200	500050	Production Line 6			1,736.11-	20,833.33-	0.00	1,736.11- L
20013		5000101200	500050	Production Machine			7,847.22-	94,166.67-	0.00	7,847.22- L
20020	160040	5000101900	500050	Cafeteria Equipments			2,380.95-	28,571.43-	0.00	2,380.95- L
20012	160045	5000101200	500050	Truck number 1			2,500.00-	30,000.00-	0.00	2,500.00- L

Posting date : 31.01.2017   **Date created: 08.03.2017**   **Period: 2017/001/01**

Figure 5.12: Depreciation run results

5.2 Manual re-postings in CCA

Manual re-posting of costs can be used to correct erroneous cost object assignments. There are two ways to do this; the preferred method is to re-post the line item using transaction KB61. This allows you to correct the posting with direct reference to the original document. The second method is to re-post costs manually using transaction KB11N. You can use this method to re-post costs between cost centers with no reference to the original posting. As a result, there is no validation that the costs you are moving actually exist in the originating cost center. This means that negative costs may appear in the sending cost center.

Usually these are CO-only postings, which means that FI does not get updated. In SAP environments, using the classic GL functionality, this will always be true. In cases where the new GL functionality is available, it is possible to update the configuration of real-time integration between FI and CO in such a way that cross-cost center posting in CO will also trigger an FI posting. This can be achieved by changing the settings on the variant for real-time integration in the system configuration to include cross-cost center postings (see Figure 5.13). Although it might seem desirable to activate this, you should consider the number of cross-cost center postings that occur to determine whether you really want all of these reflected in FI.

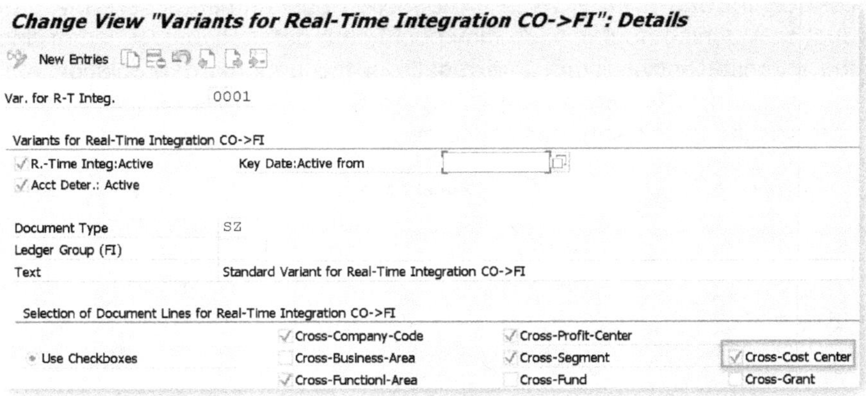

Figure 5.13: Variant for real-time integration CO-FI

The re-post line items transaction can be used if there is a controlling object assignment error in a posting and you want to re-post the document line item with the correct assignment. It can also be used to direct an original assignment to multiple CO objects. As an example, a document was posted with multiple line items, and there was an entry error in one of the lines. You can use transaction KB61 to correct the offending line. You will select the original document(s) on the initial screen by company code and fiscal year (see Figure 5.14).

Based on the documents selected, you will see the list of posted line items (see Figure 5.15) where you can see that the same cost center was posted to twice due to an entry error. Line 4 was actually supposed to go to a different cost center.

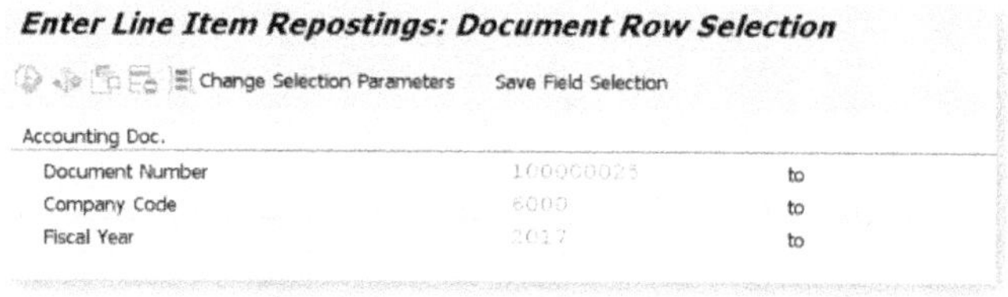

Enter Line Item Repostings: Document Row Selection

◇ ◦|○ 🗋 🖾 | ☰ Change Selection Parameters   Save Field Selection

Accounting Doc.

Document Number	100000025	to
Company Code	6000	to
Fiscal Year	2017	to

Figure 5.14: Line item re-posting – selection screen

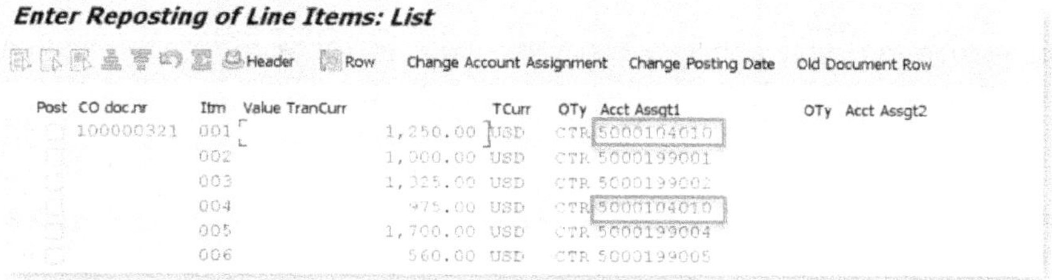

Enter Reposting of Line Items: List

🗐 🗗 🖹 🔻 🔽 🕙 🖩 🖨 Header   🖩 Row   Change Account Assignment   Change Posting Date   Old Document Row

Post	CO doc.nr	Itm	Value TranCurr		TCurr	OTy	Acct Assgt1	OTy	Acct Assgt2
	100000321	001	1,250.00	USD		CTR	5000104010		
		002	1,000.00	USD		CTR	5000199001		
		003	1,325.00	USD		CTR	5000199002		
		004	975.00	USD		CTR	5000104010		
		005	1,700.00	USD		CTR	5000199004		
		006	560.00	USD		CTR	5000199005		

Figure 5.15:Re-posting line items – list

To make a correction, simply replace the incorrect cost center in column ACCT ASSGT1 with a different cost center and post the document. You will see that a CO document has posted moving the $975.00 to the new cost center (see Figure 5.16). Note that the reference document number is populated by the CO document that is linked to the original FI document.

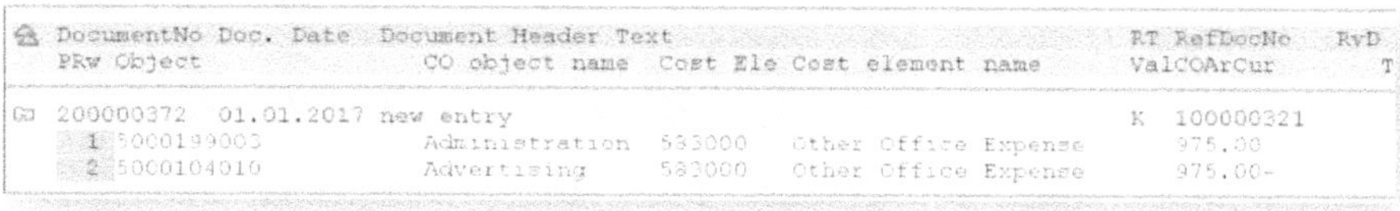

	DocumentNo	Doc. Date	Document Header Text					RT	RefDocNo	RvD
	PRw Object		CO object name	Cost Ele	Cost element name				ValCOArCur	T
GJ	200000372	01.01.2017	new entry					K	100000321	
	1 5000199005		Administration	533000	Other Office Expense				975.00	
	2 5000104010		Advertising	583000	Other Office Expense				975.00-	

Figure 5.16: Result of line item re-posting in CO.

If you are using the new GL and have set the cross-cost center flag, you will also get an FI posting, which you can see in Figure 5.17. If you have not activated this setting or are using the classic GL, then you will not get an FI posting at all. If this is the case, then the original account assignment remains in the FI document line item, even though it has been corrected in CO. For this reason, many people choose not to use the re-posting functionality in CO and instead will reverse and re-post FI documents to correct these errors so that account assignment objects remain in sync between FI and CO.

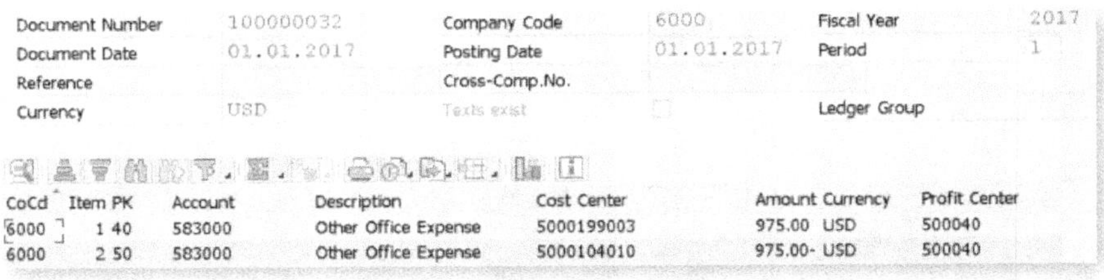

CoCd	Item	PK	Account	Description	Cost Center	Amount Currency	Profit Center
6000	1	40	583000	Other Office Expense	5000199003	975.00 USD	500040
6000	2	50	583000	Other Office Expense	5000104010	975.00- USD	500040

Document Number: 100000032 · Company Code: 6000 · Fiscal Year: 2017
Document Date: 01.01.2017 · Posting Date: 01.01.2017 · Period: 1
Reference · Cross-Comp.No.
Currency: USD · Texts exist · Ledger Group

Figure 5.17: Line item re-posting GL document

As mentioned, you can re-post a line item to more than one receiver object. You again select the original document as you saw in Figure 5.14, then in the line item list, instead of changing the cost assignment, you double click on the line you want to change to get to the individual processing screen (see Figure 5.18). Here, in the NEW ACCOUNT ASSIGNMENT section, you can enter a partial amount and account assignment and then click on the **next** button to distribute the amount. You can see and further edit the results in list mode (Figure 5.19). Once it is completed, you can post the transaction. Line item re-posting can be displayed in transaction KB63, and it can be reversed using KB64.

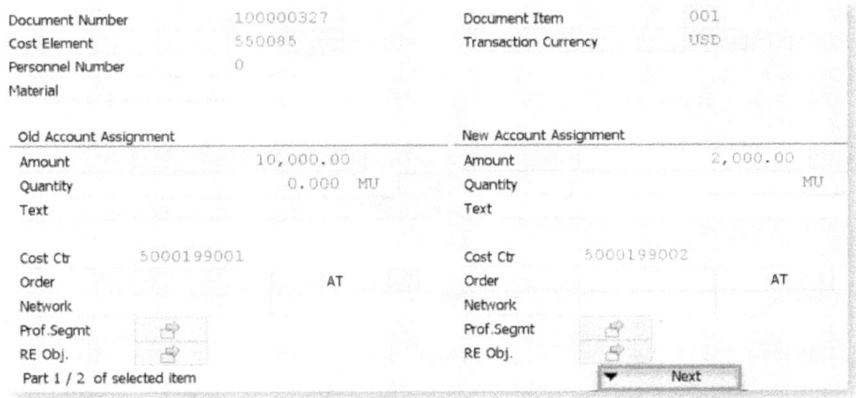

Document Number	100000327	Document Item	001
Cost Element	550085	Transaction Currency	USD
Personnel Number	0		
Material			
Old Account Assignment		**New Account Assignment**	
Amount	10,000.00	Amount	2,000.00
Quantity	0.000 MU	Quantity	MU
Text		Text	
Cost Ctr	5000199001	Cost Ctr	5000199002
Order	AT	Order	AT
Network		Network	
Prof.Segmt		Prof.Segmt	
RE Obj.		RE Obj.	
Part 1 / 2 of selected item			Next

Figure 5.18: Re-post line item multiple assignment

The second method for re-posting costs is called manual re-posting of costs. This is accessed through transaction KB11N. Here you simply need to define the date and period parameters, and then create line items to re-post costs from an old cost center (sender) to a new cost center (receiver) using a primary cost element (see Figure 5.20).

Enter Reposting of Line Items: List

Post	CO doc.nr	Itm	Value TranCurr		TCurr	OTy	Acct Assgt1
✓	100000327	001	2,000.00	USD		CTR	5000199002
✓			1,000.00	USD		CTR	5000199005
✓			4,000.00	USD		CTR	5000199003
✓			1,500.00	USD		CTR	5000199004
✓			500.00	USD		CTR	5000199001
✓			1,000.00	USD		CTR	5000104001

Figure 5.19: Re-post multiple assignments list

Enter Manual Repostings of Primary Costs

	Entry Data	Additional Info				
CO Area	6000					
Doc. Date	01.01.2017					
Postg Date	01.01.2017		Period	1		
Ref. Doc.				Confirm		
Doc. Text	Reposting of Costs					

| Scrn var. | 01SAP Cost center | | | Input Type | L List Entry | |

Items

ItmNo.	CCtr (old)	Cost Elem.	Amount		Crcy	CCtr (new)	Total Quantity
0001	5000199004	581027		2,000.00	USD	5000101901	0.000
0000					USD		

Figure 5.20: Manual cost re-posting

Similar to line item re-posting, this will create a CO-only posting (see Figure 5.21), unless you are using the new GL with the cross-cost center functionality activated. Also, note that there is no reference document number, so there is no link to an original document.

DocumentNo	Doc. Date	Document Header Text			RT	RefDocNo	
PRw Object	CO object name		Cost Ele	Cost element name	Val/COArea	Crcy	Qu
200000374	01.01.2017	Reposting of Costs					
1 5000199004	US Corporate IT		581027	Computer Support	2,000.00-		
2 5000101901	Plant IT & Comm IN		581027	Computer Support	2,000.00		

Figure 5.21 : CO document manual cost re-posting

5.3 Manual activity transactions

There are several manual processing transactions available for activity-related functions. You can perform activity allocations manually, you can re-post activity allocation documents similar to primary cost line item re-posting, you can enter activity quantities manually on sender cost centers, and you can manually enter actual activity prices.

Manual activity allocations can be performed to move activity quantities and their related costs from a sending cost center to a receiving object such as another cost center or an internal order. The prerequisites for any activity allocation are an activity type (see Section 2.5) and a planned price for that activity and sending cost center (see Section 3.4). To manually allocate activities, the activity type being used must have category 1—manual entry, manual allocation. The cost element used in the allocation is the secondary cost element assigned to the activity type.

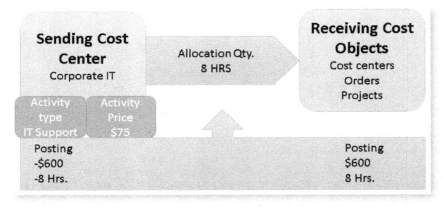

Figure 5.22: Manual activity allocation

The transaction for this is KB21N (see Figure 5.23). It is only necessary to enter the sending cost center and the receiving object, along with the activity type and the quantity being transferred. The price of the activity will be retrieved from price planning, and the cost element will be derived from the activity type. A controlling document will be created crediting the sending object and debiting the receiving object (see Figure 5.24).

Most activity allocations will occur though automatic methods such as production or plant maintenance order confirmations, template alloca-tions, time sheet entry, or indirect activity allocation. However, manual activity allocations may be useful to capture the transfer of activity quan-tities between cost objects when they are difficult to automate or when automatically posted values need to be supplemented manually.

Figure 5.23: Entering a direct activity allocation

Figure 5.24: Direct activity allocation posting

CATS

In SAP, *CATS* refer to cross application time sheet. The setup and use of CATS is beyond the scope of this book, but you should be aware that, depending on the objects being posted to, CATS is often using activity allocation in the background to transfer time from a sending cost center to another allowed cost object.

It is possible to re-post activity documents using transaction KB65. This is similar to re-posting line items using KB61, which you saw earlier. The functionality of KB65 is identical to KB61, except that instead of a posted amount, we have a posted quantity that we can redirect to a different receiver or multiple receivers.

Entering sender activities manually may be necessary if you are performing actual indirect activity allocation cycles when the activity type on the sending cost center has the category **manual entry, indirect allocation**. In this situation, the system cannot determine the activity quantity available on the sending cost center unless you manually enter it. Additionally,

135

you may just want to capture sender activity quantities for reporting purposes.

As an example, the Quality Assurance cost center provides the activity of QA testing to many of the production cost centers. They have already determined that the planned price for this is $15.00 per test. In the system, they will use an indirect activity allocation to send these activities to the sending cost centers, based on a statistical key figure representing production volumes. Before they can do that, they must capture the quantity of tests that they performed during the period. This will be done in transaction KB51N (Figure 5.25). For the posting period, you simply enter the sending cost center, the activity type, and the total quantity and post the transaction. For reference purposes, this creates a CO document, but there is no debit or credit posting to any cost center.

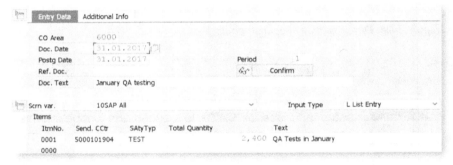

Figure 5.25: Entering sender activities

Once the sender activity has been posted, it can be used in an indirect allocation cycle, as we will see in the following chapter.

The final manual activity transaction you can perform is manual actual activity price entry. You will recall that we calculated and planned activity prices in Section 3.4. These planned prices are used in all actual activity allocations during a posting period to calculate the sending and receiving values in the cost objects. For many of the receiving cost objects, SAP gives you the opportunity to revalue the activity postings based on an actual price as part of the period end process. The question is, how do you get that actual price? There are two answers: you can have the system calculate it automatically, or you can calculate it yourself and enter it manually. You will see automatic actual price calculation later; here you will see how manual actual activity price entry works using transaction KBK6 and also see the effects of a revaluation on a receiving object.

On the initial screen for KBK6 (see Figure 5.26), you will enter the period range, the sending cost center, and the activity price. Notice that this is very like one of the initial screens in planning

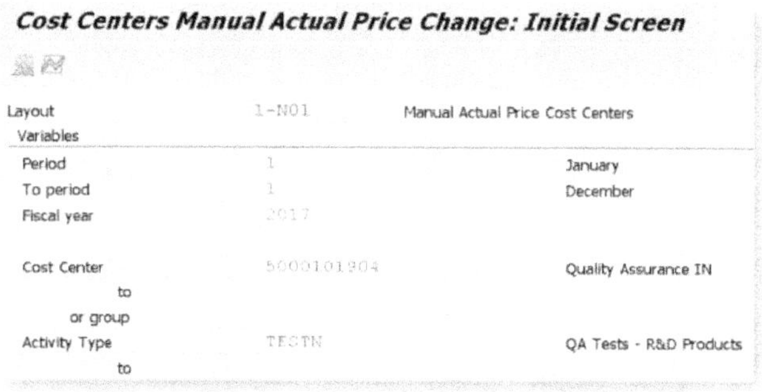

Cost Centers Manual Actual Price Change: Initial Screen

Layout	1-N01	Manual Actual Price Cost Centers
Variables		
Period	1	January
To period	1	December
Fiscal year	2017	
Cost Center	5000101904	Quality Assurance IN
to		
or group		
Activity Type	TESTN	QA Tests - R&D Products
to		

Figure 5.26: Manual activity price initial screen

On the overview screen (see Figure 5.27), you can then enter the actual fixed and/or variable price for the activity.

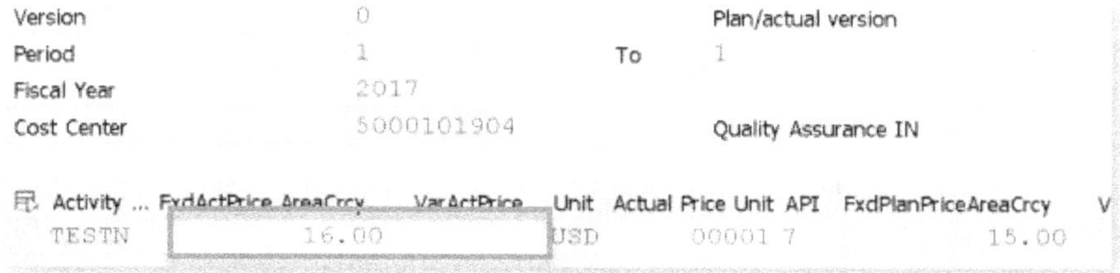

Version	0			Plan/actual version	
Period	1		To	1	
Fiscal Year	2017				
Cost Center	5000101904			Quality Assurance IN	

Activity ...	FxdActPrice AreaCrcy	VarActPrice	Unit	Actual Price Unit	API	FxdPlanPriceAreaCrcy	V
TESTN	16.00		USD	00001	7	15.00	

Figure 5.27: Enter the actual activity price

To understand what can be done with this, consider that 10 units of this activity had been allocated to an internal order being used to track testing for R&D products. During the month, those units were allocated at $15.00 per unit, but at the end of the month, the actual cost of performing the QA tests is calculated to be $16.00 per unit. That value is entered as an actual cost in KBK6. One of the period end functions for internal orders is an option to revalue at actual prices. You can use transactions KON1 or KON2 to revalue internal orders or plant maintenance orders based on actual prices. After running the revaluation, we see the resulting posting in the internal order (see Figure 5.28). The revaluation posts as a separate document because that is the option selected for the RE-VALUATION INDICATOR on the fiscal year specific settings for planning version 0 (refer back to Section 3.2 if you are unclear about this setting).

Display Actual Cost Line Items for Orders

Order	Cost Element	Cost el. descr.	Val.in rep.cur.	Quantity PUM	DocumentNo	Posting Date	Document Header Text	Partner object
300000	943500	QA Testing	150.00	10 EA	400000202	01.01.2017		5000101904/TESTN
300000	943500	QA Testing	10.00	0 EA	400000209	31.01.2017	Revaluation at actual pric	5000101904/TESTN
300000			160.00					

Figure 5.28: Internal order activity price revaluation

You should be aware that if you want the cost objects to be revalued based on actual activity prices, you would need to carry out the revaluation steps during period end processing for the relevant modules. This should be done regardless of whether the actual activity prices are calculated automatically or entered manually.

5.4 Actual statistical key figures

You saw in planning that statistical key figures often are used as tracing factors in planned allocations. The same will be true when you create actual allocations. You may want to use actual SKF values as the tracing factor instead of planned values. For this, you will need to either capture the values for actual statistical key figures manually or transfer them automatically before you can use them in allocations. You will see the automatic transfer from LIS in the next chapter; here you will see how to use transaction KB31N to enter actual SKF values. The entry screen is similar to many of the other manual entry transactions you have seen (see Figure 5.29). As usual, you will enter the dates and some text if required. Then, enter a line for each cost center and SKF with the actual quantity to be posted.

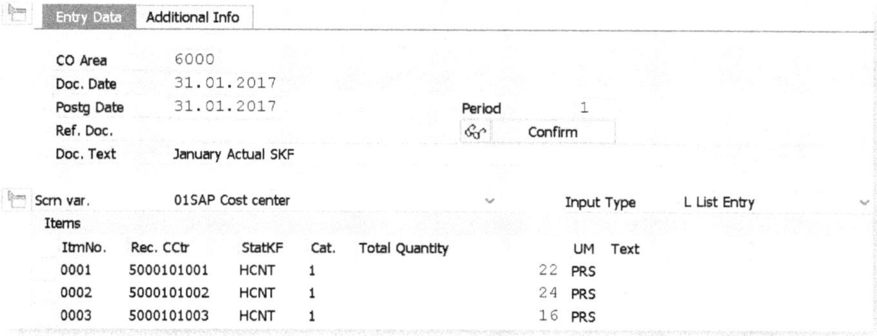

Figure 5.29: Enter actual SKF values

5.5 Manual cost allocations

Manual cost allocations can be used to post both primary and secondary costs between cost centers. It may be useful if you need to perform simple allocations on the fly and you do not want to go through the work of setting up assessment or distribution cycles. You can also use manual cost allocations to adjust secondary cost postings made with any of the cost element categories used for allocations, except for type 43, which is used for activity allocations. A manual cost allocation uses transaction code KB15N and is similar in appearance to the other manual transactions (see Figure 5.30).

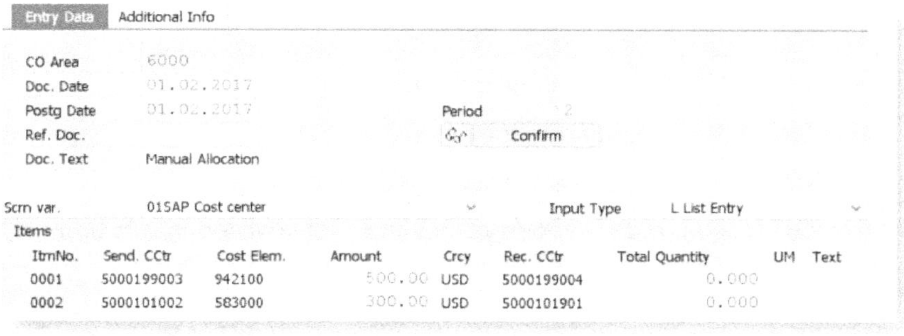

Figure 5.30: Manual cost allocation

You will enter the dates, then lines for each allocation specifying a sending cost center, a cost element, the amount, and a receiving cost center. As with other manual CO postings, this will create a CO-only posting (see Figure 5.31), unless you are posting cross-cost center postings to FI through the real-time reconciliation functionality in the new GL.

| DocumentNo Doc. Date | Document Header Text | | RT RefDocNo | Rev RvD |
PRw QTy Object	CO object name	Cost Ele Cost elem.name	Val/COArea Crcy	Qu
400000212 01.02.2017	Manual Allocation			
1 CTR 5000199003	Administration	942100 Cafeteria Costs	500.00-	
2 CTR 5000199004	US Corporate IT	942100 Cafeteria Costs	500.00	
3 CTR 5000101002	Posting IN	583000 Other Office E	300.00-	
4 CTR 5000101901	Plant IT & Comm IN	583000 Other Office E	300.00	

Figure 5.31: Manual cost allocation posting

5.6 Using BATCHMAN

At period end, you may be required to enter a significant number of manual CO postings, and you would like to avoid doing these through the standard SAP transactions presented above. Fortunately, SAP provides a tool to upload many of the manual CO postings in a batch format. This means that you can build a data file, usually in Excel, save that file as a tab delimited txt file, and upload it into SAP. This method can be used to load data for the following transactions:

▶ KB21N – Manual activity allocation

▶ KB11N – Primary cost re-posting

▶ KB15N – Manual cost allocations

▶ KB51N – Enter sender activities

▶ KB31N – Enter actual statistical key figures

▶ KB41N– Manual revenue re-posting (not covered in this book)

The transaction code BATCHMAN is used to load data for all of these transactions. This transaction uses *BAPIs,* which are essentially pre-defined interface structures that allow you to load external data into SAP. Each of the transactions listed above has two associated BAPIs, one for the document header information, and a second for the document items or lines. The BAPIs used by each transaction are shown in Figure 5.32.

You will need to know these values when you build the load file templates.

Transaction	Header BAPI	Item BAPI
KB11N – Primary Cost Reposting	BAPIRCHDR	BAPIRCITM
KB15N – Manual Cost Allocation	BAPIMAHDR	BAPIMAITM
KB21N – Manual Activity Allocation	BAPIAAHDR	BAPIAAITM
KB31N - Actual SKF	BAPISKFHDR	BAPISKFITM
KB41N – Manual Revenue Repost	BAPIRRHDR	BAPIRRITM
KB51N – Sender Activities	BAPIIAHDR	BAPIIAITM

Figure 5.32: BAPIs for manual CO transactions

Many of the companies that I work with track a lot of statistical values that they either report on or use in allocations, so they often use BATCHMAN to load actual statistical figure values as part of their period end process. The following example will demonstrate how this works; once you understand the structure of the upload file, you will be able to build and load files for any of the manual CO transactions supported by BATCHMAN.

The first thing to do is to build the upload file (see Figure 5.33). The first line in the file must contain the header BAPI name from Figure 5.32 and nothing else. The BATCHMAN program will use this to determine what type of data is contained in the file. By reading the BAPI name, the program will know that you want to load statistical key figures and not activity allocations.

The following line must contain the component or field names. Some common header components are listed in Figure 5.34. The component name in the file must exactly match what is shown in the table. Depending on the BAPI you select, you may have to use different header or item components. For example, I do not require a component for transaction currency when loading statistical key figures, but I may require that component when loading primary cost re-posting. After the component line, you will have one or more header data lines. A key thing to note is that you can load multiple documents with one file. Each header that you create in the file will post as its own document in SAP. The DOC_NO component is used to link each header line with its associated items. An internally assigned SAP document number will replace the original number in the DOC_NO component when you post the document in SAP.

After the header section, there must be at least one empty row and a line with the item BAPI name by itself. Following that will be the item component header line using some of the item components shown in Figure 5.35. I am only showing the most common components in these tables; if you require other fields, you can have developer look into the BAPI to find the correct component names. It is only necessary to include the components that you are going to use in the file. I really do not need the columns for REC_ORDER or REC_WBS_EL in my file since I do not track SKFs on these objects. The file will work equally well for cost centers if I remove those columns. You may find it involves a bit of trial and error building these files to get the correct components. Note that there will always be two common components between the header and item data, the controlling area and the document number. These serve to link the header lines to their related items.

After the item component header line, will be the lines of item data. This example will post headcount data for cost centers. It will create two documents, as there are two header lines. The first header has two line items, and the second header has only one line item. Note that some of the data items should be padded out to the SAP field length by including leading zeros in the field. I have found this to be the case with the cost center components if you do not have ten characters in the field, then the load fails.

Once you have completed the file, it must be saved as a tab delimited .txt file before it can be imported into SAP.

	A	B	C	D	E	F	G	H
1	BAPISKFHDR							
2	CO_AREA	DOC_NO	DOCDATE	POSTGDATE	DOC_HDR_TX	USERNAME	VAL_PERIOD	VAL_FISYEAR
3	6000	1	20170228	20170228	Feb Headcount	JPRINGLE	2	2017
4	6000	2	20170228	20170228	Feb Headcount	JPRINGLE	2	2017
5								
6								
7	BAPISKFITM							
8	CO_AREA	DOC_NO	STATKEYFIG	STAT_QTY	SEG_TEXT	REC_CCTR	REC_ORDER	REC_WBS_EL
9	6000	1	HCNT	25	Feb Headcount	5000102904		
10	6000	1	HCNT	50	Feb Headcount	5000102001		
11	6000	2	HCNT	25	Feb Headcount	5000102002		

Figure 5.33: SKF sample upload file

Component	Description	Component	Description
CO_AREA	Controlling Area	DOC_HDR_TX	Header Text
DOCDATE	Document Date	USERNAME	User Name
POSTGDATE	Posting Date	VAL_PERIOD	Period
DOC_NO	Document Number	VAL_FISYEAR	Fiscal Year
TRANS_CURR	Transaction Currency	PERIOD	Period

Figure 5.34: Typical header components

Component	Description	Component	Description
CO_AREA	Controlling Area	SEG_TEXT	Item text
DOC_NO	Document Number	SEN_ORDER	Sender Order
SEND_CCTR	Sending Cost Center	SEN_WBS_EL	Sender WBS element
ACTTYPE	Activity Types	COST_ELEM	Cost Element
ACTVTY_QTY	Activity Quantity	VALUE_TCUR	Amount
ACTIVITYUN	Activity Unit	QUANTITY	Quantity
REC_CCTR	Receiver Cost Center	REC_ORDER	Receiver Order
REC_WBS_EL	Receiver WBS	STATKEYFIG	Statistical Key Figure
STAT_QTY	Statistical Quantity	PERSON_NO	Personnel Number

Figure 5.35: Typical item components

To import the file, you will use the transaction code BATCHMAN and select the **execute** option to get to the transfer data screen (see Figure 5.36). There is an opportunity to run in test mode, which is useful to see any potential errors. The **presentation server** option means that the file is stored somewhere on your local computer and not on the SAP application server. When you go to look for the file, you may get a warning about seeing the file structure of the presentation server. This is just a standard SAP message and can be bypassed. Find your file and then execute the transfer. The output log will indicate if you were successful and will show the document number that was posted. As you can see in Figure 5.37, two documents posted as expected from the two header records in the upload file.

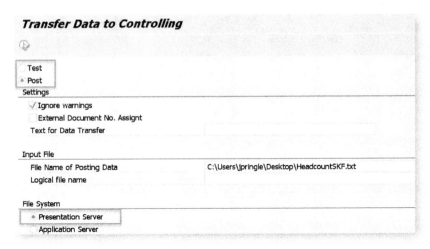

Figure 5.36: Execute BATCHMAN

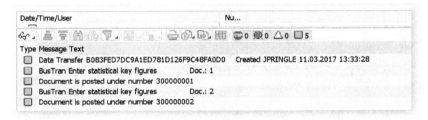

Figure 5.37: BATCHMAN posting message

You can display these documents in KB33N to see how they posted in SAP (see Figure 5.38).

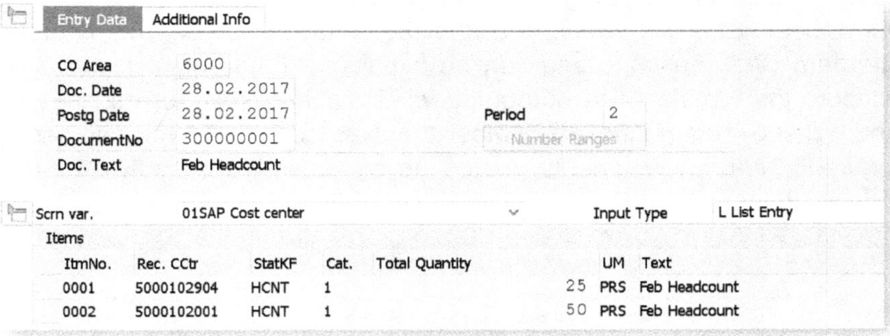

Figure 5.38: SKF document display of uploaded item

You have seen how to upload actual statistical key figures using BATCHMAN, and other than the structure of the input files, the other manual CO transactions will load in an identical manner.

5.7 Manual values in S/4 HANA

Given that FI and CO transactions now share the same table in the database, you might expect that the manual CO postings that you have just learned about would either no longer function or just be unnecessary in S/4 HANA. So far, I have found this not to be the case. I have run all the manual transaction that we have discussed in an S/4 HANA 1610 environment and have found that the transaction codes are still active and are still functioning. The major difference for the value-based transactions is that the system is posting to the universal journal when these allocations are made, meaning that both FI and CO are being updated as we would expect.

5.8 Summary

In this chapter, you have learned about the flow of actual values into CCA and you understand that overall value cannot be created or diminished within controlling. You have seen a number of manual methods for re-posting costs and moving costs around within cost center accounting and within controlling in general. You have seen how to post statistical figure values to cost centers manually and have some understanding of how they can be used. Finally, you saw a standard upload tool that can be used to import many of these manual transactions in a batch from a spreadsheet. Next, you will see that there are many additional tools to perform automatic allocations, and that these automatic tools should be the preferred option for complex periodic allocations.

6 Periodic allocations

In this chapter, you will explore the period end allocation processes that can and should be performed in cost center accounting. You will understand the difference between types of cost allocations such as distribution, assessment, and periodic re-posting and know the benefits and drawbacks of each. You will see different methods of periodic activity allocations, see the use of the accrual calculation, and understand how it can be used. You will also learn how it is possible to bring statistical key figure values from logistic information system structures on a periodic basis to use as tracing factors in allocations.

6.1 Why do allocations?

As you have seen, a lot of the activity in SAP CO involves moving costs around between different objects. Some of these movements happen on a more or less real-time basis, such as activities posted on production confirmations or confirming time against plant maintenance orders. Other cost movements are designed to occur periodically as part of the FI/CO closing steps for a fiscal period.

What is the purpose of moving all these costs? The answer is that there may be a number of reasons, and some of the major ones are:

► Expediency in data entry—it is faster to enter a shared cost in one cost center and then allocate out to other cost centers. Often, shared incoming invoices have a single amount that should be split between cost centers, making coding and entry a time-consuming job.

► Accuracy in cost reporting—resources that are shared should have their costs allocated to the using cost centers to provide accurate cost center reporting.

▶ Enhances resource usage decisions—if the using cost centers are being charged fairly for the resources they are consuming from other cost centers, they should be able to make rational decisions about the resources they are consuming. This should lead to better overall resource usage decisions for the organization.

▶ Accounting Compliance—you will want to do allocations to ensure that all the required costs are being absorbed into product costs to comply with IFRS or GAAP.

▶ Product decision making—assigning overhead costs to products may help with product and product line decisions.

Often, the issue is not with having to do the allocations, but with the methods and with the fact an allocation method may support one of the goals listed above but conflict with another one. As an example, it may be necessary to allocate all relevant overheads to a product to comply with IFRS or GAAP regardless of whether the costs are fixed or variable. For product decision-making, this may not be appropriate because fixed costs will not go away in the short term based on product mix decisions. Even if they did, there is no guarantee that a particular product is actually consuming the share of fixed costs that has been allocated.

The other perceived problem with many allocations, especially those that are not tied directly to activity consumption, is that they are largely arbitrary. Allocations based on percentages or fixed factors are most often perceived in this manner and are criticized as providing a peanut butter approach since the cost is spread on regardless of the actual consumption of activity. Cost center managers will often resent being burdened with these types of allocated costs, especially if they have no direct control over how they are charged.

The better understood and controllable the allocation is, the more likely the cost center manager will accept it. The case of rent and facilities is an obvious example. Using a tracing factor related to area occupied is well understood and likely to be perceived as fair. Depending on the situation and the overall ability to reduce total space, this may also drive overall efficiencies, as cost center managers will look to make better use of space in the long term. In general, the more an allocation can be linked to a meaningful driver or tracing factor, the more useful the results will be for decision-making.

6.2   Actual cost allocations

All the automatic allocations available for planning explained in Section 3.3 are also available for actual cost allocation.

The most common methods of actual allocations used in cost center accounting are distribution, assessment, and periodic re-posting. These all use the cycle and segment method as you saw in planning. Actual distribution and periodic re-posting use the original primary cost element to move the costs from the sending cost center(s) to the receiving objects, while assessment will use a secondary cost element with cost element type 42. Again, similar to planning, the major difference between actual distribution and re-posting is how the totals tables are updated. A distribution will update the sender cost center as a partner in the totals table, while a reposing will not. Because of this, the re-posting will save memory and may have faster run times but the totals records will be less complete. The assessment will be the most efficient of these methods as it is grouping multiple values under one secondary cost element.

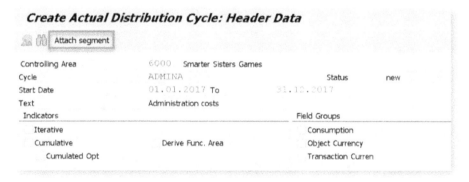

Figure 6.1: Actual distribution cycle header

The actual distribution cycle is created using transaction code KSV1. The method is similar to the planned cycle seen in Section 3.3. First, you must create the header for the actual cycle (see Figure 6.1). There are some additional indicators for actual allocations. The **iterative** indicator is the same as for the planned cycle. The **cumulative** indicator is used if you need to perform the allocations using cumulative sender amounts and tracing factors values rather than periodic values. This eases the allocation in cases where the sender values and/or tracing factors can

149

fluctuate significantly between periods and may be a legal requirement for allocations in some countries. The **derive functional area** indicator forces the functional area to be re-derived during the allocation run.

Once the header is created, you can create the first segment (see Figure 6.2).

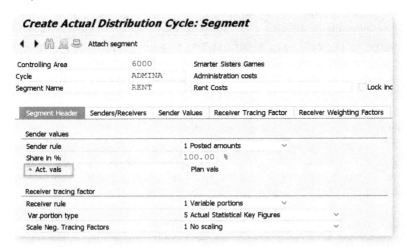

Figure 6.2: Actual distribution segment

Other than the SENDER VALUES being based on actual values, this is identical to the segment header for the planned distribution. The SENDER/RECEIVER tab is also similar to the planned distribution (see Figure 6.3). Here you are specifying the sending cost center(s) and cost element(s) along with the receiving cost objects. In this case, the office rent cost element, 581100, is the only one being distributed in this segment.

	From	To	Group
Segment Header	Senders/Receivers	Sender Values	Receiver Tracing Factor	Receiver Weighting Factors
Sender			
Cost Center	5000199003		
Functional Area			
Cost Element	581100		
Receiver			
Order			
Cost Center			USCORP
Functional Area			

Figure 6.3: Actual distribution senders and receivers

On the receiver tracing factor tab (Figure 6.4), you specify which SKF or activity type will be used as the driver in the allocation. The object you choose needs to follow from the **var portion type** that you have selected.

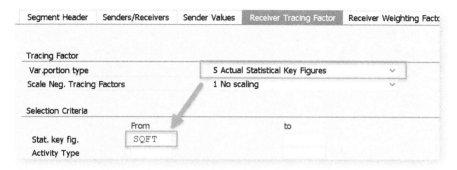

Figure 6.4: Actual distribution receiver tracing factor

Execute Actual Distribution: Initial Screen

Settings

Parameters

Controlling Area   6000

Period   1   To   1

Fiscal Year   2017

Processing

☐ Background Processing
☐ Test Run
☑ Detail Lists   List selection

Cycle   Start Date
ADMINA   01.01.2017

Figure 6.5: Run actual distribution initial screen

You can add additional segments to the cycle as required by clicking the **attach segment** button. Once you have completed and saved your cycle, you can execute it using transaction KSV5 (see Figure 6.5). Before you execute your cycles, make sure that you have posted all the actual values for your costs and for the tracing factors you are using. With plan allocations, the cycles commonly are run for the entire year, whereas with the actual allocation, you will normally be running it one period at a time as part of each period end. Multiple cycles can be executed from

151

the same initial screen. In the case of many cycles or large allocations, it may be preferable to run the allocations using **background processing** so that you can schedule the timing of the run and not tie up the foreground processes.

Once you run the distribution, you will be able to see the results (see Figure 6.6) by displaying the segments from the basic list screen. You can see that the sending cost center 5000199003 will not be cleared completely because the iterative flag was not set on the cycle header.

	Per Segment name	Cost Element	OTy	Object	PTy	Partner object	x	Val/COArea Crcy
⊙	1 RENT	581100	CTR	5000199001	CTR	5000199003		1,913.58
				5000199001	△		·	1,913.58
	1 RENT	581100	CTR	5000199002	CTR	5000199003		1,481.48
				5000199002	△		·	1,481.48
	1 RENT	581100	CTR	5000199003	CTR	5000199001		1,913.58-
	1 RENT	581100	CTR		CTR	5000199002		1,481.48-
	1 RENT	581100	CTR		CTR	5000199003		2,222.22
	1 RENT	581100	CTR		CTR	5000199003		2,222.22-
	1 RENT	581100	CTR		CTR	5000199004		1,604.94-
	1 RENT	581100	CTR		CTR	5000199005		2,777.78-
				5000199003	△		·	7,777.78-
	1 RENT	581100	CTR	5000199004	CTR	5000199003		1,604.94
				5000199004	△		·	1,604.94
	1 RENT	581100	CTR	5000199005	CTR	5000199003		2,777.78
				5000199005	△		·	2,777.78
△							··	0.00

Figure 6.6: Results of distribution posting

You will recall from Section 3.3 that assessments are similar to distribution, except that instead of moving the costs using the original primary cost element, as secondary cost element type 42 is used. This is similar to the distribution you need to create the assessment cycle header (see Figure 6.7) using transaction KSU1. You also have the options for **iterative** cycle, **cumulative** processing, and to **derive functional area**.

Create Actual Assessment Cycle: Header Data

Attach segment

Controlling Area	6000 Smarter Sisters Games		
Cycle	A6002A	Status	new
Start Date	01.01.2017 To	31.12.2017	
Text	Plant Overheads		
Indicators		Field Groups	
✓ Iterative		✓ Object Currency	
Cumulative	Derive Func. Area	Transaction Currency	
Cumulated Opt			

Figure 6.7: Assessment cycle header

152

When you attach the segments, you will see that the tabs are identical to the ones on the distribution. The only difference is on the SEGMENT HEADER tab where you have to specify the secondary cost element to be used to move the costs.

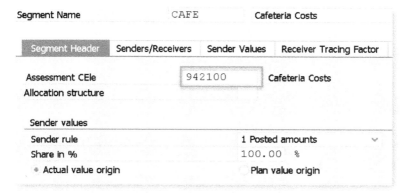

Figure 6.8: Assessment segment header

The assessment is run in a similar manner to the distribution but uses the transaction code KSU5.

Setting up and running actual periodic re-posting is again similar to the other two methods you have seen. The process for setting up and running a distribution can be followed, except using the transaction codes KSW1 to create the cycle and KSW5 to execute it.

6.3   Periodic activity allocations

In Section 3.3, you saw that planned indirect activity allocations are used to move activity quantities from a sending cost center to receiving cost centers based on some receiver tracing factor using a secondary cost element. The actual indirect activity allocation does the same thing with actual postings.

The planned indirect activity allocation that was created previously was used to allocate utility costs to production cost centers based on their machine time usage. Since we want to be able to compare our actual costs with our plan costs, an actual indirect activity allocation should be created to mirror our planned cycle. The actual indirect activity allocation

153

cycle is created using transaction KSC1 and changed using KSC2. The cycle segment format is similar to the other planned allocations you have seen.

Once you create the cycle header, you start attaching the segments. On the segment header (see Figure 6.9), remember the importance of the rule and the receiver tracing factors and how the rule relates to the activity type being used. You can refer back to Section 3.2 to review the details.

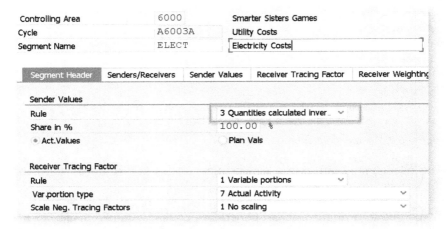

Figure 6.9: Indirect activity allocation segment header

On the SENDER/RECEIVER tab (see Figure 6.10), it is necessary to specify the sending cost center and the activity being sent, as well as the receiving objects. The activity type here is the sending activity and not the activity being used as a tracing factor. That activity will be defined on the receiver tracing factor tab (see Figure 6.11).

	From	To	Group
Sender			
Cost Center	5000101905		
Activity Type	2000		
Functional Area			
Receiver			
Order			
Cost Center			6001PROD
Functional Area			

Figure 6.10: Indirect activity allocation senders and receivers

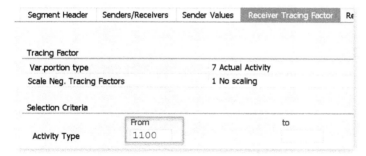

Figure 6.11: Indirect activity allocation receiver tracing factor

If you need to influence the weighting of the tracing factor as it is applied to individual receivers, it can be done on the RECEIVER WEIGHTING FACTOR tab.

Once your cycle has been saved, you can execute it using transaction code KSC5. This is similar to the execution for assessments and distributions. Activity allocations will be posted for the utility activities going from the utilities cost center to the production cost centers.

```
Cycle                  A6003A      Utility Costs
Start Date             01.01.2017
Controlling Area       6000
Version                0
Period                 001
Fiscal Year            2017
No. of messages        4        Maximum Category
```

L	I	Segment	Share in %	S	R	Senders	Receivers	No. of messages
		ELECT	100.00	3	1	1	7	2
		GAS	100.00	3	1	1	7	0
		WATER	100.00	3	1	1	7	0
*						3	21	2

Figure 6.12: Indirect activity allocation

Within each segment, you can display the postings that were created showing the receiving cost centers, the sending cost center, and activity type (see Figure 1.1and Figure 6.13).

```
|Cycle                          A6003A Utility Costs
|Valid From                     01.01.2017
|COarea currency                USD      US Dollar
```

Per	Segment name	Cost Element	OTy	Object	PTy	Partner object	Val/COArea Crcy
1	ELECT	943100	CTR	5000101001	ATY	5000101905/2000	2,560.00
	ELECT	943100	ATY	5000101905/2000	CTR	5000101001	2,560.00-
	ELECT	943100	CTR	5000101002	ATY	5000101905/2000	1,720.00
	ELECT	943100	ATY	5000101905/2000	CTR	5000101002	1,720.00-
	ELECT	943100	CTR	5000101003	ATY	5000101905/2000	1,920.00
	ELECT	943100	ATY	5000101905/2000	CTR	5000101003	1,920.00-
	ELECT	943100	CTR	5000101004	ATY	5000101905/2000	2,090.00
	ELECT	943100	ATY	5000101905/2000	CTR	5000101004	2,090.00-

Figure 6.13: Indirect activity posting

A second type of indirect activity allocation is also available, called *target=actual activity allocation*. This type of allocation is more suitable for use by business processes but can also be used by cost centers. It allows you to define a network of activities and will perform an iterative allocation using the calculated *operating rate* as the tracing factor. The operating rate is the ratio of the actual to planned activity output for a given activity type.

For an activity type to be used here, it must have the actual activity type category set to option 5, target = actual allocation (see Figure 6.14). The activity type for planning can be either 1, 2, or 3.

Names		
Name	Admin hours	
Description	Admin Hours	
Basic data		
Activity Unit	H	Hour
CCtr categories	*	
Allocation default values		
ATyp category	1	Manual entry, manual allocation
Allocation cost elem	943910	Admin Hours
Price indicator		
☐ Actual qty set	Average price	
☐ Plan quantity set	PreDistribFixedCosts	
Variance Values for Actual Allocation		
Actl Acty Type Cat.	5	Taget=actual allocation

Figure 6.14: Actual activity type category 5

The network of activities is defined during the planning process using both activity and cost input planning and activity output planning. As with many things in SAP, the final step to run the target=actual activity allocation is very simple, but it will not work unless all the preliminary planning steps are carried out. Figure 6.15 shows an example of a target=actual allocation scenario. Cost center admin provides the activity ADM, which is administration hours to the utilities cost center. The utilities cost center provides the activity ELEC, electricity to three production cost centers. Each of the production cost centers provides activity 1100, machine time to production orders. Activity types ADM and ELEC should be defined with the actual activity type category = 5 as shown in Figure 6.14. The machine time activity does not use category 5, as it will be used for direct activity postings.

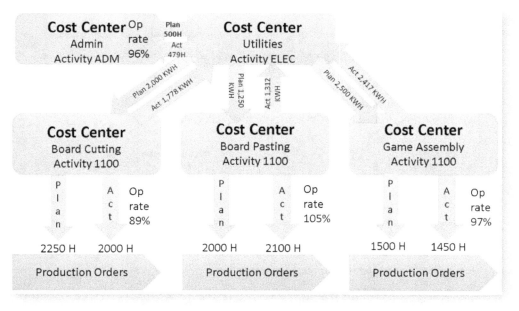

Figure 6.15: Target=actual allocation

The activity outputs and prices of all the cost centers should be planned in transaction KP26 following the procedures shown in Section 3.4. Then use transaction KP06 and plan the activity input using layout 1-102. Define both the sender and receiver cost center and activity type (see Figure 6.16).

157

Layout	1–102	Activity Input Acty-Indep./Acty-Dep.
Variables		
Version	0	Plan/actual version
From Period	1	January
To Period	12	December
Fiscal year	2017	
Cost Center	5000102905	Plant Utilities Kentucky
to		
or group		
Activity Type	ELEC	Electricity
to		
or group		
Sender cost center	5000102903	Plant General Admin Kentucky
to		
or group		
Sender activity type	ADM	Admin Hours
to		

Figure 6.16: Input planning for target=actual initial screen

In the planning overview shown in Figure 6.17 you plan the fixed and variable consumption quantities. Only variable consumption quantities will be considered for target=actual activity allocation.

Version	0		Plan/actual version	
Period	1	To	12	
Fiscal Year	2017			
Cost Center	5000102905		Plant Utilities Kentucky	

▦ Receive...	Sender Cost C...	Sender ...	Plan fixed consumpt.	Distr...	Plan vbl consumption	Distr...	Unit
ELEC	5000102903	ADM		2	6,000	2	H

Figure 6.17: Input planning variable consumption

Similar planning is carried out using sending cost center utilities, activity ELEC, the three production cost centers, and the machine time activity (see Figure 6.18). Once all the planning has been carried out, it is important to run plan reconciliation using transaction KPSI. Using an unreconciled plan in target=actual allocations can lead to incorrect results.

```
Activity Types: Receivers            Date: 11.04.2017  Page:    2 /    3

Cost Center/Group         5000102905   Utilities Ky
Person responsible        Thomas Edison
```

Partner Objects	Scheduled Activity		Valuation	
ATY 5000102001/1100 Board C	2,000	KWH	2,500.00	USD
ATY 5000102002/1100 Pasting	1,250	KWH	1,562.50	USD
ATY 5000102003/1100 Game As	2,500	KWH	3,125.00	USD
* ELEC Electricity	5,750	KWH	7,187.50	USD

Figure 6.18: Activity planning for production cost centers

Once all the production activity has been posted for the month, you can run the target=actual allocation using transaction KNMA. The results are shown in Figure 6.19. You can see that an operating rate has been calculated for each activity. For the machine activities, this is based on the ratio of the actual activity to the planned activity. For the ELEC and ADM activities, the actual quantity is derived using the operation rate as a tracing factor. This can be understood better by displaying the activity analysis (see Figure 6.20). Here you will see the operating rate for each cost center/activity and the quantity that will be posted by the allocation.

```
I◄ ◄ ► ►I   Activity Analysis   Q ▼ ⊞ ▲ ▼ ⬚ ⬚ ⬚ ⬚ Choose   Save   ⬚ ⬚ ▼ ⬚ ⬚ ⬚

Controlling Area    6000      Smarter Sisters Games
Version             0         Plan/actual version
Fiscal Year         2017
Period              001
Cost center group   KYTARG
Processing status   TestRun

Processing completed without errors
```

OTy	Object	Name	AUn	Total plan activity	Total actual acty	Oper. rate
ATY	5000102001/1100	Board Cutting	H	2,250	2,000	88.89
ATY	5000102002/1100	Pasting KY	H	2,000	2,100	105.00
ATY	5000102003/1100	Game Assembly KY	H	1,500	1,450	96.67
ATY	5000102903/ADM	Plant general Ky	H	500	478.865	95.77
ATY	5000102905/ELEC	Utilities Ky	KWH	5,750	5,506.944	95.77

Figure 6.19: Results of target=actual allocation

Period   001

Acty network	Object	C	Oper. rate	Var. plan refer.	Var. act. refer.	Fxd reference	AUn
-	ATY 5000102903/ADM	5	95.77				
└>-	ATY 5000102905/ELEC	5	95.77	500	478.850	0	H
└>-	ATY 5000102001/1100	1	88.89	2,000	1,777.800	0	KWH
└>-	ATY 5000102002/1100	1	105.00	1,250	1,312.500	0	KWH
└>-	ATY 5000102003/1100	1	96.67	2,500	2,416.750	0	KWH

Figure 6.20: Detailed activity analysis

The result is that actual activity postings are made based on the operating rates and can be compared against the plan values (see Figure 6.21).

Activity Types: Period Breakdown		Date: 11.04.2017		Page: 2 / 2
Cost Center/Group		KYTARG	Kentucky Target Actual	
Person responsible		*		
Reporting period		1 to 1 2017		

Activity Types/Periods	Act. Acty	Plan Acty	Variance	OR in %
1 January	5,550 H	5,750 H	200- H	96.52
* 1100 Machine Time	5,550 H	5,750 H	200- H	96.52
1 January	479 H	500 H	21- H	95.77
* ADM Admin Hours	479 H	500 H	21- H	95.77
1 January	5,507 KWH	5,750 KWH	243- KWH	95.77
* ELEC Electricity	5,507 KWH	5,750 KWH	243- KWH	95.77

Figure 6.21: Result of target=actual posting

6.4   Cycle overview

Within all the cycle/segment allocation methods for both plan and actual, you can use the menu option EXTRAS • CYCLE • DISPLAY OVERVIEW to see an overview of all the cycles (see Figure 6.22). You can select the cycles types to display along with whether you want to see plan, actual, or both. As well as just seeing the cycles and segments in one place, the overview is useful to search for objects within your allocations. Consider a situation where a previously active cost center has now become inactive for some reason. This cost center may exist as a sender or receiver in a number of allocations, and you would like to find where it is used and make the appropriate corrections. You could use the where-used functionality that was shown in the cost center master data in Section 2.1, or you can use the search function in the overview (see Figure 6.23) to provide similar results (see Figure 6.24).

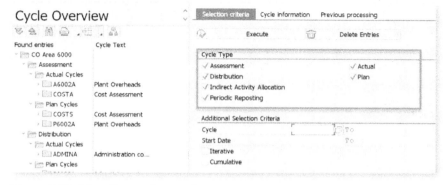

Figure 6.22: Allocation cycle overview

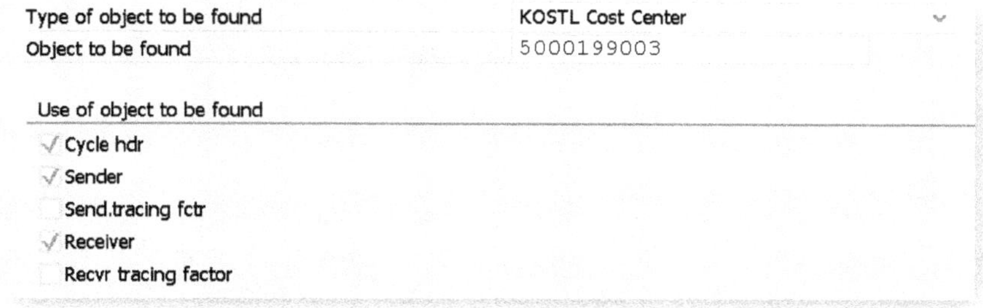

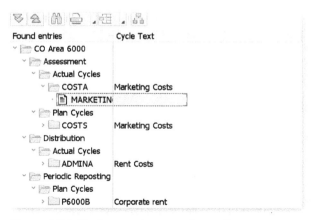

Figure 6.23: Cycle overview search

Figure 6.24: Cycle overview search results

161

The folders in the left-hand pane can be expanded to show the segments within each cycle. For each selected cycle or segment, you can display more detail on the CYCLE INFORMATION tab. For the search that was conducted, you can see that the cost center 5000199003 is a receiver in the marketing costs assessment cycle (see Figure 6.25).

Figure 6.25: Cycle overview segment detail

From the detail screen, you can use the display buttons to toggle between seeing the senders or the receivers. You will also be able to execute, edit, or display the cycles directly from the overview.

Organizing allocation sequence

 Previously the creation of a cost model or a cost map was advocated, especially when there are multiple cost allocations being performed. The cost map should take into account the timing of different allocation cycles. It is likely that some allocations will need to run prior to others to get the correct overall allocation of costs and meaningful absorption reporting. Make sure you know the relationships between all your allocation cycles and whether they are dependent on each other so that you can run them in the correct order.

6.5   Overhead allocations

Although templates and/or costing sheets can be used to perform actual overhead allocations, the use of these tools for actual allocation to cost centers is uncommon. In practice, these are used more frequently for allocating costs to various types of orders. The templates for actual cost center allocation use environments SCI and SCD, depending on whether the receiver is getting activity-independent or activity-dependent costs. In both cases, the sender needs to be a combination of cost center and activity type to provide the price. The quantity calculated on the receiving cost center can be based on any combination of elements available in the selected environment. The example in Figure 6.26 determines an actual quantity in the calculation row by multiplying together two actual statistical key figures, number of shipments (SHIPMT), and average distance of a trip (AVTRIP). This quantity is multiplied by the activity rate planned on the cost center and activity type in the second row to get a cost.

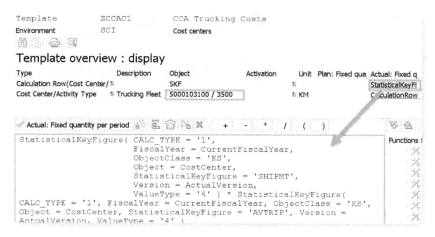

Figure 6.26: Actual allocation template for cost center

In examples of actual cost allocation using a template, the sender is usually a combination of cost center and activity type or a business process. The receiver is any object to which the template is assigned; in this case, it is a cost center (see Figure 6.27).

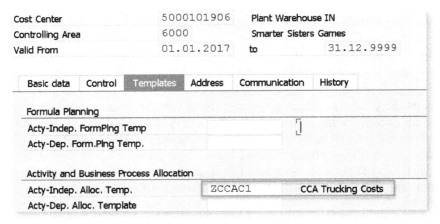

Cost Center	5000101906	Plant Warehouse IN
Controlling Area	6000	Smarter Sisters Games
Valid From	01.01.2017	to	31.12.9999

| Basic data | Control | Templates | Address | Communication | History |

Formula Planning
Acty-Indep. FormPlng Temp
Acty-Dep. Form.Plng Temp.

Activity and Business Process Allocation
Acty-Indep. Alloc. Temp. ZCCAC1 CCA Trucking Costs
Acty-Dep. Alloc. Template

Figure 6.27: Assign template to cost center

Once you have posted the necessary actual statistical key figure values
to the receiving cost centers, you can execute the actual template allocation in transaction KPAS (see Figure 6.28). This will multiply the number
of shipments by the average number of KM per trip multiplied by the
activity rate per KM of $1.25.

Cost Center		5000101906		
Version		0		Plan/actual version
Fiscal Year		2017		
Period		001		

Receiver Object	Sender object	Alloc. CElem	Total fixed/var. qty UoM ∑	Ttl Fx+Vbl value CAC CO crcy Template
CTR 5000101906	ATY 5000103100/3500	943350	43,375 KM	54,218.75 USD ZCCAC1
CTR 5000101906	△		·	54,218.75 USD
△			· ·	54,218.75 USD

Figure 6.28: Actual template allocation result

Overhead allocation requires the configuration of a costing sheet that
specifies the cost base, the overhead rates, and the credit object. If you
want to calculate and apply overhead for a receiving cost center, you can
assign the costing sheet on the TEMPLATES tab of the cost center master
data. The overhead allocation can be run using transaction KSI4. It will
result in the calculated overhead amount being posted to the receiving
cost center(s) as a debit with the corresponding credit being posted to
the credit object defined in the costing sheet.

6.6   Accrual calculation

In Section 3.2, you saw how plan accrual calculation used the percentage method to distribute irregular expenses to periods in cost center accounting. A similar process can be used to post actual accrued or imputed costs. The same overhead structure that was defined for planning can also be used for actual calculation. In addition, there are two other methods that can be used for actual accrual calculation, the *plan=actual* method and the *target=actual* method. It is also possible to use techniques such as recurring entries in FI to deal with these kinds of costs, but having the accrual methods in CO gives you more flexible options, especially when dealing with costs that need to be spread out solely for management reporting purposes.

For the percentage method, the components of the overhead structure (see Figure 6.29) are ❶ the base, which references the cost elements that form the calculation base; ❷ the O/H rate, which references the percentage rate; and ❸ the credit, which references the overhead cost element and the credited cost object.

Overhead structure		YBL	Sum wages and salaries			
Rows						
Row	Base ❶	O/H Rate	Description	Fr.	To	Credit
110	Y-B1		Wages			
120	Y-B2		Salaries			
190			Sum wages and salaries	110	120	❸
210		Y-Z1 ❷	Vacation Time	190	190	Y11
220		Y-Z2	Bonus Accrued	190	190	Y12
230		Y-Z3	Sick leave accrued	190	190	Y13

Figure 6.29: Overhead structure

You can double click on any of these three elements to see the setup involved. For example, the credit setup is shown in Figure 6.30. The credit requires an accrual primary cost element type 3 and a sending object, which can be either a cost center or an internal order. There is an SAP-delivered order type for accrual orders, which you can use or copy to create these orders.

Credit		Y11	Vacation Time	

Credit Records

CoCode	Valid to	Cost Elem.	Cost Center	Order
6000	12 9999	540500		9ABONUS

Figure 6.30: Overhead credit

Once the overhead structure is configured, you can run the actual accrual using transaction code KSA3. On the initial screen, you will select the cost centers to be included and the period parameters, then execute the calculation. The results in Figure 6.31 show that the calculated accrual is posted to the receiving cost center using the accrual cost element and, in this case, an internal order is being used to receive the credit posting.

Actual Accrual Calculation for Cost Centers

Cost Center	Activity Type	Partner Object	Cost Element	Val/COArea Crcy
5000199001		ORD 9ABONUS	540500	1,750.00
		ORD 9ABONUS	540510	2,500.00
		ORD 9ABONUS	540520	750.00
5000199002		ORD 9ABONUS	540500	1,400.00
		ORD 9ABONUS	540510	2,000.00
		ORD 9ABONUS	540520	600.00

Figure 6.31: Actual percentage based accrual results

You can use the plan=actual or target=actual methods of accruals when the accrual is known during planning and is not based on a percentage of some other value. The plan=actual method is used for activity-independent values while the target=actual method should be used for activity-dependent costs. Both of these methods require a primary cost element with a category 4 to plan and post the accrued values (see Figure 6.32). Do not confuse the target=actual accrual discussed here with the target=actual activity allocation covered earlier. They are two different things.

In the configuration settings, this cost element is assigned to a credit object, either a cost center or an internal order similar to the credit for the percentage method (see Figure 6.33).

166

Cost Element	581706	Audit fees Accrued
Controlling Area	6000	Smarter Sisters Games
Valid From	01.01.1900	to	31.12.9999

| Basic Data | Indicators | Default Acct Assgnmt | History |

Names

| Name | Audit fees Accrued |
| Description | Audit fees Accrued |

Basic Data

| CElem category | 4 | Accrual/deferral per debit = actual |

Figure 6.32: Cost element category 4

| Controlling Area | 6000 | Smarter Sisters Games |
| Cost Element | 581706 | Audit fees Accrued |

Credit Records

| CoCode | Valid to | Cost Center | Order |
| 6000 | 12 9999 | | 9AAUDIT |

Figure 6.33: Credit configuration for plan=actual or target=actual

Since these methods cannot use a base value to determine the accrued amounts, it is necessary to enter all the required planned values in KP06 as either activity-independent or activity-dependent amounts (see Figure 6.34).

Fiscal Year	2017	
Cost Center	5000199001	Corporate Finance
Cost Element	581706	Audit fees Accrued

Per...	Text	Plan Fixed Costs	Plan Variable Costs	P
1	January	8,000.00	0.00	
2	February	8,000.00	0.00	
3	March	8,000.00	0.00	
4	April	8,000.00	0.00	

Figure 6.34: Planned accrued costs

The plan=actual accrual is run from the same transaction (KSA3) as the percentage accrual. The results of the audit accrual are shown in Figure 6.35 along with the percentage accrual values. Again, the accrual will debit the receiving cost center using the accrual cost element and credit the accrual internal order with the amount originally planned for the period in Figure 6.34.

Actual Accrual Calculation for Cost Centers

Overhead Rates

Cost Center	Activity Type	Partner Object	Cost Element	Σ	Val/COArea Crcy
5000199001		ORD 9ABONUS	540500		1,750.00
		ORD 9ABONUS	540510		2,500.00
		ORD 9ABONUS	540520		750.00
		ORD 9AAUDIT	581706		8,000.00
					13,000.00

Figure 6.35: Result plan=actual accrual

The target=actual method is used for activity-dependent amounts. In activity-dependent cost planning, it is possible to separate the plan into fixed and variable costs (see Figure 6.36). The target=actual accrual will post the fixed portion similar to the plan=actual method but will post the variable cost portion based on the ratio of actual activity quantity to planned activity quantity.

Cost Center	5000101907	Plant Facilities
Activity Type	3650	Facility Maintenance
Cost Element	581121	Property Maintenance - Ac

Per... Text		Plan Fixed Costs	Plan Variable Costs	Plan fixe
1	January	15,000.00	20,000.00	
2	February	15,000.00	20,000.00	
3	March	15,000.00	20,000.00	
4	April	15,000.00	20,000.00	

Figure 6.36: Activity-dependent cost plan fixed and variable

In this example, an accrual for facility maintenance is being posted based on an hourly maintenance activity. There must be a planned activity quantity for the facilities cost center, which is entered through transaction KP26 (see Figure 6.37)

Fiscal Year	2017		
Cost Center	5000101907	Plant Facilities	
Activity Type	3650	Facility Maintenance	

Per... Text		Plan Activity	Capacity	Unit
1	January		200	H
2	February		200	H
3	March		200	H
4	April		200	H

Figure 6.37: Planned activity facility maintenance

Each month some actual quantity will be posted, which will serve as the target quantity for the variable portion of the costs. In this example, 220 hours were recorded as the actual activity quantity. Running transaction KSA3 will give the result shown in Figure 6.38. The fixed cost will be posted according to the plan amount, and the variable portion will be posted based on the plan amount adjusted for the actual quantity. The total accrued cost is $37,000, compared to the planned amount of $35,000.

Actual Accrual Calculation for Cost Centers

Overhead Rates

Cost Center	Activity Type	Partner Object	Cost Element	Val/COArea Crcy	FixValue COCurr
5000101907	3650	ORD 9ALAND	581121	37,000.00	15,000.00
				37,000.00	15,000.00

Figure 6.38: Result of target=actual accrual

6.7   Transfer actual SKF values

In the sections on automatic allocations, you have seen the value of using statistical key figures as tracing factors during cost allocations. You have seen how those values can be entered manually and how they can be loaded from Excel using BATCHMAN. Often, some of the values that you would like to use may already exist somewhere in the logistic information structures in SAP, and you would like to avoid having to re-enter these values manually as SKFs. Fortunately, the functionality exists in SAP to transfer these values periodically and avoid duplicate data entry.

In Section 2.6, you learned about statistical key figure master data and how you could link an SKF to some values in the logistic information structure. Here you will see how we can make that transfer work. The first step to create the SKF and link it to a LIS value was shown in Figure 2.37. Once you have created the SKF with the link to the LIS, there is a piece of configuration to be done, and then the transfer can be executed.

It is possible to transfer SKFs as either activity-dependent or activity-independent. You will need to decide whether you require your SKF to be activity-dependent or not when you are setting up the configuration. In the configuration, you will either define assignment of cost centers to key figures or define assignment of cost center/activity types to key figures. The pieces of configuration can be accessed through transactions KVA2 or KVD2. In this example, you will see activity-independent transfer, but the steps for the activity-dependent option are similar with the addition of an activity type.

In the configuration transaction KVA2, once you select your cost center, version, and fiscal year, you will see an overview screen (see Figure 6.39) where you will assign the SKF and create or assign a variant.

Cost Center	5000101001		Board Cutting In
Controlling area	6000		Smarter Sisters Games
Version	0		Plan/actual version
Fiscal year	2017		

VI	StatKF	Name		Variant	Description
✓	HCNT	Employee Headcount			
	PROD	Units Produced		2	Board Cutting

Figure 6.39: Assignment to SKF overview

The variant is used to limit the values being transferred from the LIS for the selected cost center. In this example, the SKF is units produced. You need to use the settings in the variant to tell what units should be transferred to each cost center. Since the cost center is board cutting related to the Indiana plant, you do not want units coming from materials that do not pass through that cost center, and you do not want units of materials that were produced in other plants. In the variant (see Figure 6.40), you can limit the selection to only get the values that you require to transfer for the selected cost center.

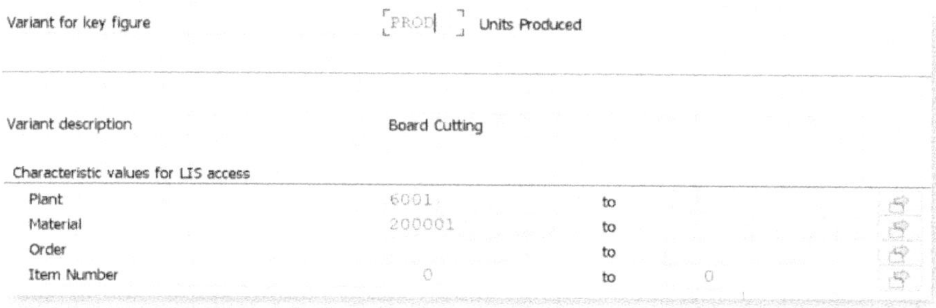

Variant for key figure	PROD	Units Produced		
Variant description	Board Cutting			
Characteristic values for LIS access				
Plant	6001	to		
Material	200001	to		
Order		to		
Item Number	0	to	0	

Figure 6.40: Variant for SKF transfer

Depending on the LIS structure linked to your SKF, you may see different characteristic values available for selection in the variant.

Once the configuration is completed, you can run the periodic transfer using transaction KVA5 for activity-independent transfer or KVD5 for activity-dependent transfer. On the initial screen of KVA5, you will enter the selection of cost centers and the period and year parameters (see Figure 6.41).

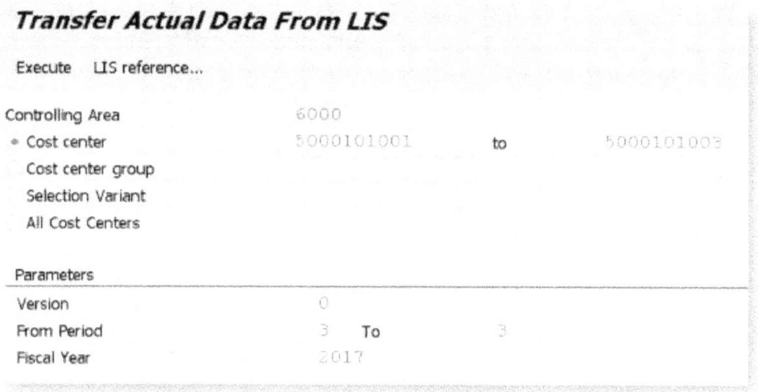

Transfer Actual Data From LIS

Execute   LIS reference...

Controlling Area	6000		
• Cost center	5000101001	to	5000101003
Cost center group			
Selection Variant			
All Cost Centers			

Parameters			
Version	0		
From Period	3 To	3	
Fiscal Year	2017		

Figure 6.41: Activity-independent transfer initial screen

You can execute in test mode to see if you have any errors, and then you can post (see Figure 6.42). The values will go to the correct cost centers based on the configuration created previously. These SKF values can now be used as tracing factors in allocations or in plan actual reporting.

Processing status   UpdateRun

Processing completed without errors

Period   003

Cost Ctr	StatKF	Statistical qty	Qty from LIS	UM	OK
5000101001	PROD	0	2,500	EA	✔
5000101002	PROD	0	1,000	EA	✔
5000101003	PROD	0	800	EA	✔

Figure 6.42: Posting transferred SKFs

6.8 Summary

In this chapter, you have seen some of the reasons why companies need to perform allocations and you have explored some of the automatic allocation tools provided by SAP. You have learned that the most commonly used allocation methods are the ones using the cycle/segment approach such as distributions, assessments and indirect activity allocations, but you have also learned about some lesser used tools such as template allocation, overhead allocation, and accrual calculation. Finally, you learned how to set up and execute a transfer of statistical key figure values from the logistic information structures to cost center accounting where they can be used in allocations as tracing factors.

7 Period end analysis and process

In this chapter, you will see methods of analyzing cost center costs at period end. Additionally, you will cover some more period end processes that were not discussed in the previous chapter. You will see how the concept of target versus actual costs can apply to cost centers and how you can use this for cost analysis. You will also learn some options for variance analysis and posting of cost center variances. You will see the process of actual price calculation as a period end step, including how cost splitting works at the activity level. Finally, you will be exposed to the concept of marginal costs and how they relate to the distribution of fixed costs. These additional period end transactions and analyses should occur after you have completed all the required allocations that were discussed in the previous chapter.

7.1   Period end analysis in CCA

It is generally the responsibility of cost accountants to analyze the performance of key cost centers as part of the period end closing process. In the preceding chapters, you have seen how to enter plan data into cost centers, how actual values flow into CCA, and how allocations are used to move them around. At a period end, with plan and actual data in place, you can now engage in analysis to understand your costs.

In CCA, SAP provides several tools for cost analysis and reporting.

- ▶ Standard plan versus actual analysis using basic reports
- ▶ Target cost analysis
- ▶ Variance analysis
- ▶ Actual price calculation
- ▶ Marginal costs

It is important to understand each of these approaches and determine which tool or combination of tools is right for your business. Some of these tools are complementary and can be used together, but some cannot be combined. For example, it is not possible to combine marginal costs with actual price calculation.

Not a last-minute thing

 Other than standard cost center reporting, most of the period end tools presented in this chapter require considerable forethought and preliminary design before you can use them. It is not possible to decide suddenly to use processes like actual activity cost calculation or marginal costing if you have not already put the right master data, configuration settings, and levels of planning in place. Activity types need to be setup with the correct indicators, and plan versions and splitting structures need to be configured correctly. Often, input planning needs include both the activity type and the cost center. If you are only engaging in activity-independent planning currently, you will not be able to benefit from most of these period end tools.

7.2   Standard analysis

Standard cost center analysis involves examining the cost center results and the differences between plan costs and actual costs and trying to understand the variances. The most useful report for this is the cost center actual/plan/variance report, which is accessed through transaction S_ALR_87013611 (see Figure 7.1).

This report is particularly useful for production cost centers or when cost centers are allocating or providing services to other cost objects. The report is split between the DEBIT section ❶, which shows the costs incurred by the cost center, and the CREDIT section ❷, which shows the costs passed on by the cost center through allocations. The balance in the cost center is shown in the OVER / UNDER-ABSORPTION ❸, which is a reflection of whether the cost center has over or under allocated its costs. For cost centers sending costs through assessments or distributions, the goal is to empty the sending cost center so that the balance at the end of a period is zero. For production cost centers where the credits are coming from activity allocations, the over/under absorbed balance may be a reflection of higher than planned input costs, an inaccurate planned activity price or activity quantities being different from plan. This balance can then be allocated to COPA to clear the cost center and support profitability reporting.

Cost Centers: Actual/Plan/Variance		Date: 05.05.2017	Page: 2 / 3	
Cost Center/Group	5000101100	CardGame Assembly IN	Column: 1 / 2	
Person responsible:	Sam Spade			
Reporting period:	2 to 2 2017			

Cost Elements	Act. Costs	Plan Costs	Var.(Abs.)	Var.(%)
540000 Salaries	61,500.00	60,000.00	1,500.00	2.50
545050 Fuel, Gas				
545145 Propane	850.00		850.00	
545210 Heating	2,145.00	1,666.66	478.34	28.70
545220 Sewage	2,998.76	3,332.45	333.69-	10.01-
550085 Subcontract Service	2,445.00	3,333.34	888.34-	26.65-
550110 Facility Costs	10,500.00	10,000.00	500.00	5.00
551155 Rental Costs	2,197.00	3,006.66	809.66-	26.93-
581020 Communications	438.00	500.00	62.00-	12.40-
640000 Depreciation Expens	10,069.45	10,069.45		
943100 Electricity	4,000.50	2,500.00	1,500.50	60.02
943110 Natural Gas	2,762.25	1,869.85	892.40	47.73
943120 Water Allocation	857.25	596.23	261.02	43.78
* Debit	100,763.21	96,874.64	3,888.57	4.01
943000 Production Labour	62,100.00-	59,999.63-	2,100.37-	3.50
943010 Machine Time	27,622.50-	36,875.01-	9,252.51	25.09-
* Credit	89,722.50-	96,874.64-	7,152.14	7.38-
** Over/Underabsorption	11,040.71		11,040.71	

Figure 7.1: Actual/plan/variance report

Looking at the variances between the plan and actual in the debit section ❹ is an indication of the basic cost efficiency of the cost center. Here you can see the absolute difference between planned and actual costs, as well as the percentage variance. However, in cost centers providing activity output, the absolute variance may not be a true indicator of efficiency, as it does not necessarily show how costs have varied because of output.

The variance between plan and actual in the credit section ❺ shows what was actually allocated from the cost center compared to the planned allocations. Again, this is absolute and does not show variation due to output.

Some indication of the impact of output can also be seen in the actual/plan/variance report, as it also displays a section showing actual versus planned activity output (see Figure 7.2).

| Cost Centers: Actual/Plan/Variance | Date: 05.05.2017 | | Page: | 3 / | 3 |

Cost Center/Group	5000101100		CardGame Assembly IN	Column:	1 /	2
Person responsible:	Sam Spade					
Reporting period:	2 to	2 2017				

Activity Types	Act. Acty	Plan Acty	Var. (Abs.)	Var. (%)
1000 Production Labour	2,300 H	2,105 H	195 H	9.25
1100 Machine Time	1,905 H	2,458 H	553- H	22.51-

Figure 7.2: Activity output actual versus plan

Combined with the cost variances, this can give some indication of the effects of output quantities on costs. This analysis will be further refined in the next section when you look at target costing reports.

7.3   Target cost analysis for cost centers

As you have seen, simply comparing the plan cost of a cost center against the actual costs is the most basic type of analysis that can be performed. You can see the variation but may have trouble explaining it. For cost centers where you plan and record activity outputs, you can use target costs to determine if the variance was due to a change in output or a change in costs. Target costs for a cost center are calculated based on the plan costs adjusted for the operating rate of the output activities. You already learned in Section 6.3 that the operating rate is the ratio of the actual activity output to the planned activity output.

Since target costing relies on comparing the planned activity output of a cost center with the actual activity output, you can only get meaningful target costs if you have performed activity-dependent planning for the cost center and activity type. This means you must enter activity-dependent planning for cost elements and activity types on costs that you expect to vary based on output. Any costs that are not planned as activity-dependent will be treated as fixed costs in the target cost analysis and will not vary by output.

You will recall from Section 3.3 that activity-dependent planning should be done using transaction KP06, planning layout 1-101 for cost element planning, and layout 1-102 for activity input planning.

Version	0		Plan/actual version	
Period	1	To	1	
Fiscal Year	2017			
Cost Center	5000101100		Card Game Assembly Indiana	

| Activity ... Cost Element | Plan Fixed Costs | Distr... | Plan Variable Costs | Distr... | Pl |
| 1000   540000 | 10,000.00 | 2 | 50,000.00 | 2 | |

Figure 7.3: Activity-dependent planning for salaries

In Figure 7.3 the cost element 540000 for salaries has been planned as activity-dependent with the activity 1000, labor. You will notice that you can plan both fixed and variable costs on this screen. This is important for target cost analysis, as only the variable costs will be adjusted based on quantity. Other than performing activity-dependent planning, there is no other specific setup or configuration required to run the actual/target/variance report using transaction S_ALR_87013625 (see Figure 7.4).

CCtrs: Act./Tgt/Var.		Date:	05.05.2017		Page:	2 /	3
Cost center/group:	5000101100		CardGame Assembly IN		Column:	1 /	6
Person responsible:	Sam Spade						
Reporting period:	2 to	2	2017				

Cost Elements		Act. Costs	Tgt Costs	Var.(Abs.)	Var.(%)
540000	Salaries	61,500.00	64,625.34	3,125.34-	4.84-
545050	Fuel, Gas				
545145	Propane	850.00		850.00	
545210	Heating	2,145.00	1,666.66	478.34	28.70
545220	Sewage	2,999.76	3,332.45	333.69-	10.01-
550085	Subcontract Service	2,445.00	3,333.34	888.34-	26.65-
550110	Facility Costs	10,500.00	10,000.00	500.00	5.00
551155	Rental Costs	2,197.00	3,006.66	809.66-	26.93-
581020	Communications	438.00	500.00	62.00-	12.40-
640000	Depreciation Expens	10,069.45	10,069.45		
943100	Electricity	4,000.5	1,937.29	2,063.21	106.50
943110	Natural Gas	2,762.2	1,448.97	1,313.28	90.64
943120	Water Allocation	857.25	462.03	395.22	85.54
*	Debit	100,763.21	100,382.19	381.02	0.38
943000	Production Labour	62,100.00	65,550.01-	3,450.01	5.26-
943010	Machine Time	27,622.5	28,575.00-	952.50	3.35-
*	Credit	89,722.50-	94,125.01-	4,402.51	4.68-
**	Over/Underabsorption	11,040.71	6,257.18	4,783.53	76.45

Figure 7.4: Actual / target / variance report

The actual/target/variance report shown in Figure 7.4 is similar in layout to the actual/plan/variance report that you saw in Figure 7.1. It is productive to compare the two reports to understand what the actual/target report is showing.

The first thing to note is that the credit entries ❶ are adjusted to reflect the actual operating rate. The second ❷ is in the debit section; any costs that you have planned as activity-dependent will vary based on the activity output. Notice that in the debit section for any activity-independent costs such as rental costs the target cost, will equal the plan cost. Overall, what this report can tell you is what my variance would be if my plan values had been based on my actual activity output.

When you compare actual versus target, you can see variance considering output. For example, in Figure 7.1, there is an unfavorable variance on the salaries account; however, when this is adjusted for actual output in Figure 7.4, we have actually performed better than you would expect based on the actual operating rate. In the next section, you will see how you can use variance analysis to further analyze the differences between actual and target costs.

Pages and columns in reports

Often when reports such as the actual/target variance report are shown on the screen, there may be additional columns or report sections that do not all fit on the first page. This is indicated by the page 2/3 and column 1/6 shown in the report header. You can generally scroll up or down to see various pages, and you can use the ⌗Column button to see and navigate to the various column sections in the report. Alternately, you can use the next/previous buttons |◀ ◀ ▶ ▶| to move between sections.

7.4 Variance analysis

The difference between actual and target costs can be further analyzed using variance analysis. Unlike target cost analysis, which only requires activity-dependent planning, there are a number of prerequisite steps required for variance analysis.

For variance analysis and for actual price calculation, it will be necessary to run *actual cost splitting* as part of the process. If you have already used cost splitting during plan activity price calculation, then the configuration of the splitting structures will already be in place. You will recall that a splitting structure (see Figure 7.5) is required with assignments that allow us to assign particular cost elements or groups to activity types (see Figure 7.6). In this simple example, there are only two activity types, labor and machine time. All the compensation-related costs are collected in a cost element group called **labor,** and this is linked to assignment 1 in the structure. A second cost element group called **other** containing all the other plant costs was also created and is linked to assignment 2 in the structure.

Dialog Structure	Structure Name	P1 Production Structure		
˅ Splitting Structures				
˅ Assignments	Assignments			
Selection for assignment	Assgnmnt	Text	Rule	Text
˅ Splitting rules	1	Labor	P1	Production
Selection for rules	2	Other	P1	Production

Figure 7.5: P1 splitting structure

Structure Name	P1	Production Structure	
Assignment	1	Labor	
Splitting Rule	P1	Production	
Controlling Area	6000	Smarter Sisters Games	
Selection for assignment			
Field Label	From Value	To Value	Group
Cost Element			LABOR
Activity Type	1000		

Figure 7.6: Cost element to activity type assignment

The reason that splitting is required for variance analysis is due to the fact that most actual costs in cost center accounting are posted only to the cost center and not to the cost center/activity combination. For the calculation of variances and actual prices, SAP requires that these actual costs be split between the activity types that are output by the cost centers.

An additional configuration step is required to configure the *target cost version* (see Figure 7.7). Here it is important to assign the *variance variant* that will activate the target cost version. The variance variant is configured separately and serves to determine which variance categories will be included in the variance calculation.

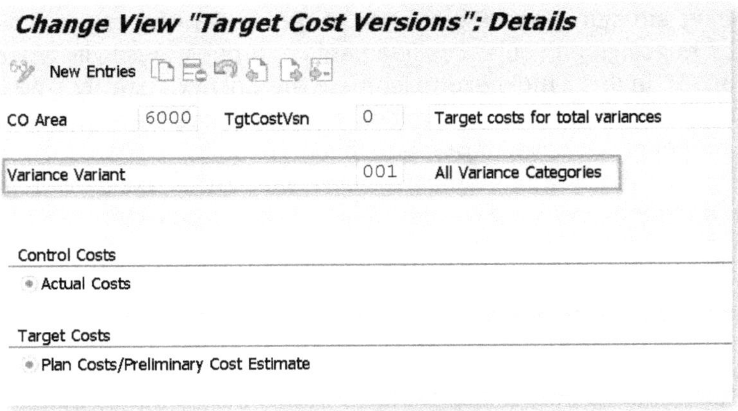

Change View "Target Cost Versions": Details

New Entries

CO Area	6000	TgtCostVsn	0	Target costs for total variances

Variance Variant	001	All Variance Categories

Control Costs
- Actual Costs

Target Costs
- Plan Costs/Preliminary Cost Estimate

Figure 7.7: Target cost version configuration

Transaction KSS1 is used to perform variance calculation. It is not necessary to run transaction KSS2 for actual cost splitting independently as it is run automatically as part of the variance calculation. Technically, this transaction runs through four steps to calculate the final variance values.

▶ Importing the data and calculating the target costs.

▶ Splitting the actual costs based on target values—this assign actual costs to activities in cases where the cost element is directly planned on the activity type.

▶ Splitting based on the splitting rules—the costs which were not assigned to activities in the previous step are now assigned using the splitting structure.

▶ Variance calculation—variances are calculated at this step.

The transaction can be run for all cost centers, cost center groups, individual cost centers, and pre-defined selection variants. As this is a periodic process, it is run for one period at a time. The initial layout of the report in Figure 7.8 shows the same overall values from Figure 7.4 split between the two activity types, labor and machine time. In this layout, you can see the target costs, the actual costs from the debit side (control costs), the actual allocations from the credit side (allocated actual costs), and the over / under-absorption (variance) broken down by activity. The calculated operating rate of the activity also is displayed. This shows that the overall variance is unfavorable, a debit balance of $11,040.71, and

180

that it is made up of a favorable variance in the labor activity (1000) and an unfavorable variance in the machine activity (1100).

Variance Calculation for Cost Centers: List [Test Run]

Cost Elements Variance Categories

Period	2	Fiscal year	2017	Messages		0 ◇ Currency		USD
Version	0 Target costs for total variances (0)				∨	20 Controlling area currency		∨

Cost Center	Description	Acty Type	Oper. Rate Σ	Target Costs Σ	Control Costs Σ	Allocated Actl Costs Σ	Variance	Var.(%) tgt cts
5000101100	CardGame Assembly IN	1000	109.25	64,625.34	61,500.00	62,100.00	600.00-	0.93-
5000101100	CardGame Assembly IN	1100	77.49	35,756.85	39,263.21	27,622.50	11,640.71	32.56
				100,382.19	100,763.21	89,722.50	11,040.71	

Figure 7.8 : Variance calculation standard layout

In the case of this report, there are many columns of information available for display, so you may find it useful to create meaningful layouts to assist in your analysis. In addition to the standard SAP-delivered variant, you might want to consider some of the options shown in Figure 7.9.

Layout	Layout description	Default setting
/VAR001	Variance Categories	
/VAR002	Input & Output Side	
/VAR003	Input Variance Categories	
/VAR004	Output Variance Categories	
/VAR005	Standard Version with totals	✓
1SAP	Standard Version	

Figure 7.9: Additional layouts for variance reporting

The additional layouts can provide different levels of analysis into the variances. For example, variances are always broken down between input and output, so the next level of analysis would be to examine the input and output variance as shown in Figure 7.10. Here you can see that the favorable labor variance is more on the input side, while the unfavorable machine time variance is more on the output side.

Period	2	Fiscal year	2017	Messages		0 ◇ Currency	USD
Version	0 Target costs for total variances (0)				∨	20 Controlling area currency	∨

Cost Center	Description	Acty Type	Oper. Rate Σ	Var. InSd Σ	Output Variance Σ	Variance
5000101100	CardGame Assembly IN	1000	109.25	3,125.34-	2,525.34	600.00-
5000101100	CardGame Assembly IN	1100	77.49	3,506.36	8,134.35	11,640.71
				381.02	10,659.69	11,040.71

Figure 7.10: Input and Output side variances

In addition to grouping by input and output side, SAP also gives you a number of pre-defined categories to subdivide the variances. These categories are defined in the configuration of the variance variant. In Figure 7.7 you saw that a variance variant needs to be assigned to the target cost version. The configuration settings of this variance variant are shown in Figure 7.11. As mentioned, the variance categories shown on the variance variant are pre-defined by SAP and cannot be changed. The only modification you can make is to un-check categories, which means that SAP will not calculate variance for that category and will instead place those variances in the remaining variances categories.

Figure 7.11: Variance variant configuration

On the input side, actual costs are compared against target costs and split into the following categories:

▶ Input price variance, which reflects variances caused by a difference between planned and actual activity rates;

▶ Resource usage variance in a cost center appears if you post actual costs to a cost element with no planned costs;

▶ Input quantity variance reflects an over or under consumption of activity quantities; and

▶ The remaining input variance will contain any variances that cannot be determined in the other categories.

You can create a display variant to examine the breakdown of the input side variance based upon the categories above (see Figure 7.12) to gain further insight into input variance composition.

| Period | 2 | Fiscal year | 2017 | Messages | 0 | Currency | USD |
| Version | 0 Target costs for total variances (0) | | | 20 Controlling area currency | | | |

Cost Center	Description	Acty Type	Input Price Var	Input Qty Variance	Resource-Usage Var.	Remaining Input Var.	Input-Side Variances
5000101100	CardGame Assembly IN	1000	0.00	0.00	0.00	3,125.34-	3,125.34-
5000101100	CardGame Assembly IN	1100	628.66	3,143.05	850.00	1,115.35-	3,506.36
			628.66	3,143.05	850.00	4,240.69-	381.02

Figure 7.12: Input variance categories

On the output side, the allocated actual costs (credits from activity allocations) are compared against the target costs or the plan costs and split into the following categories:

▶ Output price variance occurs when the output activity rate for the actual activity allocation differs from the planned rate.

▶ Output quantity variance occurs if there is a difference between actual allocated costs and target costs possibly due to a manual entry of actual values on a sending cost center, which are different from those posted by indirect activity allocation.

▶ Fixed cost variance (shown on the variance analysis as lot size variance) applies to cost elements which are planned as fixed costs, usually activity-independent, and occurs when the actual operating rate is different from the planned operating rate.

▶ The remaining output variance will contain any variances which cannot be determined in the other categories.

You can also create a display variant to give further details on the output variance based on the categories.

| Period | 2 | Fiscal year | 2017 | Messages | 0 | Currency | USD |
| Version | 0 Target costs for total variances (0) | | | 20 Controlling area currency | | | |

Cost Center	Description	Acty Type	Oper. Rate	Output Price Var.	Output Qty Var.	Lot Size Variance	Remaining Variance	Output-Side Variance
5000101100	CardGame Assembly IN	1000	109.25	3,450.41	0.00	925.07-	0.00	2,525.34
5000101100	CardGame Assembly IN	1100	77.49	952.21	0.00	7,182.12	0.02	8,134.35
			186.74	4,402.62	0.00	6,257.05	0.02	10,659.69

Figure 7.13: Output variance categories

It is possible to further subdivide each variance category into a fixed and variable component, and you could create layouts to display the costs at that level.

It is also possible to display the variance at the level of individual cost elements by clicking on the Cost Elements button (see Figure 7.14). Here you can also create layouts to display the variances based on input or output and by category. The report also shows how the costs were split and what occurred in the steps leading up to the variance calculation itself.

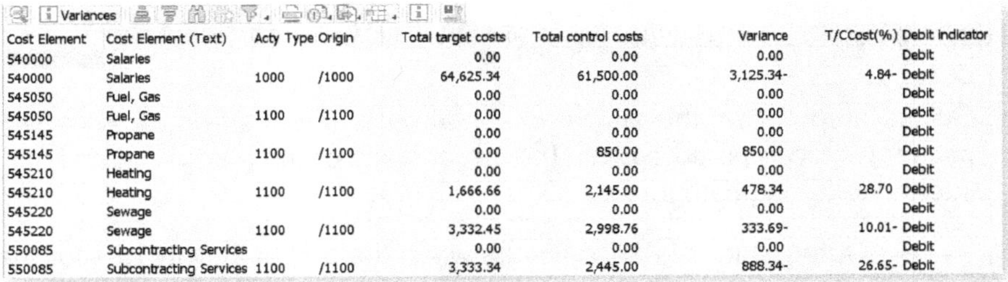

Cost Element	Cost Element (Text)	Acty Type	Origin	Total target costs	Total control costs	Variance	T/CCost(%)	Debit indicator
540000	Salaries			0.00	0.00	0.00		Debit
540000	Salaries	1000	/1000	64,625.34	61,500.00	3,125.34-	4.84-	Debit
545050	Fuel, Gas			0.00	0.00	0.00		Debit
545050	Fuel, Gas	1100	/1100	0.00	0.00	0.00		Debit
545145	Propane			0.00	0.00	0.00		Debit
545145	Propane	1100	/1100	0.00	850.00	850.00		Debit
545210	Heating			0.00	0.00	0.00		Debit
545210	Heating	1100	/1100	1,666.66	2,145.00	478.34	28.70	Debit
545220	Sewage			0.00	0.00	0.00		Debit
545220	Sewage	1100	/1100	3,332.45	2,998.76	333.69-	10.01-	Debit
550085	Subcontracting Services			0.00	0.00	0.00		Debit
550085	Subcontracting Services	1100	/1100	3,333.34	2,445.00	888.34-	26.65-	Debit

Figure 7.14: Variances at the cost element level

Once you have displayed the variances at the cost element level, you can select the processing step from the drop-down menu (see Figure 7.15). By selecting a step, the cost element report will change to show what happened at that step. These four splitting and calculation steps were described previously.

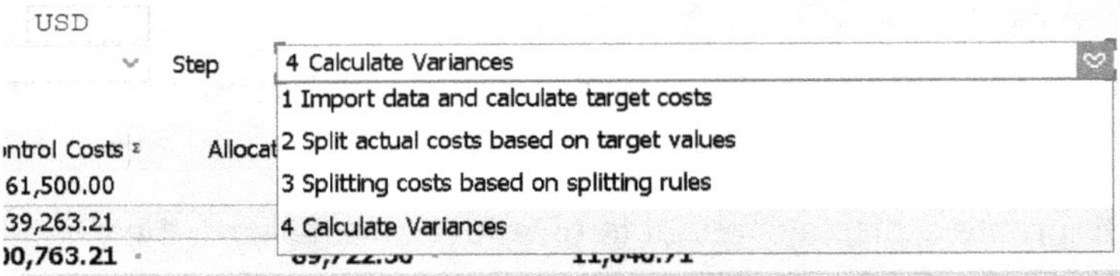

USD

Step: 4 Calculate Variances

1 Import data and calculate target costs
2 Split actual costs based on target values
3 Splitting costs based on splitting rules
4 Calculate Variances

Control Costs 61,500.00 / 39,263.21 / 0,763.21

Figure 7.15: Select processing step

Finally, in the cost element view, you can click on the ⓘ Variance Categories button to obtain documentation through the variance tree (see Figure 7.16). Here you select any of the items in the tree, and by clicking on the 🔍 button, you can obtain documentation about that particular item.

When running the variance analysis, you should run in test mode first. All the reporting that you have seen will be available in test mode. When you run with the test mode removed, the splitting and the variances will be posted and will be available in standard reports such as S_ALR_87013627 – Cost Centers: Variances and S_ALR_87013628 – Cost Centers: Splitting.

184

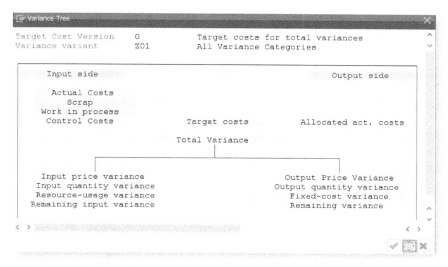

Figure 7.16: Variance tree

7.5   Actual price calculation

You can use actual activity price calculation to determine what the real activity rate would be based on the actual costs and actual outputs of your cost centers. It is possible to perform an actual *cost component split* to determine what caused the actual price change. Finally, you can use the actual prices to revalue the activity allocations that have occurred during the month at planned rates, effectively moving the variances from the sending cost center to the original receiving objects.

To be able to use actual price calculation, the actual price indicator in the activity type needs to be set to either 5 or 6, based on the values shown in Figure 7.17.

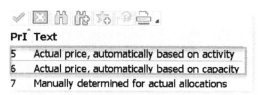

Figure 7.17: Actual price indicator

In addition, price calculation settings for version 0, the plan/actual version, needs to be in place. Most of these settings have been covered in Section 3.2; the only additional things you might consider are assigning a cost component structure and activating the cost component split in object currency. This is only required if you wish to see the actual cost component split as part of the actual activity price calculation.

The following provides an example of actual cost splitting. In this case, the cost center is 5000101200, and it has been providing production activities to a repetitive manufacturing cost collector throughout the period (see Figure 7.18).

Cost Centers: Actual/Plan/Variance	Date: 09.05.2017		Page: 2 / 3	
			Column: 1 / 2	
Cost Center/Group	5000101200	Video Game Assembly		
Person responsible:	Billy Bishop			
Reporting period:	5 to 5 2017			

Cost Elements	Act. Costs	Plan Costs	Var. (Abs.)	Var. (%)
540000 Salaries	134,900.00	133,950.00	950.00	0.71
545145 Propane	1,900.00	1,666.66	233.34	14.00
545220 Sewage	1,950.00	2,000.00	50.00-	2.50-
550085 Subcontract Service	12,050.00	12,000.00	50.00	0.42
550110 Facility Costs	20,750.00	20,000.00	750.00	3.75
581020 Communications	5,033.00	5,230.00	197.00-	3.77-
640000 Depreciation Expens	12,083.34	12,083.34		
943100 Electricity	4,444.44	3,000.00	1,444.44	48.15
943110 Natural Gas	2,844.44	1,600.00	1,244.44	77.78
943120 Water Allocation	866.67	1,170.00	303.33-	25.93-
* Debit	196,821.89	192,700.00	4,121.89	2.14
943000 Production Labour	126,666.65-	133,950.00-	7,283.35	5.44-
943010 Machine Time	55,555.55-	58,750.00-	3,194.45	5.44-
* Credit	182,222.20-	192,700.00-	10,477.80	5.44-
** Over/Underabsorption	14,599.69		14,599.69	

Cost Centers: Actual/Plan/Variance	Date: 09.05.2017		Page: 3 / 3	
			Column: 1 / 2	
Cost Center/Group	5000101200	Video Game Assembly		
Person responsible:	Billy Bishop			
Reporting period:	5 to 5 2017			

Activity Types	Act. Acty	Plan Acty	Var. (Abs.)
1000 Production Labour	4,444 H	4,700 H	256-
1100 Machine Time	2,222 H	2,350 H	128-

Figure 7.18: Production cost center actual activity out

You may analyze this cost center using the target/actual/variance report, and you may perform the variance analysis. In this case, you also want to recalculate the activity rates based on actual costs and revalue the product cost collector based on the actual activity prices. This is a two-step process; first, you should calculate and post the actual activity prices, and then you can optionally use them to revalue the production object.

The actual price calculation transaction is KSII. Similar to variance analysis, cost splitting will be performed during the calculation of actual prices. However, the determination of fixed and variable cost in the split will not be posted when you post actual prices. If you require this posting for some purpose, then you should run and post actual cost splitting KSS2 prior to running actual price calculation. The results of the actual cost calculation for the cost center are shown in Figure 7.19.

OTy	Object	Name	AUn	Activity Quantity	Total price	Price (Fixed)	PUnit
ATY	5000101200/1000	Video Game Assembly	H	4,444.444	3,035.25	0.00	100
ATY	5000101200/1100	Video Game Assembly	H	2,222.222	2,786.49	2,419.49	100

Figure 7.19: Actual activity price calculated

If you have assigned a cost component structure in the planning version, then you can use the menu option GOTO • COMPONENTS to display the cost component split. There will be a separate cost component display for each line the list. The cost component for machine time activity 1100 is shown in Figure 7.20.

Cost Center	5000101200	Video Game Assembly
Activity Type	1100	Machine Time
Price indicator	5	Actual price, automatically based on activity

CComp	Name of Cost Comp.	Val/COArea Crcy	FixValue COCurr	Variable value
100	Labor Costs	0.00	0.00	0.00
101	Prod Overhead Costs	36,650.00	36,650.00	0.00
103	Admin Costs	5,033.00	5,033.00	0.00
104	Depreciation	12,083.34	12,083.34	0.00
105	Utilities	8,155.55	0.00	8,155.55
*		61,921.89	53,766.34	8,155.55

Figure 7.20: Cost component split for machine time

You can use the activity price report, transaction KSBT, to display both the plan and the actual activity prices (see Figure 7.21). The highlighted column contains the indicator for plan versus actual values.

Cost Center Group	VIDEO
Activity Type	1000 To 1100
Version	0 Plan/actual version
Fiscal Year	2017
Period	5 To 5
Price unit	1

Cost Center	ActTyp	Cost ctr short text	Act. type short text	COC	A	Total pri	Variable pri	Price (Fixed)	P	AUn	VT	ObCur
5000101200	1000	Video Game Assembly Prod Labour		USD	P	28.50	28.50	0.00	1	H	1	USD
5000101200	1000	Video Game Assembly Prod Labour		USD	A	30.35	30.35	0.00	5	H	4	USD
5000101200	1100	Video Game Assembly Machine Time		USD	P	25.00	25.00	0.00	1	H	1	USD
5000101200	1100	Video Game Assembly Machine Time		USD	A	27.86	3.67	24.19	5	H	4	USD

Figure 7.21: Plan and actual activity price display

The final optional step is to revalue the receivers of the activity postings based on the new actual price. The result of this is to move the variance from the cost center to the original activity receivers. In Figure 7.18 you can see that there is a $14,599 balance on the cost center. This can be analyzed as variance in the cost center and passed on to another object through revaluation.

The original receiver for the activities from this cost center was a product cost collector, which is an object used to capture production costs in repetitive manufacturing. The same revaluation functionality is available for other objects, but the transaction codes will vary. The costs in the cost collector before the revaluation posting are shown in Figure 7.22.

Description	Production
Company Code	6000 Smarter Sisters US
Material	300004 Super Sergio Video Game
Order Type	YBMR BP: Product Cost Collector

Cost Element	Cost Element (Text)	Origin		Total actual costs	Currency
510000	Consumption - Raw Materials	6001/100074		139,372.85	USD
510010	Consumption - Semi Finished Goods	6001/200002		1,250,012.50	USD
510020	Consumption - Finished Goods	6001/300004		1,740,000.00-	USD
943000	Production Labour	5000101200/1000		126,666.65	USD
943010	Machine Time	5000101200/1100		55,555.55	USD
				168,392.45-	**USD**

Figure 7.22: Cost collector costs before revaluation

The revaluation at actual activity prices is a function in the period end closing activities for cost object controlling. For product cost collectors, the transaction is CON1 for individual processing or CON2 for mass processing. Running CON1 for the above material will post the $14,599 from the cost center and activity type to the cost collector order (see Figure 7.23).

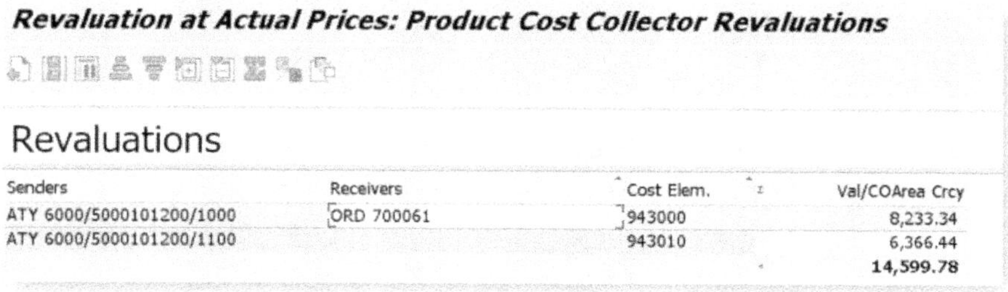

Revaluation at Actual Prices: Product Cost Collector Revaluations

Revaluations

Senders	Receivers	Cost Elem.	Val/COArea Crcy
ATY 6000/5000101200/1000	ORD 700061	943000	8,233.34
ATY 6000/5000101200/1100		943010	6,366.44
			14,599.78

Figure 7.23: Actual revaluation posting

Now display the costs on the cost collector and notice the difference in the activity amounts (Figure 7.24). Then display the sending cost center and see that the revalued activities have essentially made the balance zero. In this way, the variance is moved from the cost center to the production object, will be subsequently dealt with during the period end variance process for repetitive manufacturing, and will likely be settled to COPA.

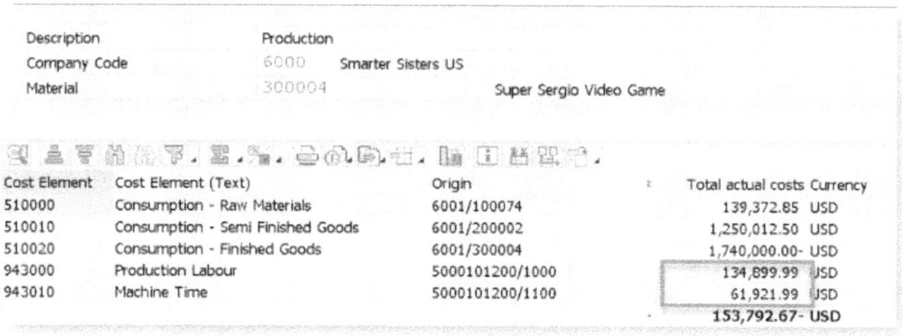

Description	Production		
Company Code	6000	Smarter Sisters US	
Material	300004	Super Sergio Video Game	

Cost Element	Cost Element (Text)	Origin	Total actual costs	Currency
510000	Consumption - Raw Materials	6001/100074	139,372.85	USD
510010	Consumption - Semi Finished Goods	6001/200002	1,250,012.50	USD
510020	Consumption - Finished Goods	6001/300004	1,740,000.00-	USD
943000	Production Labour	5000101200/1000	134,899.99	USD
943010	Machine Time	5000101200/1100	61,921.99	USD
			153,792.67-	USD

Figure 7.24: Cost collector costs after revaluation

Cost Centers: Actual/Plan/Variance		Date: 09.05.2017		Page:	2 / 3
				Column:	1 / 2
Cost Center/Group	VIDEO		Video Games		
Person responsible:	Billy Bishop				
Reporting period:	5 to 5 2017				

Cost Elements		Act. Costs	Plan Costs	Var. (Abs.)	Var. (%)
540000	Salaries	134,900.00	133,950.00	950.00	0.71
545145	Propane	1,900.00	1,666.66	233.34	14.00
545220	Sewage	1,950.00	2,000.00	50.00-	2.50-
550085	Subcontract Service	12,050.00	12,000.00	50.00	0.42
550110	Facility Costs	20,750.00	20,000.00	750.00	3.75
581020	Communications	5,033.00	5,230.00	197.00-	3.77-
640000	Depreciation Expens	12,083.34	12,083.34		
943100	Electricity	4,444.44	3,000.00	1,444.44	48.15
943110	Natural Gas	2,844.44	1,600.00	1,244.44	77.78
943120	Water Allocation	866.67	1,170.00	303.33-	25.93-
* Debit		196,821.89	192,700.00	4,121.89	2.14
943000	Production Labour	134,899.93-	133,950.00-	949.93-	0.71
943010	Machine Time	61,921.99-	58,750.00-	3,171.99-	5.40
* Credit		196,821.98-	192,700.00-	4,121.98-	2.14
** Over/Underabsorption		0.09-		0.09-	

Figure 7.25: Cost Center after activity revaluation

7.6   Marginal costing

In general, marginal cost refers to the cost required to produce an additional unit of output. In a specified range of output, this is usually the same as the variable cost. Within that defined range of output, fixed cost will not change if we produce an extra unit, so the marginal cost of that additional unit is only the variable costs required to produce it.

In activity allocations where the sender is a cost center, and the receiver is either another cost center or a business process, marginal costing can be achieved through a function called *pre-distribution of fixed costs*. If you choose to use this function, then the fixed costs that are planned on a sending cost center, and activity types get pre-distributed to the receiver cost centers as actual postings as part of planning. Any actual activity allocations posted later will only occur at the variable activity price. This way inefficiencies or fixed cost variances in the sender cost center are not transferred to the receiving cost centers through the activity allocation. The theory is that fixed costs should not be allocated proportionally because they do not vary with increases in activity but are dependent on time.

You can set the indicator for pre-distribution of fixed cost as a default on the activity type, or you can enter it during activity price planning in transaction KP26 using layout 1-204 to display and change indicators (see Figure 7.26). You can change the indicator here as long as you have not posted any plan values for the period.

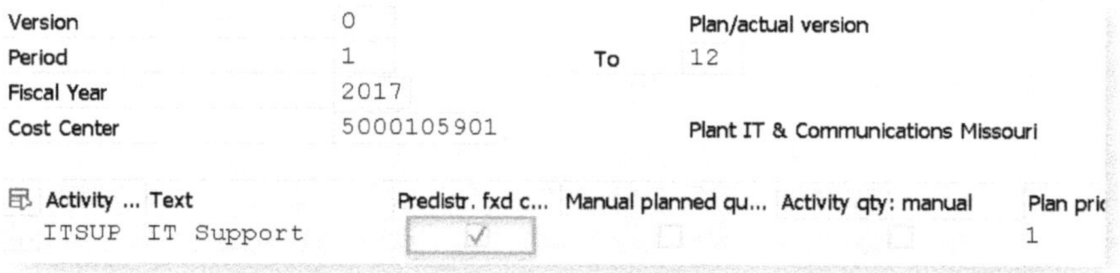

Version	0		Plan/actual version	
Period	1	To	12	
Fiscal Year	2017			
Cost Center	5000105901		Plant IT & Communications Missouri	

Activity ... Text	Predistr. fxd c...	Manual planned qu...	Activity qty: manual	Plan pric
ITSUP IT Support	✓			1

Figure 7.26 : Pre-distribution indicator in planning

For pre-distribution of fixed costs to work properly, the cost planning on the sender should be activity-dependent. This allows you to enter the plan for each cost element as a combination of fixed and variable amounts in KP06 using layout 1-101, as seen in Figure 7.27.

Version	0		Plan/actual version	
Period	1	To	12	
Fiscal Year	2017			
Cost Center	5000105901		Plant IT & Communications Miss	

Activity ... Cost Element	Plan Fixed Costs	Distr...	Plan Variable Costs	Distr...	Plan
ITSUP 540000	420,000.00	2	180,000.00	2	

Figure 7.27 : Activity-dependent plan with fixed and variable costs

The receiving cost centers will then plan their activity inputs from the sending cost center/activity type. This planning can be either activity-dependent or activity-independent. You can use transaction KP06 and layout 1-102 (see Figure 7.28). The assumption is that the receiving cost center's plans for activity input will drive the planned activity output of the sending cost center.

Version	0		Plan/actual version		
Period	1	To	12		
Fiscal Year	2017				
Cost Center	5000105200		Video Game Assembly Missouri		

⊞ Sender Cost C...	Sender ...	Plan fixed consumpt.	Distr...	Plan vbl consumption	Distr...	Unit
5000105901	ITSUP	15,000	2	0	2	H

Figure 7.28: Plan inputs on the receiving cost centers

Once you have planned the inputs on the receiving cost centers, you must run plan reconciliation, transaction KPSI, to ensure that the activity inputs in the receiving costs centers match with the planned activity output of the sending cost center. This transaction will post the difference between the receiver's plan values and the sender's plan values back to the sender. In Figure 7.29 you can see that the sender has originally planned zero activity, and the receivers are planning to use 21,000 hours, so now that value will be posted to the sender's plan.

Processing completed without errors

Display status   Total for all per.

OTy	Object	Name	AUn	Total plan activity	New plan activity	Activity difference
ATY	5000105901/ITSUP	Plant IT & Comm MI	H	0	21,000	21,000

Figure 7.29: Plan reconciliation

Following plan reconciliation, you can perform plan activity price calculation using transaction KSPI. On the initial screen, you have the option to perform pre-distribution of fixed costs as part of the activity price calculation (see Figure 7.30). If you do not select the indicator here, you can run pre-distribution of fixed costs in a separate transaction code, KSFX. The plan price calculation will determine the fixed and variable portions of the planned price based on the activity-dependent cost plan of the sender and the reconciled activity quantity (see Figure 7.31).

192

Controlling Area   6000
* Cost center group   5000105
All Cost Centers
Parameters
Version   0   Plan/actual version
Period   1   To   12
Fiscal Year   2017

Processing
   Background Processing
   Test Run
✓ Detail Lists
✓ With fixed cost predistr.

Figure 7.30: Plan price calculation – initial screen

Value Date	01.01.2017

✓ With fixed cost predistr.

Processing status   UpdateRun

Document number from 200000668
                200000667
                300000100   to   300000111
Period   001

OTy	Object	Name	AUn	Activity Quantity	Total price	Price (Fixed)	PUnit
ATY	5000105901/ITSUP	Plant IT & Comm MI	H	1,750	7,171.43	4,300.00	100

Figure 7.31: Plan price results with fixed cost pre-distribution

Now we will see what has actually occurred in the cost centers due to the plan price calculation and the pre-distribution of fixed costs. First, look at the sending cost center (see Figure 7.32). You will see that all fixed and variable costs previously planned have been allocated out to two receiving cost centers based on the planned activity inputs of those two cost centers fully absorbing the costs in the sending cost center's plan.

193

Fiscal Year	2017
Period	1 To 12
Version	000 Plan/actual version
Cost Center	5000105901 Plant IT & Comm MI

Cost element/description	OTy	Partner object	∑	Value report curr. ∑	Variable value in ∑	Fxd val./rep.cur.	Total quantity UoM
540000 Salaries				600,000.00	180,000.00	420,000.00	
550085 Subcontract Services				180,000.00	180,000.00	0.00	
550110 Facility Costs				45,000.00	0.00	45,000.00	
551086 Duty & Demurrage				135,000.00	75,000.00	60,000.00	
551210 Transportation				42,000.00	24,000.00	18,000.00	
581020 Communications				210,000.00	30,000.00	180,000.00	
581025 Computer S/Hardware				84,000.00	24,000.00	60,000.00	
581030 Consultants				90,000.00	90,000.00	0.00	
581115 Meals & Enter				120,000.00	0.00	120,000.00	
ITSUP IT Support				1,506,000.00	603,000.00	903,000.00	
Activity-Dependent Costs				1,506,000.00	603,000.00	903,000.00	
Debit				1,506,000.00	603,000.00	903,000.00	
943400 IT Support		CTR 5000105200		1,075,714.56-	430,714.56-	645,000.00-	15,000- H
943400 IT Support		CTR 5000105300		430,285.80-	172,285.80-	258,000.00-	6,000- H
ITSUP IT Support				1,506,000.36-	603,000.36-	903,000.00-	
Activity Allocation				1,506,000.36-	603,000.36-	903,000.00-	
Credit				1,506,000.36-	603,000.36-	903,000.00-	
Under/Over-Absorbed Overhead				0.36-	0.36-	0.00	

Figure 7.32: Sending cost center planning

Looking at a cost center plan actual report you will see that the planned fixed costs of $903,000 have been pre-distributed from the sending cost center as actual cost credits (see Figure 7.33).

Column:

Cost Center/Group	5000105901	Plant IT & Comm MI
Person responsible:	Lucius Fox	
Reporting period:	1 to 12 2017	

Cost Elements	Act. Costs	Plan Costs	Var.(Abs.)
540000 Salaries		600,000.00	600,000.00-
550085 Subcontract Service		180,000.00	180,000.00-
550110 Facility Costs		45,000.00	45,000.00-
551086 Duty & Demurrage		135,000.00	135,000.00-
551210 Transportation		42,000.00	42,000.00-
581020 Communications		210,000.00	210,000.00-
581025 Computer S/Hardware		84,000.00	84,000.00-
581030 Consultants		90,000.00	90,000.00-
581115 Meals & Enter		120,000.00	120,000.00-
* Debit		1,506,000.00	1,506,000.00-
943400 IT Support	903,000.00-	1,506,000.36-	603,000.36
* Credit	903,000.00-	1,506,000.36-	603,000.36
** Over/Underabsorption	903,000.00-	0.36-	902,999.64-

Figure 7.33: Sender actual fixed costs are pre-distributed

If you look in one of the receiving cost centers, you will see actual cost debits resulting from the pre-distribution of the fixed costs (see Figure 7.34). In the receiver, the plan debits include both the fixed and variable portions. At this point, the actuals only include the pre-distributed fixed costs.

194

Column:

Cost Center/Group	5000105200		Video Game Assembly
Person responsible:	Billy Bishop		
Reporting period:	1 to 12 2017		

Cost Elements	Act. Costs	Plan Costs	Var.(Abs.)
943400 IT Support	645,000.00	1,075,714.56	430,714.56-
* Debit	645,000.00	1,075,714.56	430,714.56-
** Over/Underabsorption	645,000.00	1,075,714.56	430,714.56-

Figure 7.34: Receiver actual fixed costs are pre-distributed

When you perform actual activity allocation during a period, the activities will only be valued at the variable rate on the sender. The variable price per hour was calculated previously in KSPI as $28.71 per hour (this is the difference between the total price and the fixed price in Figure 7.31 divided by the price unit of 100). Figure 7.35 shows the results of an actual activity allocation between the plant IT cost center and the video games assembly cost center. You can see that based on the posted amount and quantity a rate of $28.71 was used.

Layout	1SAP	Primary cost posting	
COarea currency	USD	USD	
Valuation View/Group	0	Legal Valuation	

DocumentNo Doc. Date Document Header Text		RT RefDocNo Rev RvD	
PRw OTy Object	CO object name	Cost Elem. CElem.name Val/COArea Crcy	Quantity PUM
400000417 31.01.2017			
1 ATY 5000105901/ITSUP	Plant IT & Comm MI / IT Suppo. 943400	IT Support 43,071.45-	1,500- H
2 CTR 5000105200	Video Game Assembly 943400	IT Support 43,071.45	1,500 H

Figure 7.35: Result of marginal cost posting

The cost center actual/plan variance report shows what this means (see Figure 7.36). The actual cost debit has increased due to the actual activity posting. Drilling down to the actual cost line items shows that this value is made up of the initial pre-distribution of fixed costs and the actual activity allocation posted at the variable rate (see Figure 7.37). When you compare the actual costs to the plan costs in this case, you can assume that variance is only due to greater activity, and since fixed costs are held constant, there is no fixed cost variance.

As previously stated, pre-distribution of fixed cost can only occur between cost centers or between a cost center and a business process. If pre-distribution of fixed costs is flagged, then the object type of the receiver will determine whether the activity allocation will occur at the vari-

195

able rate or the total rate. For cost center and business processes, the activity will be allocated at the variable rate; for all other receiver cost object types such as orders or WBS elements, the allocation will use both fixed and variable rates.

			Column:	1 /	2
Cost Center/Group	5000105200	Video Game Assembly			
Person responsible:	Billy Bishop				
Reporting period:	1 to 1 2017				

Cost Elements	Act. Costs	Plan Costs	Var.(Abs.)	Var.(%)
943400 IT Support	96,821.45	89,642.88	7,178.57	8.01
* Debit	96,821.45	89,642.88	7,178.57	8.01
** Over/Underabsorption	96,821.45	89,642.88	7,178.57	8.01

Figure 7.36: Actual costs after activity allocation

Year	Per Cost Center	DocumentNo	Cost Element	Cost elem.name	D/C	Σ	Val.in rep.cur.	Σ	Quantity	PUM	Document Header Text
2017	1 5000105200	400000417	943400	IT Support	D		43,071.45		1,500	H	
2017	1 5000105200	300000100	943400	IT Support	D		53,750.00		0	H	Predistribution of fixed costs 740
	5000105200						96,821.45		1,500	H	
							96,821.45		1,500	H	

Figure 7.37: Line item detail of actual IT support

Marginal costing can be used in conjunction with target/actual reporting and with cost center variance analysis. It should not be used with actual price calculation, as the results of actual price calculation will overwrite the planning data from the pre-distribution of fixed costs.

7.7   Summary

In this chapter, you have seen some of the tools made available by SAP for periodic analysis of cost center results. The most basic approach is simply actual/plan variance reporting using standard reports. In this chapter, you have learned that with a bit of forethought and preparation you can make use of more advanced reporting and analysis tools such as target costing, variance analysis, actual price calculation with revaluation, and marginal costing. You now understand each of these tools and how they can be used. You also understand which tools can be used together and which conflict with each other.

8 Manufacturing and cost center accounting

CCA functions can be utilized to their fullest in a manufacturing environment. In a manufacturing company, the cost centers form part of a cost accounting system, which culminates in standard product costing, valuation of inventory, and variance analysis. This chapter will present a typical manufacturing scenario comprising master data requirements, integrated planning, month-end processes, and reporting. In Chapter 3, a typical overall planning scenario was presented, which included CCA. In this chapter, you will see aspects of that scenario in detail and understand how all the pieces fit together.

8.1 Master data

In Chapter 2, you saw the key pieces of master data associated with cost center accounting including the cost center, the cost element and the activity type. Now you will see some master data from other modules where the cost center and the activity type are also required in the setup. The *work center* is the key piece of logistical master data, relying on a cost center and activity types to function. The work center is used mostly in production planning and plant maintenance. Various categories of work centers distinguish their usage. Commonly used categories are: 0001-Machine, 0005-Plant Maintenance, and 0008-Processing unit. Work centers in category 0001 are used most commonly in standard production using production orders, and in repetitive manufacturing, category 0005 work centers are used in plant maintenance. Category 0008 work centers (also called *resources*) are used in process manufacturing.

All of these types of work centers should be linked to the cost center providing the activity for the work being performed. Only one cost center can be assigned per work center, but the same cost center can provide activities to multiple work centers. For all three categories, the cost center is assigned on the costing tab of the work center (see Figure 8.1). Here you will also assign the activities being provided from the assigned cost center. Some activity planning needs to exist for the cost center/activity type combination before SAP will allow you to make the assignment to the work center.

| Plant | 6001 | Indiana Mfg Plant |
| Work center | 1020 | Board Games Final Assemby/Packing |

| Basic Data | Default Values | Capacities | Scheduling | Costing | Technology |

Validity

| Start date | 24.11.2016 | End Date | 31.12.9999 |

Link to cost center/activity types

| Controlling Area | 6000 | | Smarter Sisters Games |
| Cost Center | 5000101003 | | Game Assembly IN |

Activities Overview

Alt. activity descr.	Activity Type	Activity Unit	Re...	Formula...	Formula description
Setup					
Machine	1100	MIN	✓	YBPI01	BP: Machine time
Labor	1000	MIN	✓	YBPI02	BP: Labor time

Figure 8.1: Work center costing tab

The other tabs on a work center are important for aspects of production planning such as capacity management and scheduling but have little impact on costing. However, for the integrated planning scenario capacity settings have to be maintained correctly. Specifically, for the capacity category being used, the flag to include in long-term planning (LTP) should be set (see Figure 8.2).

Available capacity

Factory calendar ID	US	USA	
Active version	1	Normal available capacity	
Base unit of meas.	MIN	Minute	

Standard available capacity

Start	08:00:00			
Finish	18:00:00	Capacity utilization	100	
Length of breaks	00:15:00	No. of indiv. cap.	6	
Operating time	9.75	Capacity	3,510.00	MIN

Planning details

| ✓ Relevant to finite scheduling | Overload | % |
| Can be used by several operations | ✓ Long-term planning |

Figure 8.2: Capacity setting for machine

The work center usually represents a place within the manufacturing site where the work is being performed. This might be a machine, a workstation, or a production line. Often a product will have to pass through a succession of work centers before it is completed. This succession of work centers for a product is called a *task list*. There are varieties of task lists, depending on how you are manufacturing the product. When production orders are used, the task list type is usually a *routing*; in repetitive manufacturing, a *rate routing* is more commonly used, and in process manufacturing, the task list is part of the *recipe*. The task lists always are created with reference to a single product or material while many materials may pass through a work center.

Figure 8.3 shows a standard routing; the work centers are sequenced into *operations* or lines in the routing. Each line has a base quantity and the input quantities of the activities required to produce that base quantity. The cost center is assigned indirectly to each line through the work center.

Material	300000		Oligopoly Game			Grp.Count1							
Sequence	0												

Operation Overv.

Oper...	Work center	Plnt	Cont...	Description	Base Quan...	Un...	Machine	Unit	Activity	...	Labor	Unit	Activity ..
0010	1020	6001	YBP1	Assembly	1,000	EA	60	MIN	1100		60	MIN	1000
0020	1030	6001	YBP1	Bagging	1,000	EA	30	MIN	1100		30	MIN	1000

Figure 8.3: Standard routing

At a high level, the cost of an internally manufactured product will have three main components: input materials, production activities, and some allocation of overheads. The work centers, task lists, cost centers, activity types, and planned activity rates all combine to determine the production activities portion of the product cost. The material portion comes from a combination of the bill of material, with the costs of the input materials and the overhead allocation will come from costing sheets or templates. The cost centers are not involved in the material cost of the product, so that master data is not relevant for this book. The cost center involvement in planned overhead or template allocation was fully covered in Section 3.3 and will not be repeated here so we can move on to planning.

8.2 Manufacturing planning scenario

You will now see a possible planning scenario involving COPA, sales and operations planning, long-term planning, and cost center planning. The system configuration for the areas outside of cost center accounting will not be explained in detail as they are beyond the scope of this book. Instead, you understand how planned quantities and values flow between the different modules. Since planning is generally a forward-looking activity, all the planning examples will be for the next fiscal year, in this case, 2018.

In this scenario, the first step is to project the planned sales quantities for the next year. This can be carried out in logistics using standard SOP or flexible planning and then transferred to COPA, or it can start in COPA and then be transferred to logistics. In this example, COPA will be the starting point. COPA planning is carried out in the *planning framework*, transaction KEPM.

The planning framework will require you to create a *planning level*. This is where you tell SAP the COPA *characteristics* you will be planning on directly. You may decide to plan sales of product by customer. In that case, you would need to include both product and customer than characteristics in the planning level. Beneath the planning level will be the *planning package*. The characteristics from the planning level will be inherited into the planning package. Here you will select the range of values for the selected characteristics that you want to plan in that package. You might decide to have a package by planning version and fiscal year or by some other combination of selection criteria.

There are some characteristics that you will be need to have in the planning level such as company code, plant, sales organization, period year, record type, and version. You should then decide on the characteristics that define your level of planning and include them. In this case, the characteristics product, division, and sales unit of measure were included (see Figure 8.4). Note that it will not be necessary to plan every characteristic in COPA, as many will be planned automatically from other primary characteristics due to the process of *characteristic derivation*. This means that characteristics that can be derived from planned characteristics do not have to be manually planned themselves. For example, you do not have to include material group in the planning since SAP can derive the value of the material group from the product.

Planning levels	Description	Status
Planning levels		
Z5000	Sales Planning	
SS000	Version 0 Planning	
SS001	Version 1 Planning	
SS00018	Sales Planning V0 2018	

Plan. package	SS00018	Sales Planning V0 2018

Selection | Description

Selection

Characteristic	From	To
Company Code	6000	
Division		
Period/year	001.2018	012.2018
Plant	6001	
Product	300000	300999
Record Type	F	
Sales Org.	6000	
Unit Sales qty	EA	
Version	0	

Figure 8.4: Planning levels and packages with characteristics

For each planning package, there will be a number of pre-defined *planning methods*. The methods are essentially the planning actions that you might want to perform such as enter plan, display plan, copy plan, valuate plan, and more. You will use the enter plan method to create the sales quantity plan. Entering the plan requires a layout similar to cost center planning. This layout is built in report painter, and it must include all the characteristics from the planning level. The layout is assigned to the method through the creation of a parameter set, which not only includes the planning layout but also some other settings relating to control and output. Running the parameter set will allow you to enter the plan (see Figure 8.5). You can use the 📝 button to display and edit the values at a period level. Changes made at the period level will be reflected at the overall level. Within COPA planning, there is also a flexible Excel upload transaction which allows you to plan all your sales quantities in Excel and load them into the COPA planning framework. This works similarly to the uploads you have seen for cost center planning, so it will not be covered here.

Sales Org.	6000	US Sales
Unit Sales qty	EA	each
Currency type	BO	Operating concern ⟨

D... Product	Sales quantity
10 300004	1,094,000
20 300000	1,145,500
300012	990,000
300014	1,180,000
300016	1,025,000
30 300007	1,337,500
300008	660,000
*D *Product	7,432,000

Figure 8.5: Sales quantity plan in COPA

Once the sales quantities have been entered and saved, they can be transferred to logistics for planning. On the logistics side, we can use two options, standard sales and operations planning (SOP), which largely is pre-configured by SAP, or *flexible planning* using existing or custom de-signed info-structures. The standard SOP uses the LIS structure S076 and has pre-defined characteristics and layouts. With flexible planning, you can use other standard info structure or ones that are self-defined. This gives you the option to plan on any available organizational level or characteristics and define your own layouts for the planning screens.

In this example, flexible planning is being used in logistics, so you will use the transaction KE1K to transfer the COPA plan (see Figure 8.6). You select the periods and the assignment and then click the Selection Criteria button and make any required selection restriction before you execute the transfer. The *assignment* is defined in system configura-tion and serves to map COPA characteristics and value fields into LIS structure elements.

Transfer to LIS: Initial Screen

Selection Criteria

Plan Data

| From Period | 001.2018 to   012.2018 |
| Assignment | Z001 |

Options

| ✓ Test run | Background Processing |

Figure 8.6: Transfer to LIS

You can now use transaction MC95 to see the transferred plan to the logistic info structure in flexible planning (see Figure 8.7). Note that there will be some setup and configuration of the LIS structures which will need to be done by a production planning expert before this can work.

Material Group	9020		Material		*			
Plant	6001							
Version	A00	Active version				Active		
Sales forecast								
Aggregate Information	Un	0 - Column	M 01.2018	M 02.2018	M 03.2018	M 04.2018	M 05.2018	M 06.2018
Sales forecast qty	EA		469750	504250	523667	555667	581666	611667
Actual sales qty	EA							
PrvYrAct sales qty	EA							

Figure 8.7: Transferred plan in LIS flexible planning

The first view in MC95 is the overall values. You can use the button to see the details by material (see Figure 8.8).

Material Group	9020		Material		300000			
Plant	6001							
Version	A00	Active version				Active		
Sales forecast								
Detailed Information	Un	0 - Column	M 01.2018	M 02.2018	M 03.2018	M 04.2018	M 05.2018	M 06.2018
Sales forecast qty	EA		47500	58000	59000	80000	90000	110000
Actual sales qty	EA							
PrvYrAct sales qty	EA							

Figure 8.8: MC95 material detail

Planning data can be edited in logistics using transaction MC94; however, it would be preferable to go back to COPA planning to make the changes and then transfer them to maintain consistency.

The sales and operations plan creates independent requirements for the finished materials, which can be read by long-term planning (LTP). Long-term planning is a form of simulative material requirements planning (MRP) which allows you to create longer term, usually 1 year, periodic requirement plans. The LTP uses its own planning scenarios and versions that are distinct from operative MRP; however, firm requirements from LTP can be transferred to operative MRP, LTP uses the existing master data, material masters, BOMs, resources, and task lists. Like operative MRP, LTP will plan all the materials and activities based on those master data elements and will perform a full BOM explosion and include all sub-component levels in planning.

There are many possible uses for the output of LTP, including purchasing, inventory management, production scheduling, and capacity planning. They are all beyond the scope of this book. The concern here is with the ability of LTP to plan cost center activity requirements. As stated, LTP will read the material and production master data. It will look at the required material output quantities from the sales plan and will determine all the inputs required to fulfill that plan. It will calculate all the input activity requirements from the task lists and related work centers or resources. This activity requirement can then be transferred back to activity planning in CCA.

LTP can be executed manually using transaction MS01 or can be run as a background job using transaction MSBT. There are two key reports to see the LTP results. MS04 is a stock requirements list generated by the planning scenario and will show all the material requirements needed to fulfill the sales plan. CM38 is more interesting from the standpoint of activity planning since it shows the planned activity requirements by work center and gives a preview of the values that will be transferred to activity planning in CCA.

The selection screen for CM38 is shown in Figure 8.9. You will note that there are no drop-down selection options for the fields. In this case, you will have to use the F4 key to find values or simply type a known value into the field.

Capacity Planning: Selection

Standard overview   Detailed cap. list   Variable overview

			Operator
Planning Scenario Long-Term Pl	2
Work Center	1020
Capacity Planner Group	MOB
Plant	6001

Figure 8.9: Selection screen for capacity planning

The standard overview option will display the planned activity quantity versus the capacity of the work center (see Figure 8.10). This will allow the production planners to make capacity decisions for the work centers, such as how to deal with the overcapacity for the first ten months and the under capacity in the last two periods. The values in the requirements column will be transferred to activity planning in CCA when the transfer is executed.

Work center   1020   Board Games Final Assemby/Pack   Plant
Capacity cat.: 001   Machine

Month	Requirements	AvailCap.	CapLoad	RemAvailCap	Unit
01.2018	1,070.52	1,228.50	87 %	157.98	H
02.2018	1,081.82	1,111.50	97 %	29.68	H
03.2018	1,082.82	1,287.00	84 %	204.18	H
04.2018	1,103.82	1,228.50	90 %	124.68	H
05.2018	1,113.82	1,287.00	87 %	173.18	H
06.2018	1,133.82	1,228.50	92 %	94.68	H
07.2018	1,119.82	1,228.50	91 %	108.68	H
08.2018	1,113.82	1,345.50	83 %	231.68	H
09.2018	1,103.82	1,111.50	99 %	7.68	H
10.2018	1,143.82	1,287.00	89 %	143.18	H
11.2018	1,173.82	1,170.00	100 %	3.82-	H
12.2018	1,188.82	1,170.00	102 %	18.82-	H
Total >>>	13,430.58	14,683.50	92 %	1,252.92	H

Figure 8.10: Work center requirements versus capacity

The capacity displayed in CM38 will depend on the capacity category defined on the work center; in this case, all the work centers are maintained with the capacity based on machine time. The transaction KSPP is used to transfer the planning from logistics to activity planning in CCA (see Figure 8.11). When the transfer occurs, both machine and labor activities will be transferred, even though capacity is based on machine time.

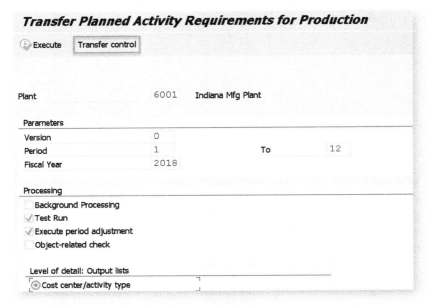

Figure 8.11: Activity plan transfer initial screen

Prior to performing the transaction, the transfer control settings must be maintained for your controlling area, fiscal year and CO planning version (see Figure 8.12)

CoAr	Version	Version Name	Fiscal Year	
6000	0	Plan/actual version	2016	
6000	0	Plan/actual version	2017	
6000	0	Plan/actual version	2018	

Figure 8.12: Transfer control overview

Behind the overview level, you will assign the source of the plan transfer. In this case, you are transferring from LTP and from the plan scenario 2 (see Figure 8.13).

Figure 8.13: Transfer control detail

Back at the initial screen, you can execute the transfer. There is a test run option to enable you to see the values before executing the transfer (see Figure 8.14).

Transfer Planned Activity Requirements for Production

Cost Ctr	ActTyp	Activity scheduled	UM
5000101001	1000	6,608	H
5000101001	1100	3,304	H
5000101002	1000	5,484.500	H
5000101002	1100	5,484.500	H
5000101003	1000	13,430.584	H
5000101003	1100	13,430.584	H
5000101004	1000	11,703.186	H
5000101004	1100	11,703.186	H
5000101100	1000	14,330.357	H
5000101100	1100	2,388.392	H
5000101110	1000	4,776.784	H
5000101110	1100	2,388.392	H
5000101200	1000	44,084.445	H
5000101200	1100	22,042.224	H
* Total		161,159.134	H

Figure 8.14: Planned activity requirements transfer

Once you execute without the test mode, the activity requirements will appear in cost center activity planning as scheduled activities in the production cost centers (see Figure 8.15).

207

Version	0		Plan/actual version							
Period	1	To	12							
Fiscal Year	2018									
Cost Center	5000101001		Board Cutting Indiana							

Activity ...	Plan Activity	Distr...	Capacity	Distr...	Unit	P... V...	Price unit	Pla... P... A...	Alloc. cost ele...	T	EquiNo	Scheduled Activity	I...
1000		2	5,396.500	2	H	00001 1			943000	1	1	6,608	
1100		2	5,396.500	0	H	00001 1			943010	1	1	3,304	
*Activ			10,793								2	9,912	

Figure 8.15: Transferred scheduled activities

You can convert the scheduled activities into planned activity by running the plan reconciliation transaction KPSI that you have seen previously. Once you execute the plan reconciliation, the scheduled activity quantity will be copied to the plan activity quantity.

Version	0		Plan/actual version							
Period	1	To	12							
Fiscal Year	2018									
Cost Center	5000101001		Board Cutting Indiana							

Activity ...	Plan Activity	Distr...	Capacity	Distr...	Unit	Price... Va...	Price unit	Pla... P... A...	Alloc. ...	T	Eq...	Scheduled Activity
1000	6,608	2	5,396.500	2	H	00001 1			94300.1			6,608
1100	3,304	2	5,396.500	0	H	00001 1			94301.1			3,304
*Activ	9,912											9,912

Figure 8.16: Activity planning after plan reconciliation

While the sales and production planning activities are going on, the cost center managers will be engaged in their cost planning activities. These may include all the planning activities that you saw in Section 3.3. Once all the activity quantity planning and input cost planning is completed, then the system can calculate the activity prices following the procedures set out in Section 3.4.

Following the calculation of the activity prices, it will be possible to calculate the standard costs of all the manufactured materials for the upcoming year by performing a *costing run* using transaction CK40N. You can then go back to the COPA planning framework in KEPM and use the *valuate* planning method to read pricing conditions and the created cost estimates and generate a valuated sales plan with revenue and cost of sales values based on the original planned quantities.

8.3 Manufacturing execution scenario

In this section, you will see how cost centers are involved in a typical manufacturing execution scenario. The examples will be restricted to what is known as *make-to-stock* manufacturing. The more complex scenarios of *make to order* or *engineer to order* will not be covered in this book. It is possible to use production orders, process orders, or repetitive manufacturing to manufacture stock materials. Each uses its own distinct object for manufacturing and cost collection, the production order, the process order, or the product cost collector. From the standpoint of the cost center, these objects are identical in that they all serve to receive activity and overhead costs from cost centers.

Usually the production scenario will start with MRP creating planned orders, which are then converted into operative production, or process orders. Even in a repetitive manufacturing situation, you may still run MRP and generate planned orders; however, you will record production and costs against a product cost collector. The creation of the production order triggers a number of events, including material reservations, material and capacity checks, and order cost planning. The cost planning in the production object will calculate the planned activity inputs for that object and will show the related activity type and sending cost center.

However, the actual involvement of the cost center starts with the confirmation of the production activities. There are a number of transactions available for this, depending on the production cost object and the process you wish to follow. For a production order, the transaction CO11N is one option that can be used to enter confirmations by activity (see Figure 8.17). Depending on whether you are issuing materials to the production order manually or through a *backflush* process, you may also get material postings from your confirmation. These can be viewed and possibly edited by clicking on the ⬚ Goods Movements button. Posting the confirmation will create a controlling posting (see Figure 8.18). These postings will occur based on the planned rate of the activity and the actual activity quantity recorder in the confirmation. You will see that the production object is debited for the cost of the activity and the cost center/activity type is credited.

Order	1000080	terial	300000	
Operation	0010	Sequence	0	Assembly
Suboperation				
Capacity Cat.		Split		
Work Center	1020	Plant	6001	Board Games Final

Confirm.type	Partial confirmation	v	Clear open reservations	

Quantities

	To Be Confirmed	Unit
Yield	100,000	EA
Scrap		
Rework		
Reason for Var.		

Activities

	To Be Confirmed	Unit	R
Setup			
Machine	6,000	MIN	
Labor	6,000	MIN	

Figure 8.17: Confirming activity quantities

Layout   /GL DISPLA /GL display
CoArea currency   USD   USD
Valuation View/Group   0   Legal Valuation

DocumentNo Doc. Date Document Header Text		RT RefDocNo		
PKw OTy Object CO object name	Cost Elem. CElem.name Val/COArea Crcy	Total quantity PUM O		
	R 601			
400000502 30.05.2017				
1 ATY 5000101005/1100 Game Assembly IN / Machine Ti	943010	Machine T	1,800.00-	6,000- MIN
2 ORD 1000080 Oligopoly Game	943010	Machine T	1,800.00	6,000 MIN
4 ATY 5000101003/1000 Game Assembly IN / Prod Labour	943000	Prod Labo	2,850.00-	6,000- MIN
5 ORD 1000080 Oligopoly Game	943000	Prod Labo	2,850.00	6,000 MIN

Figure 8.18: Posting from confirmation

The production activities continue in this manner throughout the period generating goods movements and activity postings. The next involvement of cost centers is during the period end process for cost object controlling. The process and some of the transaction codes are slightly different between order-based costing (production or process orders) and period-based costing (repetitive manufacturing), but the overall concepts are the same. This example will continue to use the production order you have already seen above. The period end menu (see Figure 8.19) for product cost by order has a number of steps that should be completed in the correct order to complete the period end for production or process orders.

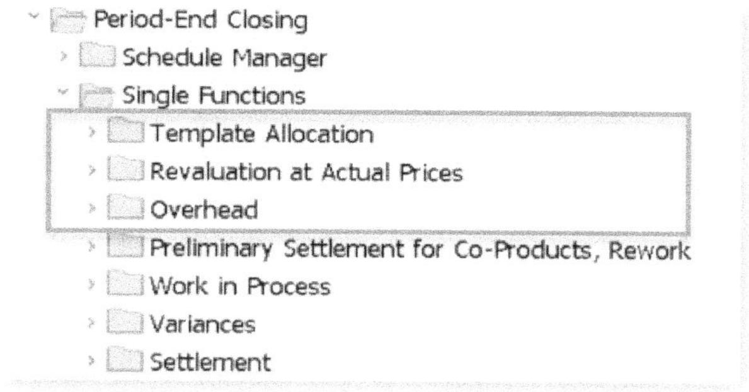

Figure 8.19: Period end menu for order costing

The first four steps in the menu may be optional depending on your business and how your SAP solution is designed. The first three steps are the ones that involve cost center accounting.

You have seen how template allocations can work for allocating costs to cost centers in Section 6.5. Here the templates are used to allocate costs from cost centers and activities to production objects. Conceptually, this is similar to what you saw previously; however, the templates for production use different environments that obviously contain different elements to be used in the calculations.

To use templates for production objects, they need to be assigned to a costing sheet using configuration transaction KTPF (see Figure 8.20). If you are using overhead keys to assign to overhead groups and materials, then you will need to assign an overhead key. In this example, overhead keys and groups are not used.

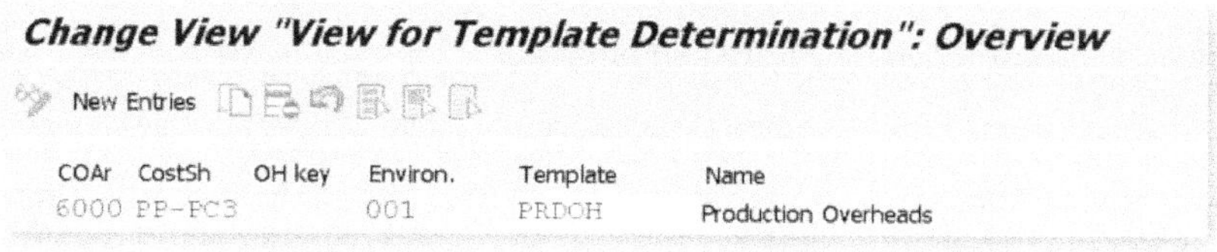

Figure 8.20: Assign template to costing sheet

It is then through the assignment of the costing sheet to products (using overhead keys and groups) or directly to production orders that the template is accessed. The assigned costing sheet can be seen on the control tab of the production order (see Figure 8.21).

211

General	Assignment	Goods Receipt	Control	Dates/Qties	Master Data	Long Text	Administration

Order

| Reference order | | | | Deletion flag |
| Reserv./PReq | 3 Immediately | ∨ | | |

Costing

CstgVariantPlan	YGP1		CstgVariantActl	YGP2
Costing Sheet	PP-PC3		Overhead key	
RA Key	YBMF01		Variance Key	000001
PlannedCostCalc	2 Determine Planned Costs When Saving ∨			

Figure 8.21: Costing sheet assignment on production order

The costing sheet and other costing related parameters will populate into the production order based on default values that are defined by order type and plant in the system configuration (see Figure 8.22). There are two costing variants assigned to the order type; the first is used for order planning, and the second is used for order actual values.

Plant	6001	Order Type		YBM1	MTS Production Order
Default Rule		PP1	Production Mat.Full settlement		
RA Key		YBMF01	BP WIP actual cost		

Costing

Prel./Vers.Cstg	YGP1	BP: Prod. Order Planned
Val. Var.	Y06	BP: Prod. Order: Planned
Simul. Costing	YGP2	BP: Prod. Order Actual
Val. Var.	Y07	BP: Prod. Order: Actual

Figure 8.22: Default values by plant and order type

The costing variants have valuation variants assigned that contain, among other things, the costing sheet to be defaulted into the order (see Figure 8.23).

During the period end process, the template allocation step can be run either individually or collectively to transfer costs from the cost center/activity type to the production order (see Figure 8.24). Since the template uses activities, this appears as an activity posting in the cost center in the credit section of the actual/plan/variance report.

212

Figure 8.23: Valuation variant for production order actual

Actual Template Allocation: Order

Result

Processing completed with no errors

Receiver Object	Sender object	AllocCElem	Tot. F&V qty UoM	Ttl Fx+Vbl value	CAC CO crcy	Template
ORD 1000081	ATY 5000101903/OVHD	943015	100,000 H	10,000.00	USD	PRDOH
ORD 1000081				10,000.00	USD	
				10,000.00	USD	

Figure 8.24: Actual template posting

The next period end step is revaluation at actual prices. This step only makes sense if you are calculating actual activity prices as described in Section 7.5. You can refer back to that section to see the relevant steps and it affects CCA.

The final step in the cost object controlling period end involving cost centers is overhead allocation. Again, you have seen this concept before. The actual overhead is calculated and allocated using a costing sheet. The concept and elements of the costing sheet were explained in Section 3.3 when you learned about automatic planning. You have also seen how and where the costing sheet is assigned on the production order when you looked at actual template allocation. The costing sheet and its components are defined in configuration (see Figure 8.25). The components are:

▶ The base—what range or group of cost elements is the overhead being calculated on;

▶ The overhead rate—what is the rate, is it for actual or plan and what is the percentage or quantity value; and

213

► The credit—what cost center gets the credit and what secondary cost element is used to move the costs.

Dialog Structure								
˅ 🗀 Costing sheets	Procedure		YPP-PC BP: Costing Sheet Production					
˅ 🗀 Costing sheet rows								
· 🗀 Base	**Costing sheet rows**							
· 🗀 Overhead rate	Row	Base	Overhead r...	Description		From	To Row	Credit
· 🗀 Credit	10	Y001		Material				
	20		Y101	Material overhead		10		Y10
	30	Y002		Production				
	40		Y102	Production overhead		30		Y20
	50			Production overhead				

Figure 8.25: Costing sheet

The credit is most relevant to us since it is the link to cost center accounting (Figure 8.26). When actual overhead allocation is run, the costs will be moved from the cost center defined here to the production cost objects.

Controlling Area		6000	Smarter Sisters Games			
Credit		Y10	Credit Material 1			
Credit						
Valid to	Cost Elem.	O... Fxd %	Cost Center	Order	Bu
31.12.9999	941000		+ 5000101906		

Figure 8.26: Credit cost center

Actual overhead can be run individually or collectively for the production objects; there are various transaction codes depending on whether you are using orders or repetitive manufacturing. The costs will be allocated from the credit cost center to the production object using the defined cost element based on the rules and rates defined in the costing sheet (see Figure 8.27).

The final possibility in the period end manufacturing scenario is that you have completed all your period end steps and you have a remaining under or over absorbed balance in the production cost centers (see Figure 8.28). This will likely be the case if you are not doing actual activity price calculation and order revaluation. In this case, you have the option of leaving this balance in the cost centers or assessing the remaining amount to COPA.

Actual Overhead Calculation: Order Debits

Debits

Senders	Receivers	Cost Elem.	Σ	Val/COArea Crcy
CTR 5000101906	ORD 1000081	941000		6,100.00
CTR 5000101903		941010		513.00
				6,613.00

Figure 8.27: Actual overhead posting

```
Cost Centers: Actual/Plan/Variance       Date: 02.06.2017          Page:

                                                                    Column:
Cost Center/Group           5000101001            Board Cutting In
Person responsible:         Vincent Crane
Reporting period:             5  to    5  2017
```

Cost Elements		Act. Costs	Plan Costs	Var.(Abs.)
540000	Salaries	6,500.00	5,999.25	500.75
550110	Facility Costs	25,432.00	23,333.34	2,098.66
581020	Communications	23,987.00	22,915.50	1,071.50
640000	Depreciation Expens	17,361.12	17,361.12	
943100	Electricity	3,600.00	2,812.50	787.50
943110	Natural Gas	2,304.00	2,133.34	170.66
943120	Water Allocation	702.00	715.01	13.01-
* Debit		79,886.12	75,270.06	4,616.06
943000	Production Labour	5,700.00-	5,999.25-	299.25
943010	Machine Time	66,500.00-	69,270.81-	2,770.81
* Credit		72,200.00-	75,270.06-	3,070.06
** Over/Underabsorption		7,686.12		7,686.12

Figure 8.28: Cost center with under-absorbed costs

If you want to assess the value to COPA, you will need to build an assessment cycle using KEU1. This has some similarities to the cost center assessments that you have already seen, but there are also some differences since you are moving costs into COPA. There is still a cycle header (see Figure 8.29). The key fields are the SENDER SELECTION TYPE and the TRACING FACTOR BASIS. You also have to specify the sending controlling area since an *operating concern* in COPA can contain multiple controlling areas. The SENDER SELECTION TYPE defines if you are sending total costs or costs split into fixed and variable components. The TRACING

FACTOR BASIS determines if the tracing factors that you will use are based on costing-based or account-based COPA.

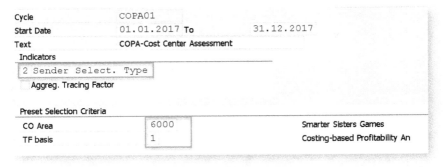

Figure 8.29 : COPA assessment header

As with other assessments, once you have completed the cycle header, you will add segments.

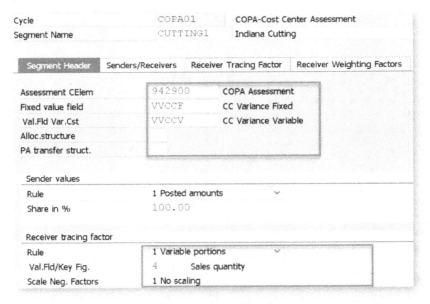

Figure 8.30: COPA assessment – segment header

On the segment header, you will need an ASSESSMENT COST ELEMENT. This is the cost element that will be used in CCA. If you are using cost-ing-based COPA, you will need either *value fields* or a *PA transfer struc-ture* to define where the values will post in COPA. Finally, you will define the receiver tracing factor. The concept is similar to the cost center as-sessments that you have seen, but there are a number of different op-tions available based on COPA values. In this example, the variances are being allocated to profitability segments based on sales quantity.

The SENDERS/RECEIVERS are defined on the next tab (see Figure 8.31). The senders will be cost centers and cost elements. Make sure the range or group of cost elements that you use encompasses all the post-ings to your cost center, including secondary postings, so that only the remaining variance is picked up in the allocation.

The receivers will be some combination of characteristics from COPA (this example is based on costing-based COPA). In many cases, the **group** option for the COPA characteristic requires the creation of a *set*. Fortunately, SAP has provided us with a link to create the set so that we can avoid going to the normal GS01 transaction. To use this link, type a group name in the group box next to the characteristic that you want to use before pressing enter use the menu EXTRAS • CREATE GROUP. This will allow you to create a group directly that you can use in your assessment.

Segment Header	Senders/Receivers	Receiver Tracing Factor	Receiver Weighting Factors	
	From		To	Group
Sender				
Cost Center	5000101001			
Cost Element	500000		999999	
Receiver				
Product				BOARDGAMES
Procurement				
Company Code	6000			

Figure 8.31: COPA assessment senders and receivers

The RECEIVER TRACING FACTOR tab (see Figure 8.32) contains the param-eters for the tracing factor that you selected on the header screen. The important things to select are the RECORD TYPE and the PLAN ACTUAL INDI-CATOR. In this example, the record type is "F," which means it is coming from billing data, and the plan actual indicator is "0" meaning actual data.

MANUFACTURING AND COST CENTER ACCOUNTING

Segment Header	Senders/Receivers	Receiver Tracing Factor	Receiver Weighting Factors

Receiver tracing factor

Val.Fld/Key Fig.	4 Sales quantity	Part type
Scale Neg. Factors	1 No scaling	⌄

Selection criteria

	From	to	Group
Record Type	F		
Plan/Act. Indic	O		
Reference Versi			

Figure 8.32: COPA assessment – receiver tracing factor

The final tab for RECEIVER WEIGHTING FACTORS is similar to the cost center assessments you have seen, so it will not be covered again here. You can add additional segments as required and then save your cycle.

The COPA assessment is run from transaction KEU5. The initial screen is the same as other allocations that you have seen. Simply select your cycle and the time periods, then execute the assessment. The costs will be posted from the selected cost center(s) to the profitability characteristics that you defined (see Figure 8.33).

Display CO-PA: Actual Assessment Receiver List

|◄ ◄ ► ►| ⬛ ⬛ ⬛ ⬛ ⬛ Basic list ⬛ Segments ⬛

Cycle	COPA01	COPA-Cost Center Assessment
Start Date	01.01.2017	
Period	005	

Cost Ctr	Cost Elem.	CoCd	Product	Fixed Costs	Total Costs	Tracing Factor	COCr
5000101001	942900	6000	300000	0.00	2,105.79	1,000,000	USD
5000101001	942900	6000	300012	0.00	1,694.63	800,000	USD
5000101001	942900	6000	300014	0.00	2,316.36	1,100,000	USD
5000101001	942900	6000	300015	0.00	1,579.34	750,000	USD
* Posting period 005				0.00	7,696.12		USD
**				0.00	7,696.12		USD

Figure 8.33: COPA assessment receiver postings

After the assessment has been, run the over or under-absorbed balance in the cost center will have been allocated to COPA, and the cost center balance will be zero (see Figure 8.34).

```
Cost Centers: Actual/Plan/Variance        Date: 04.06.2017           Page:

                                                                     Column:
Cost Center/Group          5000101001              Board Cutting In
Person responsible:        Vincent Crane
Reporting period:          5   to    5   2017
```

Cost Elements	Act. Costs	Plan Costs	Var. (Abs.)
540000 Salaries	6,500.00	5,999.25	500.75
550110 Facility Costs	25,432.00	23,333.34	2,098.66
581020 Communications	23,987.00	22,915.50	1,071.50
640000 Depreciation Expens	17,361.12	17,361.12	
943100 Electricity	3,600.00	2,812.50	787.50
943110 Natural Gas	2,304.00	2,133.34	170.66
943120 Water Allocation	702.00	715.01	13.01-
* Debit	79,886.12	75,270.06	4,616.06
942900 COPA Assessment	7,686.12-		7,686.12-
943000 Production Labour	5,700.00-	5,999.25-	299.25
943010 Machine Time	66,500.00-	69,270.81-	2,770.81
* Credit	79,886.12-	75,270.06-	4,616.06-
** Over/Underabsorption			

Figure 8.34: Cost center assessed to COPA

8.4   Summary

In this chapter, you have seen the potential of SAP cost center functionality for a typical manufacturing company. You have learned some more about planning and how COPA planning, sales and operations planning, long-term planning, and cost center activity planning can be combined with an integrated planning process. You have learned about the role of the cost center in the actual manufacturing process and how it contributes costs and activities to production. This included direct activity postings, as well as template and overhead allocations. Finally, you have seen how over or under-absorbed cost center balances can be allocated to COPA through periodic assessments.

9 Reporting in cost center accounting

In this chapter, you will see some standard reporting options for CCA. Since there are probably over 50 standard reports in the information system for CCA, the focus will be on those that have proven to be the most useful over a number of implementation projects. This will be a somewhat subjective exercise, and you should use your own judgement to investigate any of the other reports not covered in this chapter. In cases where there are no standard SAP reports, you will also see some possibilities for using report painter to create your own cost center reports.

9.1 Standard reporting

Each sub-module within CO has its own information system tree in the SAP menu. Within the cost center information system under REPORTS FOR COST CENTER ACCOUNTING, there are eight sub-folders containing a variety of standard reports (see Figure 9.1).

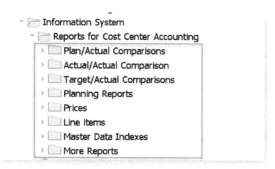

Figure 9.1: CCA standard reporting menu

9.1.1 Plan/actual comparisons

As the description indicates, reports in this section compare plan versus actual values for various objects in CCA (see Figure 9.2). Some reports are called *range* reports. These present the plan/actual comparison for the total of the object. The remaining reports present the cost center values broken down by cost element and possibly some other character-istic.

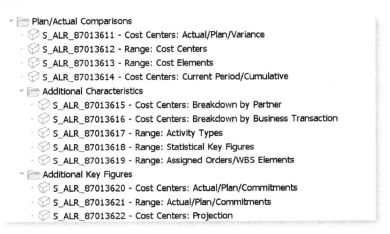

Figure 9.2 : Plan/actual comparison reports

You have already seen one of the most useful reports in this section, S_ALR_87013611 – Cost Centers: Actual/Plan/Variance, in Section 7.2. Other useful reports are the range reports for activity types and statistical key figures. These give you the opportunity to compare plan and actual values for those objects. The reports containing commitments are also useful to see what future costs will be coming into your cost centers and to compare actual plus commitment to your plan. The *breakdown* reports allow you to see the cost center values broken down by either *partner* or *business transaction*. The breakdown by partner is useful since it will show you, for each cost element, the breakdown of the costs by the sending cost object. The breakdown by business transaction will show the costs broken down by the transaction that created them, as shown in Figure 9.3. The report can be expanded to display the cost elements within each section.

Breakdown by Trans.			Date: 16.05.2017	Page:	2 / 2
Cost Center/Group 6000 Top Level				Column:	1 / 2
Person responsible:					
Reporting period: 1 to 3 2017					

Transactions/Cost Elements	Act. Costs	Plan Costs	Var.(Abs.)	Var.(%)
* Primary Costs	1,464,665.31	4,130,179.10	2,665,513.79-	64.54-
* Transfer				
* Distribution	10,000.00		10,000.00	
* Accrual Calculation	25,000.00		25,000.00	
* Activity Allocation	381,612.08	511,786.91	130,174.83-	25.44-
* Manual Allocation	1,498.00		1,498.00	
** Debit	1,882,775.39	4,641,966.01	2,759,190.62-	59.44-
** Credit	1,232,298.43-	4,022,118.79-	2,799,820.31	69.36-
*** Over/Underabsorption	650,476.91	619,847.22	30,629.69	4.94

Figure 9.3 : Breakdown by business transaction

9.1.2 Actual/actual comparison

There are only two reports in this section (see Figure 9.4). These are of limited use in a manufacturing scenario compared to the plan/actual reports. The first report shows the costs by cost element with four quarterly columns and a fiscal year total. The second shows annual amounts for the selected current year, prior year, and the year before the prior year.

> ˅ ▭ Actual/Actual Comparison
> · ◌ S_ALR_87013623 - Cost Centers: Quarterly Comparison
> · ◌ S_ALR_87013624 - Cost Centers: Fiscal Year Comparison

Figure 9.4: Actual/actual comparison reports

9.1.3 Target/actual comparisons

Again, you have seen some of the reports from this section already in Section 7.3 and Section 7.4. If you are able to determine operation rates for your cost centers and activities, then you will be able to use the target actual reports. The most useful of these is S_ALR_87013625 – Cost Centers: Actual/Target/Variance, which you have already seen. The variance analysis reports will only contain data if you have been able to per-form variance analysis as shown in Section 7.4 and have posted the variances in transaction KSS1.

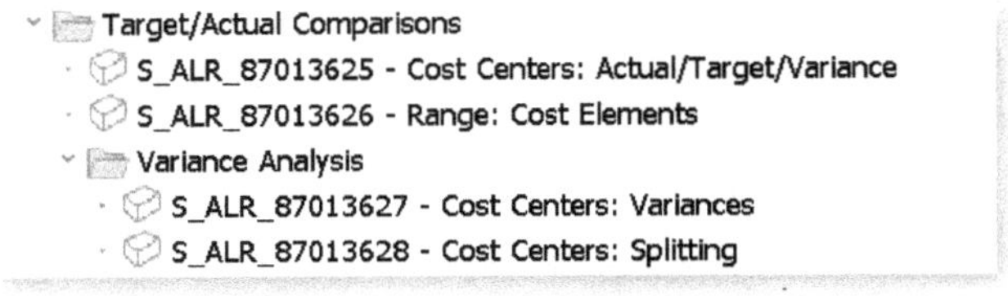

∨ ▭ Target/Actual Comparisons
    · ⬡ S_ALR_87013625 - Cost Centers: Actual/Target/Variance
    · ⬡ S_ALR_87013626 - Range: Cost Elements
  ∨ ▭ Variance Analysis
    · ⬡ S_ALR_87013627 - Cost Centers: Variances
    · ⬡ S_ALR_87013628 - Cost Centers: Splitting

Figure 9.5: Target/actual and variance reports

9.1.4 Planning reports

There are three reports in the planning section, and they are all useful for different reasons.

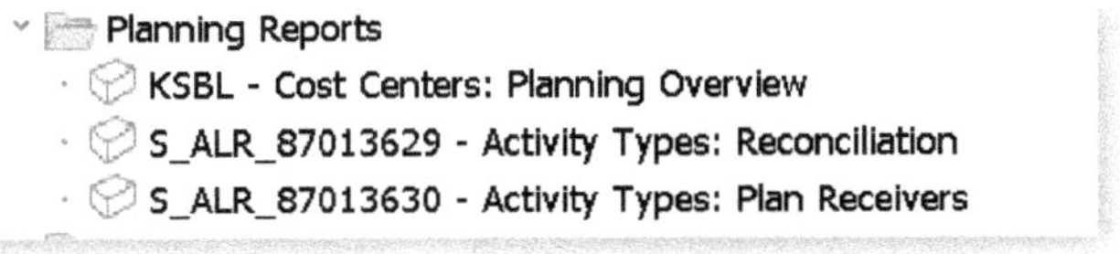

∨ ▭ Planning Reports
    · ⬡ KSBL - Cost Centers: Planning Overview
    · ⬡ S_ALR_87013629 - Activity Types: Reconciliation
    · ⬡ S_ALR_87013630 - Activity Types: Plan Receivers

Figure 9.6: Planning reports

The planning overview report allows you to review the planning data for each cost center (see Figure 9.7). You can see primary and secondary costs, which costs are activity-dependent versus activity-independent, activities costs, and quantities coming in and going out. You can see the total plan debits, total plan credits, and the over- or under-absorbed bal-ance.

On the initial selection screen for this report, you can use the ⊕ Execute Multiple button to run this report for multiple cost centers in the background. This will create a background job that will output the report for a group of cost centers based on a selected layout and either print them directly or place them in the print spool for later processing.

Controlling Area	6000 Smarter Sisters Games	
Fiscal Year	2017	
Period	1 To 12	
Version	000 Plan/actual version	
Cost Center	5000101100 CardGame Assembly IN	

Cost element/description		OTy	Partner object	Σ	Value report curr. Σ	Variable value in Σ	Fxd val./rep.cur.	Total quantity UoM
545210	Heating				20,000.00	0.00	20,000.00	
545220	Sewage				39,989.40	0.00	39,989.40	
550085	Subcontract Services				40,000.00	0.00	40,000.00	
550110	Facility Costs				120,000.00	0.00	120,000.00	
551155	Rental Costs				36,080.00	0.00	36,080.00	
581020	Communications				6,000.00	0.00	6,000.00	
640000	Depreciation Expense				120,833.33	0.00	120,833.33	
Primary Costs				·	**382,902.73** ·	**0.00** ·	**382,902.73**	
Activity-Independent Costs				··	**382,902.73** ··	**0.00** ··	**382,902.73**	
540000	Salaries				720,000.00	600,000.00	120,000.00	
1000	Production Labour			·	**720,000.00** ·	**600,000.00** ·	**120,000.00**	
943100	Electricity	ATY	5000101905		30,000.00	30,000.00	0.00	15,000 KWH
943110	Natural Gas	ATY	5000101905		22,086.40	22,086.40	0.00	17,254.973 M3
943120	Water	ATY	5000101905		7,042.45	7,042.45	0.00	18,057.580 L
1100	Machine Time			·	**59,128.85** ·	**59,128.85** ·	**0.00**	
Activity-Dependent Costs				··	**779,128.85** ··	**659,128.85** ··	**120,000.00**	
Debit				···	**1,162,031.58** ···	**659,128.85** ···	**502,902.73**	

Figure 9.7: Plan overview report

The activity type reconciliation report allows you to see if your plan is reconciled. The report shows the columns PLAN and SCHEDULED. The PLAN column shows the amount planned directly by the sending cost center. The SCHEDULED column will show the amount of activity being requested by other objects. This may be from other cost centers or from planned production activities transferred from long-term planning. You will also be able to see the CAPACITY of the activity in the cost center, which may be useful if you are calculating activity price based on capacity rather than activity. Since many period end functions required a reconciled plan, it is a good practice to refer to this report throughout the planning cycle. The plan in Figure 9.8 is unreconciled now as there is a variance between scheduled activity and plan activity.

Activity Types: Reconciliation		Date: 18.05.2017			Seite: 2 / 2
Cost Center Group	5000101905	Utilities IN			
Reporting period	1 to 12 2017				

Cost Centers/Activity Types	Plan	Scheduled	Variance	in %	Capacity
2000 Electricity	56,000 KWH	53,000 KWH	3,000 KWH	5.35	40,000 KWH
2010 Natural Gas	35,000 M3	33,255 M3	1,745 M3	5.54	40,000 M3
2020 Water	60,000 L	54,058 L	5,942 L	9.90	80,000 L
* 5000101905 Utilities IN	×	×	×	×	×
** Total	×	×	×	×	×

Figure 9.8: Plan reconciliation report – unreconciled plan

Once the plan is reconciled using transaction KPSI, there will be no variance between the two columns (see Figure 9.9). This is the desired state.

Cost Centers/Activity Types	Plan		Scheduled		Variance	in %	Capacity	
2000 Electricity	33,000	KWH	33,000	KWH			40,000	KWH
2010 Natural Gas	32,255	M3	32,255	M3			40,000	M3
2020 Water	54,058	L	54,058	L			80,000	L
* 5000101905 Utilities IN	*		*				*	
** Total	*		*				*	

Activity Types: Reconciliation — Date: 18.05.2017 — Seite: 2 / 2
Cost Center Group 5000101905 Utilities IN
Reporting period 1 to 12 2017

Figure 9.9: Plan reconciliation report – reconciled plan

The planned activity type receivers report allows you to see all the activity receivers and quantities from the standpoint of a sending cost center (see Figure 9.10). This is useful if you are a cost center manager and you want to see who will be consuming your activities.

Activity Types: Receivers   Date: 16.05.2017   Page: 2 / 3
Cost Center/Group   5000102905   Utilities Ky
Person responsible   Thomas Edison

Partner Objects	Scheduled Activity		Valuation	
ATY 5000102001/1100 Board C	24,000	KWH	30,000.00	USD
ATY 5000102002/1100 Pasting	15,000	KWH	18,750.00	USD
ATY 5000102003/1100 Game As	30,000	KWH	37,500.00	USD
* ELEC Electricity	69,000	KWH	86,250.00	USD

Figure 9.10: Activity receivers report

9.1.5 Prices

This section has only one report, KSBT, which allows you to display cost center activity prices. This is a particularly useful report to display all the activity prices for cost centers or groups in one list and to display some of the indicators from planning.

Cost Center Group 6001PROD
Activity Type
Version 0 Plan/actual version
Fiscal Year 2017
Period 1 To 12
Price unit 1

Cost Center	ActTyp	Cost ctr short text	Act. type short text	COCr	Total pri	Variable pri	Price (Fixed)	P	AUn	V	A
5000101001	1000	Board Cutting In	Prod Labour	USD	28.50	28.50	0.00	1	H	1	P
5000101001	1100	Board Cutting In	Machine Time	USD	35.00	35.00	0.00	1	H	1	P
5000101002	1000	Pasting IN	Prod Labour	USD	28.50	28.50	0.00	1	H	1	P
5000101002	1100	Pasting IN	Machine Time	USD	15.00	15.00	0.00	1	H	1	P

Figure 9.11: Activity price report

9.1.6 Line items

This group of reports contains all the detailed line item reports available for cost center accounting (see Figure 9.12), including the reports to display actual CO documents.

```
∨ 📂 Line items
   · 🗒 KSB1 - Cost Centers: Actual Line Items
   · 🗒 KSB1N - Cost Centers: New Actual Line Items
   · 🗒 KSB2 - Cost Centers: Commitment Line Items
   · 🗒 KSBP - Cost Centers: Plan Line Items
   · 🗒 KSBPN - Cost Centers: New Plan Line Items
   · 🗒 KSB5 - CO Documents: Actual Costs
   · 🗒 KSB5N - Controlling Documents: Actual Costs: New
   · 🗒 KABP - CO Plan Documents
```

Figure 9.12: Cost center line item reports

You can display line items for actual postings, commitments, and plan postings. Since the line item reports are displayed in an ALV format, they are very easy to sort, filter, subtotal, and export into a spreadsheet to perform further analysis.

The new line item reports include a hierarchy feature similar to the report painter reports so that you can display line items for each level of the hierarchy (see Figure 9.13).

Line Item Display in Hierarchy View

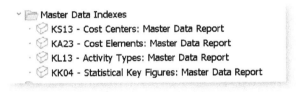

Figure 9.13 : KSB1N with hierarchy display

9.1.7 Master data indexes

This group of reports (see Figure 9.14) allows you to create listings of the master data objects in CCA and display any of the master data fields in the report layout. All of the master data elements covered in Chapter 2 can be displayed using these reports. These reports are also output in an ALV grid format, making them easy to export to spreadsheets.

- Master Data Indexes
  - KS13 - Cost Centers: Master Data Report
  - KA23 - Cost Elements: Master Data Report
  - KL13 - Activity Types: Master Data Report
  - KK04 - Statistical Key Figures: Master Data Report

Figure 9.14: Cost center master data reports

9.1.8 More reports

This group contains a variety of different reports that have not been included in any of the other folders (see Figure 9.15).

The most useful reports in this section are the period breakdown reports for statistical key figures and activity types that will let you see the values posted to these objects by period over the course of the year. If you have assigned a cost component split to your cost centers in planning, then there is a report to display cost centers based on the cost component split. The only other report that may be useful is the rolling year report, which allows you to report on a cost center for a year based on selected rolling year values (see Figure 9.16). This is one of the few reports that has been designed to report across fiscal year boundaries rather than within a specific fiscal year.

Figure 9.15: More reports

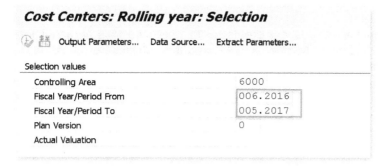

Figure 9.16 : Selection for rolling year

The remaining reports may prove useful in certain scenarios and situations, but other than the ones that I have described, I do not use many of the reports in this section. If there are specific cost center reporting requirements not met by any of the standard reports in these sections, then the alternatives are to engage a programmer to develop a report or examine the options within the report painter tool.

9.2 Report painter options

SAP provides a number of tools to allow you to create your own reports. Sometimes, if the reporting requirement is particularly complex, you have to have a developer build a report. In other cases, especially in FI/CO, you may be able to use the tools that are provided to build your own reports. In CCA, the *report writer* and *report painter* tools are most commonly used. The report painter is particularly useful since it is less complex and could be used by experienced users without need for technical or functional consulting assistance. Let's look at the report painter structure shown in Figure 9.17 to understand how it works.

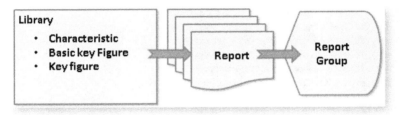

Figure 9.17 : Report painter structure

All report painter reports are created with reference to a *library*. There are many pre-defined libraries in SAP, and it is possible to create libraries, although that is beyond the scope of this book. The library is a collection of *characteristics*, *basic key figures*, and *key figures* contained in a reporting table. The characteristic is a non-numeric value that you can use in your report such as a cost element or a cost center. The basic key figure is a numeric value field, such as an amount in controlling area currency or quantity. The key figure is a pre-defined combination of a basic key figure and one or more characteristics such as actual costs in the current period.

Once the reports have been created, they must be assigned to a *report group* before you can run them. Sometimes there is only one report assigned to a report group; other times, there are multiple reports in a group. In the report group, you can also define drilldowns from your report into other reports through functionality called *report to report interface,* which allows you to assign other reports to call or drill into from your report painter report.

For cost center accounting, there are a number of SAP-delivered libraries containing the standard SAP reports highlighted in Figure 9.18. You can view these in transaction GRR3. The libraries are represented by the folders, and the reports associated with the libraries can be found by opening the folders. The majority of the delivered reports are in library 1VK; the other libraries contain some reports for the advanced period end processes that you saw in Chapter 7.

1AB	Cost Centers: Variance Analysis	JPRINGLE	05.05.2017	CCSS
1C1	Obsolete, do not use anymore!	SAP	21.05.1993	CCSS
1CT	Cost Centers: Special Reports	SAP	24.03.2000	RWCOOM
1EI	EIS Interface CO-OM	SAP	27.05.1999	CCSS
1GK	Cost Centers: Marginal Costing	JPRINGLE	17.04.2017	CCSS
1KS	Cost Centers: Cost Component Split	SAP	08.09.1998	KKBE
1O1	Obsolete, do not use anymore!	SAP	27.05.1993	CCSS
1OW	OIW Library	SAP	27.05.1999	CCSS
1RU	Cost Centers: Summarizaton Area	JPRINGLE	11.04.2017	CCSS
1VK	Cost Centers: Absorption Costing	JPRINGLE	11.05.2017	CCSS

Figure 9.18: Relevant libraries for CCA

You can display libraries in transaction GR23 and see what characteristics, basic key figures, and key figures are contained within a library (see Figure 9.19).

Characteristics	Basic key figures	Key figures	History...	Use...

Library	1VK
Table	CCSS
	Report Table for Overhead Cost Controlling
Description	Cost Centers: Absorption Costing
Component ID	CO-OM-IS-CC
Original Language	DE German

Report/report interface

No reports assigned to the library

Configure...

Figure 9.19: Library for cost centers absorption costing

231

By clicking on the outlined buttons shown in Figure 9.19 you can display the components of the library. As an example, you can see some of the characteristics in library 1VK shown in Figure 9.20. The check box on the left of the NAME indicates that the component can be used in reports for this library. You can use the other buttons to display the available KEY FIGURES and BASIC KEY FIGURES. The USE button will display a list of reports that are using this library.

Library	1VK	
Table	CCSS	Report Table for Overhead Cost Controlling
Description	Cost Centers: Absorption Costing	

Characteristics

Name	Default set	Short text	Pos
✓ KOKRS		Controlling Area	1
✓ KOSTL		Cost Center	2
✓ KSTAR		Cost Element	3
✓ AUFNR		Order Number	4
✓ POSID		Work Breakdown Structure Element (WBS Element)	5
✓ LSTAR		Activity Type	6
✓ STAGR		Statistical key figure	7
✓ GJAHR		Fiscal Year	8
✓ PERBL		Period	9
✓ WRTTP		Value Type	10
✓ VERSN		Version	11
✓ VALUTYP		Valuation	12
✓ BELKZ		CO Debit/Credit Indicator	13

Figure 9.20: Characteristics in library 1VK

The basic building of a report painter report is simple. The view for building the report is graphical in nature, meaning that the finished report will resemble that structure when you finally execute it. The report is built using rows and columns where the rows are based on a characteristic or combination of characteristics, and the columns are usually a combination of characteristics, basic key figures, and/or key figures. Beyond that, it is possible to add formula columns and rows and to enhance the formatting of the rows, columns, and sections of the report. There are more advanced features that can be incorporated into a report painter report that are not described here, but you can explore them if you are interested in creating your own reports in SAP.

Review and copy from an existing SAP report

 Other than the line item reports, all the existing cost center reports in the information system have been built using report painter. These can serve as a valuable resource when you want to create your own reports. You may simply want to review them to see how certain types of reports have been built, or you may also use them as templates to copy from if they are similar to the reports you are trying to create.

The transactions for creating or changing report painter reports are GRR1 and GRR2. The report in Figure 9.21 was created in report painter, and the editing view of that report can be seen in Figure 9.22.

```
Period Comparison-U                                    Date:14.05

Cost Center/Group          5000101100    CardGame Assembly IN
Report Currency:           USD Dollars
Fiscal Year                2017

Cost Elements                    January      February

   540000  Salaries              61,500        61,500
   545050  Fuel, Gas
   545145  Propane                  850           850
   545210  Heating                2,145         2,145
   545220  Sewage                 2,999         2,999
   550085  Subcontract Services   2,445         2,445
   550110  Facility Costs        10,500        10,500
   551155  Rental Costs           2,197         2,197
   581020  Communications           438           438
   640000  Depreciation Expense  10,069        10,069
   943000  Production Labour     (65,550)      (62,100)
   943010  Machine Time          (28,575)      (27,623)
   943100  Electricity            3,810         4,001
   943110  Natural Gas            2,438         2,762
   943120  Water Allocation         743           857
*  TOTAL COSTS                    6,010        11,041
```

Figure 9.21: Sample custom report painter output

Report Section Standard layout	ZPCOMP-U 0001 1-BTC2	Period Comparison-U Period Comparison		Horizontal page 1 /	
Format group:	O	O	O	O	O
Cost Elements	January	February	March	April	
* TOTAL COSTS	XXX,XXX,XXX	XXX,XXX,XXX	XXX,XXX,XXX	XXX,XXX,XXX	

Figure 9.22: Creating a report painter report

Once you build your report painter reports and assign them to report groups, you can either run them from the transaction GR55 or, even better, have a custom transaction code assigned to the report group so that access can be more easily controlled through security.

9.3 Summary

In this chapter, you have seen all the reports available in the information system for cost center accounting. The most useful reports in each section have been discussed either in this chapter or in previous chapters in the books. Finally, you have been given some idea of the capabilities of the report painter tool and how capable users can produce their own custom reports using it.

You have finished the book.

A   The Author

John Pringle is a SAP FI/CO Competency Group Lead and Solution Architect with Illumiti, an SAP Partner and a leading SAP systems integration and management consulting company based in Toronto, Canada. He is the product owner for the SAP all-in-one Mining Solution, one of Illumiti's all-in-one SAP solutions. John has been working in SAP consulting for over 15 years and has previously worked for PwC, IBM, and Accenture. He has implemented SAP solutions in a number of industries, including mining, automotive, food processing, semi-conductor manufacturing, and industrial and building products. He is SAP-certified in CO and is experienced in implementing most areas within SAP FI/CO, as well as areas in PS, MM, SD, and PP. Prior to his consulting career, John worked in a variety of business and accounting roles for over 10 years and has also been part of the client team in several large system implementations, which gives him a unique perspective on the issues faced by both consultants and the business. John has an MBA in Finance and International Business from Schulich School of Business in Toronto and is a CMA and CPA.

B Index

A

ACDOCA 19
Activity analysis 159
Activity dependent planning 68
Activity independent planning
   68
Activity planning 63
Activity type
   Definition of 53
Actual accrual calculation 165
Actual allocations
   Reasons for 147
Actual assessment 152
Actual cost component split
   185
Actual distribution 149
Actual indirect activity allocation
   153
Actual overhead allocation 164
Actual periodic reposting 153
Actual Statistical Key Figures
   138
Actual template allocation 163
Allocation cycle overview 160
Alternative hierarchies 45
Ambiguity check 44
Analysis for office 109
Automatic cost input planning
   83

B

Backflush 209
BAPI' 140
BATCHMAN 140

B

BPC category 112
BPC planning areas 111
Business area 33

C

Characteristic derivation 200
Chart of accounts 15
Commitment management 35
Company code
   Assisgnment 14
   Definition of 13
Compatibility views 18
Controlling
   Main funtions of 14
   time-based object 29
Controlling area
   definition of 13
COPA Assessment 215
COPA planning framework 200
Copy a cost center group 49
Copy actual to plan 105
Copy plan to plan 104
Cost center
   Basic data 31
   Company code assignment 32
   Cost center category 32
   Cost center numbering 28
   Definition of 11
   History 37
   Lock indicators 35
   Master Data 28
   Record quantity 34
   Standard hierarchy 42
   Where-used list 38
Cost center group 45

Cost element
  category 51
  Definition of 50
Cost planning 63
Costing sheet
  definition of 36
  elements 86
Costing variant 212

D

Dependency planning 81
Depreciation 128
Direct activity allocation 53
Distribution key 76

E

Embedded planning 109
Enter sender activities 135
Equivalence numbers 99

F

Fiori 23
Flexible Excel upload 72
Flexible planning 202
Formula planning 83
Full absorption costing 97
Functional area 33

G

Generic file 73

I

Imputed costs 85
Independent requirements 204
Indirect activity allocation 54
Input side variances 182
Integrated excel planning 72
Integrated planning indicator 66

L

Line item reposting 129
Long term planning 204

M

Manual activity allocation 134
Manual actual activity price 136
Manual cost allocation 139
Manual cost input planning 68
Manual cost planning 68
Manual reposting of costs 129,
  132
Marginal cost 190

O

Operating rate 156
Operations 199
Output side variances 183
Overhead costs
  Definition of 11
Overhead structure 86

P

Plan cost splitting 99
Plan reconciliation 81
Plan revaluation 105
Plan versions 65
Planned accrual calculation 85
Planned activity 208
Planned assessment 87
Planned distribution 87
Planned indirect activity
  allocation 87
Planned periodic reposting 87
Planner profiles 69
Planning areas 69
Planning cycle 61
Planning layouts 69

Planning level 200
Planning package 200
Pre-distribution of fixed costs 190
Price determination methods 67
Primary cost element
  Definition of 16
Product cost collector 188
Production confirmation 209
Profit center 33
Purely iterative prices 56

Q

Quantity based commitment 126

R

Rate routing 199
Recipe 199
Report painter
  Library 230
Report Painter
  Report Group 230
Report to report interface 231
Routing 199

S

S4/HANA 17
Sales and operations planning 202
SAP Business Client 22
SAP Simple Finance 17
Scheduled activities 207
Secondary cost element
  definition of 16
Segment 33
Splitting rule 101

Splitting structure 100
Statistical key figure planning 63
Statistical key figures 57

T

Target cost version 179
Target costs 176
Target=actual activity allocation 156
Task list 199
Template
  Definition of 36
  Environment 83
  Planning example 83
Tracing factor 58
Transaction code
  CPT1 – Create template 83
  GRR1 – Create report painter report 233
  KA06 – Create secondary cost element 52
  KB15N – Manual cost allocation 139
  KB21N – Manual activity allocation 134
  KB31N – Actual SKF 138
  KB61 – Line item reposting 129
  KB65 – Repost activity documents 135
  KBK6 – Manual activity price 137
  KK01 – Create statistical key figure 58
  KL01 – Create activity type 54
  KN11N – Manual cost reposting 129
  KP06 – Cost element planning 75
  KP26 – Activity price planning 96

KP46 – SKF planning 104
KPAS – Actual template allocation 164
KPSI – Plan reconciliation 81
KPT6 – Formula planning 85
KS01 – Create cost center 28
KSA3 – Actual Accrual Calculation 166
KSA8 – Planned accrual calculation 86
KSC7 – Create planned indirect activity allocation cycle 93
KSCB – Execute planned indirect activity allocation 95
KSH1 – Create cost center group 45
KSI4 – Actual overhead allocation 164
KSS1 – Variance calculation 180
KSS4 – Planned cost splitting 103
KSU7 – Create planned assessment cycle 92
KSUB – Execute planned assessment 92
KSV7 – Create planned distribution cycle 88
KSVB – Execute planned distribution 90

KVA5 – Transfer actual SKF 171
OKB9 – Default account assignment 52
OKEON Standard hierarchy for cost centers 43
Transction code
  KB51N – Sender Activities 136
Transfer actual SKF values 169
Transfer planned depreciation 107

U
Universal journal
  Benefits I 20
  Concept of 18

V
Value based commitment 126
Variance analysis 178
Variance Categories 182
Variance variant 179

W
Web Dynpro 23
WIP 16
Work center 197

D Disclaimer

This publication contains references to the products of SAP SE.

SAP, R/3, SAP NetWeaver, Duet, PartnerEdge, ByDesign, SAP BusinessObjects Explorer, StreamWork, and other SAP products and services mentioned herein as well as their respective logos are trademarks or registered trademarks of SAP SE in Germany and other countries.

Business Objects and the Business Objects logo, BusinessObjects, Crystal Reports, Crystal Decisions, Web Intelligence, Xcelsius, and other Business Objects products and services mentioned herein as well as their respective logos are trademarks or registered trademarks of Business Objects Software Ltd. Business Objects is an SAP company.

Sybase and Adaptive Server, iAnywhere, Sybase 365, SQL Anywhere, and other Sybase products and services mentioned herein as well as their respective logos are trademarks or registered trademarks of Sybase, Inc. Sybase is an SAP company.

SAP SE is neither the author nor the publisher of this publication and is not responsible for its content. SAP Group shall not be liable for errors or omissions with respect to the materials. The only warranties for SAP Group products and services are those that are set forth in the express warranty statements accompanying such products and services, if any. Nothing herein should be construed as constituting an additional warranty.

More Espresso Tutorials Books

Martin Munzel:

New SAP® Controlling Planning Interface

▶ Introduction to Netweaver Business Client

▶ Flexible Planning Layouts

▶ Plan Data Upload from Excel

http://5011.espresso-tutorials.com

Michael Esser:

Investment Project Controlling with SAP®

▶ SAP ERP functionality for investment controlling

▶ Concepts, roles and different scenarios

▶ Effective planning and reporting

http://5008.espresso-tutorials.com

Stefan Eifler:

Quick Guide to SAP® CO-PA (Profitability Analysis)

▶ Basic organizational entities and master data

▶ Define the actual value flow

▶ Set up a planning environment

▶ Create your own reports

http://5018.espresso-tutorials.com

Paul Ovigele:

Reconciling SAP® CO-PA to the General Ledger

▶ Learn the Difference between Costing-based and Accounting-based CO-PA

▶ Walk through Various Value Flows into CO-PA

▶ Match the Cost-of-Sales Account with Corresponding Value Fields in CO-PA

http://5040.espresso-tutorials.com

Tanya Duncan:

Practical Guide to SAP® CO-PC (Product Cost Controlling)

▶ Cost Center Planning Process and Costing Run Execution

▶ Actual Cost Analysis & Reporting

▶ Controlling Master Data

▶ Month End Processes in Details

http://5064.espresso-tutorials.com

Ashish Sampat:

First Steps in SAP® Controlling (CO)

▶ Cost center and product cost planning and actual cost flow

▶ Best practices for cost absorption using Product Cost Controlling

▶ Month-end closing activities in SAP Controlling

▶ Examples and screenshots based on a case study approach

http://5069.espresso-tutorials.com

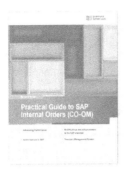

Marjorie Wright:

Practical Guide to SAP® Internal Orders (CO-OM)

► Concepts and daily postings to internal orders

► Master data configuration

► Streamlining period-end close activities

► Reporting options and summarization hierarchies in SAP CO

http://5139.espresso-tutorials.com

Ashish Sampat:

Expert Tips to Unleash the Full Potential of SAP® Controlling

► Optimize SAP ERP Controlling configuration, reconciliation, and reporting

► Transaction processiong tips to ensure accurate data capture

► Instructions for avoiding common month-end close pain points

► Reporting and reconciliation best practices

http://5140.espresso-tutorials.com

John Pringle:

Practical Guide to SAP® Profit Center Accounting

► Fundamentals of SAP Profit Center Accounting (PCA)

► Concepts, master data, actual data flow, and planning basics

► Differences between PCA in classic and new GL

► Reporting for Profit Center Accounting (PCA)

http://5144.espresso-tutorials.com/

Janet Salmon & Claus Wild:

First Steps in SAP® S/4HANA Finance

► Understand the basics of SAP S/4HANA Finance

► Explore the new architecture, configuration options, and SAP Fiori

► Examine SAP S/4HANA Finance migration steps

► Assess the impact on business processes

http://5149.espresso-tutorials.com

www.ingramcontent.com/pod-product-compliance
Lightning Source LLC
LaVergne TN
LVHW022307060326
832902LV00020B/3320